Drive Around

Andalucía
and the Costa Del Sol

YOUR GUIDE TO GREAT DRIVES

Titles in this series include:

- Andalucía and the Costa del Sol
- Bavaria and the Austrian Tyrol
- Brittany and Normandy
- Burgundy and the Rhône Valley
- California
- Catalonia and the Spanish Pyrenees
- Dordogne and Western France
- England and Wales
- Florida
- Ireland
- Italian Lakes and Mountains with Venice and Florence
- Languedoc and Southwest France
- Loire Valley
- Provence and the Côte d'Azur
- Scotland
- Tuscany and Umbria
- Vancouver and British Columbia
  and

- Selected Bed and Breakfast in France (annual edition)

For further information about these and other Thomas Cook publications, write to Thomas Cook Publishing, PO Box 227, The Thomas Cook Business Park, 15–16 Coningsby Road, Peterborough PE3 8SB, United Kingdom.

Drive Around

Andalucía
and the Costa Del Sol

The best of Andalucía's Mediterranean coastline plus Gibraltar, the vibrant Moorish cities of Granada, Córdoba and Sevilla, the white villages of the interior and the mountain villages of the Sierra Nevada.

Patricia Harris and David Lyon

Thomas Cook
Publishing

www.thomascookpublishing.com

Published by Thomas Cook Publishing,
a division of Thomas Cook Tour Operations Limited
PO Box 227, The Thomas Cook Business Park
15–16 Coningsby Road
Peterborough PE3 8SB
United Kingdom

Telephone: +44 (0)1733 416477
Fax: +44 (0)1733 416688
E-mail: books@thomascook.com

For further information about
Thomas Cook Publishing, visit our website:
www.thomascookpublishing.com

ISBN 1-841574-48-1

Text: © 2005 Thomas Cook Publishing
Maps and diagrams:
Road maps supplied and designed by Lovell Johns Ltd., OX8 8LH
Road maps generated from Bartholomew Digital Database
© Bartholomew Ltd., 1999
City maps prepared by RJS Associates, © Thomas Cook Publishing

Head of Thomas Cook Publishing: Chris Young
Series Editor: Charlotte Christensen
Production/DTP Editor: Steve Collins
Project Administrator: Michelle Warrington

Written and researched by: Patricia Harris and
David Lyon
Update research by: Mary McLean

About the authors

Authors Patricia Harris and David Lyon are independent travel writers and photographers, restaurant reviewers and art critics. Their work appears regularly in a wide range of English-language periodicals and in Spanish in the Organisation of American States' publication *Américas*. They are restaurant critics for the Microsoft website *Boston Sidewalk*, contributors to the *Expedia* travel website and Madrid correspondents for the *Visa Infinite* website. They contributed Maine and Massachusetts chapters to *Signpost New England*, and Québec chapters to *Touring Eastern Canada*, both from Thomas Cook Publishing.

Acknowledgements

Patricia would like to thank Sr Sibursky, who taught Spanish at Manchester High School in Manchester, Connecticut, and focused her interest on Spanish-speaking cultures. The authors especially thank Pilar Vico of the Tourist Office of Spain in New York for her guidance, encouragement and long-term faith. They also thank her colleague, Margaret Walenga, for assistance with current information and with arrangements for their research trips. They are also indebted to Antonio Alonso of Marketing Ahead, the Paradores de Turismo, Diana Serop of Costa del Sol Tourism and Turespaña.

Contents

About Drive Around Guides

Thomas Cook's Drive Around Guides are designed to provide you with a comprehensive but flexible reference source to guide you as you tour a country or region by car. This guide divides Andalucía into touring areas – one per chapter. Major cultural centres or cities form chapters in their own right. Each chapter contains enough attractions to provide at least a day's worth of activities – often more.

Star ratings
To make it easier for you to plan your time and decide what to see, the main sights and attractions are given star ratings. A three-star rating indicates an outstanding sight or major attraction. Often these can be worth at least half a day of your time. A two-star attraction is worth an hour or so of your time, and a one-star attraction indicates a site that is good, but often of specialist interest. The stars are intended to help you set priorities, so that travellers with limited time can quickly find the most rewarding sights.

Chapter contents
Every chapter has an introduction summing up the main attractions of the area, and a ratings box, which will highlight the area's strengths and weaknesses – some areas may be more attractive to families travelling with children, others to wine-lovers visiting vineyards, and others to people interested in finding castles, churches, nature reserves, or good beaches.

Each chapter is then divided into an alphabetical gazetteer, and a suggested tour. You can select whether you just want to visit a particular sight or attraction, choosing from those described in the gazetteer, or whether you want to tour the area comprehensively. If the latter, you can construct your own itinerary, or follow the author's suggested tour, which comes at the end of every area chapter.

The gazetteer
The gazetteer section describes all the major attractions in the area – the villages, towns, historic sites, nature reserves, parks or museums that you are most likely to want to see. Maps of the area highlight all the places mentioned in the text. Using this comprehensive overview of the area, you may choose just to visit one or two sights.

One way to use the guide is simply to find individual sights that interest you, using the index, overview map or star ratings, and read what our authors have to say about them. This will help you decide

Symbol Key
- ❶ Tourist Information Centre
- ❷ Advice on arriving or departing
- ❿ Parking locations
- ❺ Advice on getting around
- ❺ Directions
- ❶ Sights and attractions
- ❶ Accommodation
- ❶ Eating
- ❺ Shopping
- ❾ Sport
- ❺ Entertainment

Practical information

The practical information in the page margins, or sidebar, will help you locate the services you need as an independent traveller – including the tourist information centre, car parks and public transport facilities. You will also find the opening times of sights, museums, churches and other attractions, as well as useful tips on shopping, market days, cultural events, entertainment, festivals and sports facilities.

whether to visit the sight. If you do, you will find plenty of practical information, such as the street address, the telephone number for enquiries and opening times.

Alternatively, you can choose a hotel, perhaps with the help of the accommodation recommendations contained in this guide. You can then turn to the overall map on page 10 to help you work out which chapters in the book describe those cities and regions that lie closest to your chosen touring base.

Driving tours

The suggested tour is just that – a suggestion, with plenty of optional detours and one or two ideas for making your own discoveries, under the heading *Also worth exploring*. The routes are designed to link the attractions described in the gazetteer section, and to cover outstandingly scenic coastal, mountain and rural landscapes. The total distance is given for each tour, as is the time it will take you to drive the complete route, but bear in mind that this indication is just for the driving time: you will need to add on extra time for visiting attractions along the way.

Many of the routes are circular, so that you can join them at any point. Where the nature of the terrain dictates that the route has to be linear, the route can either be followed out and back, or you can use it as a link route, to get from one area in the book to another.

As you follow the route descriptions, you will find names picked out in bold capital letters – this means that the place is described fully in the gazetteer. Other names picked out in bold indicate additional villages or attractions worth a brief stop along the route.

France

Spain

Portugal

Accommodation and food

In every chapter you will find lodging and eating recommendations for individual towns, or for the area as a whole. These are designed to cover a range of price brackets and concentrate on more characterful small or individualistic hotels and restaurants. In addition, you will find information in the *Travel Facts* chapter on chain hotels, with an address to which you can write for a guide, map or directory. The price indications used in the guide have the following meanings:

€   budget level
€€   typical/average prices
€€€   de luxe

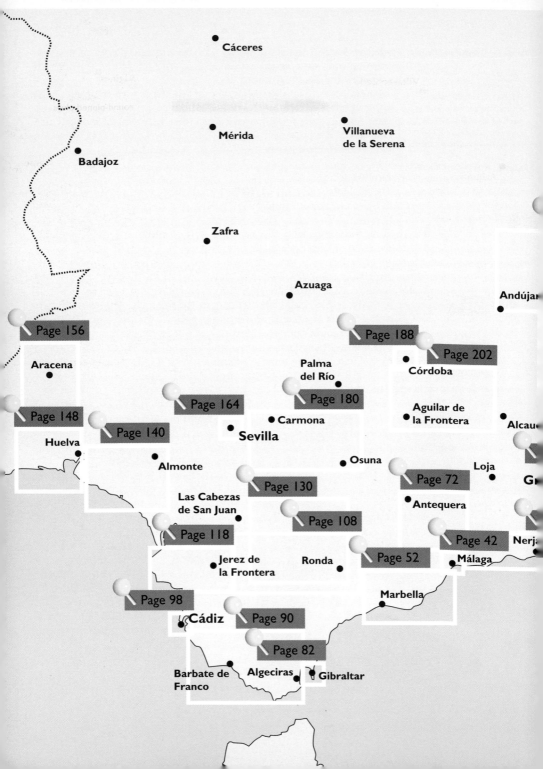

Cáceres

Mérida

Villanueva
de la Serena

Badajoz

Zafra

Azuaga

Andújar

Page 156

Page 188

Page 202

Aracena

Palma
del Río

Córdoba

Page 148

Page 164

Page 180

Aguilar de
la Frontera

Alcau

Page 140

Huelva

Carmona

Sevilla

Almonte

Osuna

Loja

G

Page 130

Page 72

Las Cabezas
de San Juan

Antequera

Page 118

Page 108

Page 42

Nerj

Jerez de
la Frontera

Ronda

Page 52

Málaga

Page 98

Marbella

Cádiz

Page 90

Page 82

Barbate de
Franco

Algeciras

Gibraltar

Requena

Valencia

Villarrobledo

Alginet

Gandía

Albacete

Xativa

Almansa

Denia

Alcoy

Calpe

Valdepeñas

Benidorm

Hellín

Alicante

224

Elche

Caravaca
de la Cruz

Murcia

Villacarrillo

Torrevieja

Page 212

San Javier

Huéscar

La Manga

Lorca

Cartagena

Baza

Aguilas

Guadix

2

Page 246

Gérgal

Page 274

Garrucha

Torvizcón

Canjáyar

Mojácar

Page 258

Almería

Motril

Adra

Page 266

Introduction

We are always struck by how many sightseers in Andalucía hail from other parts of Spain. We watched one day as a bus tour pulled up at Almería's *alcazaba*, depositing a large group of pensioners to make the uphill walk, many of them arm in arm, to the fortress. Pausing to rest in the shade of a tree, one woman turned to her comrade and sighed, 'Tomorrow – Granada!'

Andalucía holds a special place in the hearts and minds of Spaniards, many of whom make at least one pilgrimage to see where their country took full form and where so many essential aspects of Spanish culture took root. Moreover, they are usually eager to share that heritage with visitors, amplifying the limited interpretation available at many sites.

A rich past anchors Andalucía. People apologise for the slow progress in erecting buildings by explaining that excavation for the foundation seems to have unearthed another ruin. There is a tendency for museums to treat everything before Julius Caesar as archaeology, everything since as history. Wherever you go in Andalucía, the past is

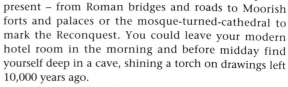

present – from Roman bridges and roads to Moorish forts and palaces or the mosque-turned-cathedral to mark the Reconquest. You could leave your modern hotel room in the morning and before midday find yourself deep in a cave, shining a torch on drawings left 10,000 years ago.

The largest of Spain's autonomous regions, Andalucía is divided into eight provinces named after their capital cities. Its diversity is sweeping. One day you can stroll the elegant boulevards south of Sevilla's historic district, admiring the phantasmagoric architecture of Plaza de España and the green symmetries of Parque María Luisa. The next morning you might have to turn off the engine in your car to let a herd of goats pass down a narrow road into a mountain village where only the electricity cables and television antennae indicate that anything has changed since Moorish days.

Andalucía contains landscapes as different as the parched high desert of Almería and the moist, verdant canopies of the cork oak forest in Cádiz and Málaga provinces. Vast reaches of rubble-strewn scrubland hum with honeybees extracting pollen from sage, rosemary and cactus flowers, while the silence of the hills is so intense in parts of the Sierra Aracena that you can hear the springs burble from the hillside. The interior mountain ranges are green with natural parks where walking paths link tiny hamlets and more difficult hiking trails scale craggy peaks. Yet the landscape can change in a blink. After hours of navigating the contours of mountain roads, drivers can suddenly swoop down a hill onto the coastal plain where white, brown or even jet-black sandy beaches stretch along the ocean to the horizon.

Spaniards often pronounce anything brimming with colour and passion to be ¡muy Andalucía! That joy and exuberance permeates the region, accessible to any traveller who remains receptive. Step out of your hotel and you could find yourself swept up in a procession of musicians and floats marking a saint's day or celebrating a harvest. Glance into an open doorway and you might see four generations of a family talking and eating in their central patio. The famous Andalucían alegría shines forth equally at a flamenco performance in a fancy nightclub, or in the impassioned arpeggios of a young guitarist playing to tourists on a street corner. The Andalucían love affair with flowers finds expression in extravagant gardens with fountains and pools – and in the strident gitanilla cascading from an old tin can. Few places in the world are so devoted to domestic ornament: a riot of painted tiles in every doorway, a web of iron bars to create the grille for a window, a carved wooden lintel, a plaster cast coat of arms, a filigree window ledge.

The sensuality of Andalucían life is the root of local pride and identity. Walking down a village street you are suddenly dazzled by three colours of bougainvillaea or assailed by the sweet scent of the blossoms of bitter orange. Enter a bar where bottles of sherry, Montilla and Málaga line the wall and the hams of Sierra Aracena and Las Alpujarras hang overhead and there's likely to be a sign on the till: Aquí hablamos Andaluz, 'Here we speak Andalucían'.

We were in a petrol station/grocery store near Bobadilla in northern Málaga province when the cashier suddenly spoke to us in English with a lilting Irish accent. When we commented on her language skills, she explained that she had studied English in Dublin after finding the pace of London altogether too hectic. 'I'm Andalucían,' she shrugged – a statement that needed no further explanation.

You will enjoy your stay in Andalucía most if you adopt the deliciously measured pace of life. Sit in the shade and relax with friends over a meal through the heat of the afternoon. Enjoy the respite instead of fretting that the churches, museums and shops on your itinerary are closed for a couple of hours. Dine late at night when the air is cool and everyone can linger, since the day's business is done. If you feel starved waiting for a restaurant to open at 10 o'clock at night, do as the Andalucíans do: sidle up to a string of tapas bars and taste, taste, taste until you find the food and the convivial crowd to suit your mood.

Travel facts

Accommodation

Spain ranks hotels from one to five stars and *hostales* and *pensiones* from one to three. Most hotels have a restaurant on the premises, with the exception of *hoteles-residencias,* which typically serve breakfast only. Common in smaller towns and still found in cities are *hostales* (basic hotels) and *pensiones* (or guesthouses), which often have shared baths and sometimes include breakfast in the rate. Symbols in this book indicate price level:

€	budget
€€	average
€€€	de luxe

Rooms tend to be small except at the most luxurious resorts and hotels designated *gran lujo.* Twin beds are more common than a double bed, or *cama matrimonial.* Even fairly upmarket properties place more emphasis on public areas than private rooms. Except where noted, listed accommodations have private baths.

Most camping areas in Spain are self-contained, offering a bar, restaurant, grocery store and, often, swimming pool and other recreational facilities. They are graded from first class (most amenities) to third class (fewest), but even third-class camping usually offers hot showers, electrical hookups and a cafeteria. Many towns prohibit 'uncontrolled camping', although camping outside campsites is legal except in environmentally protected sites, tourist resorts and on beaches. For information and reservations, contact: *Federación Española de Empresarios de Camping; General Oraa 52, 28006, Madrid; tel: (91) 562–9994.*

Airports

Most international flights arrive either at Málaga airport or at Madrid-Barajas airport with connecting flights to Málaga or other Andalucían airports in Almería, Córdoba, Granada, Jerez and Sevilla. Technically, these are all international airports but only Madrid-Barajas and Málaga handle large jets.

Children

Spaniards dote on their children until they are old enough to walk, at which point they are expected to be quiet and well-mannered in public. Hotels and restaurants are accommodating, and reduced admissions are usually available at attractions.

Hotel chains:

Paradores de Turismo
Requena 3, 28013 Madrid, España; tel: (91) 516–6666; fax: (91) 516–6658; e-mail: info@parador.es; www.parador.es.
State-run chain of well-located hotels in mainly historic buildings. Special promotions sometimes available.

Tugasa
Parque González Hontoría s/n, 11405 Jerez de la Frontera Cádiz, España; tel: (95) 630–5611 or (95) 630–5955; fax: (95) 630–5559; e-mail: tugasa@tugasa.com; www.tugasa.com. Small chain of hotels and tourist villas operated by Cadiz provincial tourism provides good choices in the white villages (pueblos blancos), heart of the Frontera and smaller towns of sherry country.

Hoteles con Encanto (Charming Hotels)
c/ Capitulaciones 29620 Torremolinos Málaga, España; tel: (95) 205–2560; fax: (95) 205–2206; e-mail: info@charminghotels-spain.com; www.charminghotels-spain.com
Centralised booking service for hotels with regional character also assists with trip planning.

**Hoteles Rurales de
Andalucía** c/ Ramal Hoyo
s/n, Edificio El Congreso I,
Local 82–83, 29620,
Torremolinos, Malaga;
tel: (95) 237–8775;
fax: (95) 237–8784; e-mail:
info@ahra.es; www.ahra.es.
Centralised booking service
for extensive association of
hotels, typically family-run
and featuring regional
cuisine.

Turismo Rural
tel: (90) 244–2233;
fax: (95) 027–1678 or
(95) 456–0003; e-mail:
info@ruar.es; www.ruar.es.
Network of rural lodgings,
including camping, selected
to allow travellers to
experience natural sites
and village life more closely.

NH Hoteles
Santa Engracia 120, 28003
Madrid, España, tel: (90)
211–5116 (reservations
within Spain), fax: (91)
442–4402, tel: (91)
398–4400 (reservations
outside Spain); e-mail:
nh@nh-hoteles.com;
www.nh-hoteles.es. Chain of
good-value business hotels
includes several in
Andalucía.

Sol Melía Hoteles,
Andalucía Office, Paseo
Colorado 26, 29620
Torremolinos, Málaga,
España; tel: (95) 238–4922;
fax: (95) 238–4923;
www.solmelia.com. Hotel
chain includes some of the
best resort hotels on the
Costa del Sol and urban
business hotels.

Climate

The best times to visit are Apr–Jun and Sept–Oct, when temperatures are moderate and rain is minimal. Eastern Andalucía, especially along the coast, is extremely dry in all seasons, while precipitation is common at all times in mountainous regions. Daily high temperatures above 35 degrees centigrade are the norm in Jul–Aug, both on the coast and in the interior.

Currency

Spain is one of the 25 European Union countries to use a single currency, the euro. Coins are issued in denominations of 1, 2, 5, 10, 20 and 50 euro cents and 1 and 2 euros. Notes are issued in denominations of 5, 10, 20, 50, 100, 200 and 500 euros.

Customs regulations

Non-EU visitors may bring in no more than 200 cigarettes or 50 cigars or 250 grams of tobacco, plus two bottles of wine and one bottle of liquor. Dogs and cats are admitted as long as they have up-to-date vaccination records from their home country. Travellers going from one EU country to another have no restrictions, although it is advisable to check before travelling.

Check with customs authorities before leaving home to determine limits and restrictions for bringing home purchases made in Spain. Pay close attention to agricultural restrictions on plants, animals and food products.

Drinking

Beer, wine, soft drinks and bottled water are available everywhere (although tap water is safe to drink). Patrons must be 18 years old to purchase alcoholic beverages although this is not strictly enforced. Every town has at least one bar that opens by 0700, where the customers drinking coffee and brandy are about equally split. Except at resorts catering to Americans, coffee is strong, dark and small, while café con leche is one-third strong coffee and two-thirds steamed milk. Tea (té) is usually served as hot water with a tea bag.

Electricity

Electric appliances run on 220 volts AC 50 HZ. Standard European-pattern round-pinned plugs are used.

Entry formalities

A National ID Card or passport is acceptable for citizens of EU member states, Switzerland, Andorra, Monaco and Liechtenstein. All other visitors must present a passport. For tourist visits up to 90 days, nationals from the US, Canada, Australia and New Zealand do not need a visa. South Africans must obtain a visa. Applications for a visa must be made at the Spanish Consulate in the applicant's country of residence. It is advisable to check the current legislations before travelling.

Eating out

Breakfast is usually from 0800–1000; lunch from 1400–1530 is, for many Spaniards, the major meal of the day. In cities, *tapas* are widely available throughout the day. Dinner is served from 2030–2300, often later in urban centres. This schedule has evolved to enable diners to evade the afternoon heat and enjoy the cooler evenings. Travellers wishing to dine on their own schedules should seek out *cafeterías* and bars offering *tapas* and *raciones*. A *tapa* is usually a small plate of meat, fish or snack food, whereas *raciones* are larger plates meant to either serve as a meal or be shared. Food and drink served at a table usually costs 10–15% more than if consumed at the bar.

Most establishments display a menu at the entrance. This *carta* is not to be confused with the set *menú del día*, usually offered at midday, that offers a good price on limited choices of appetiser, main dish and dessert with beverage. For regional home cooking, seek out establishments serving *comidas caseras*.

Symbols used in this book indicate the price level of a meal with appetiser, main dish, dessert and beverage:

€	budget
€€	average
€€€	de luxe

Festivals

Andalucían festivals can be unforgettable but require planning and advance booking, as hotels tend to sell out far in advance. Consider staying 20km or more away and visiting festivities as a day trip. Many festivals in Andalucía are tied to the Christian religious calendar, including **Carnaval** leading up to Lent and **Semana Santa**, the week before Easter.

Ferias begin in April or May and last through the summer, as do performing arts festivals. Re-enactments of **battles between the Moors and Christians** are usually held near the feast of San Antonio in mid-June in Almería and Jaén provinces. The entire province follows the tradition of setting up flower-covered crosses, *Cruces de Mayo*, in plazas and patios, joining the liturgical tradition to the national holiday of Labour Day. **Córdoba's Patio Festival** provides a wonderful opportunity to view the city's fabled patios, festooned with flowers.

Throughout the year groups of pilgrims descend on Andalucían holy sites to honour the local manifestation of the Virgin Mary. The largest, the Pentecost weekend **Romería del Rocío**, attracts up to 500,000 participants and spectators.

Insurance

Experienced travellers carry insurance that covers their belongings, holiday investment (including provision for cancelled or delayed flights and weather problems) and health (including immediate evacuation home in case of medical emergency). Thomas Cook and other travel agencies offer comprehensive policies.

Tourist Offices in Europe:

UNITED KINGDOM
Spanish Tourist Office
22–23 Manchester Square London W1U 3PX;
tel: (0207) 486–8077;
fax: (0207) 486–8034;
e-mail:
londres@tourspain.es;
www.tourspain.es

SPAIN
In addition to regional offices mentioned in appropriate chapters:

Oficina de Turismo de la Junta de Andalucía
(Andalusian Regional Tourist Board)
Paseo de la Castellana 15 – 2° drch.
28046 Madrid, España;
tel: (91) 308–0440;
fax: (91) 308–0427;
www.andalucia.org

Food

Andalucía produces the only sherry in the world and arguably the best olive oil and dry-cured hams. All three figure prominently in the local cuisine. Coastal specialities focus on fish, of which the small ones are fried (often whole) or grilled and the large ones baked – either drizzled with olive oil or whole in a bed of salt. The fresh anchovy, or *boquerón*, is a staple; preserved in olive oil and vinegar, it is a ubiquitous *tapa*. Tuna, both as fresh steak or poached and crumbled into salads, is found on almost every menu. Dry-cured tuna, known as *mojama*, is a delicacy produced along the Costa de la Luz. Vegetables are not a major part of Andalucían cuisine, with the exceptions of artichokes, asparagus and fresh tomatoes. Oranges and other citrus fruits grow in the south, strawberries in the west, cherries in Las Alpujarras and peaches and apples throughout the region. Grapes are nearly all reserved for wine. Andalucían desserts are limited, usually comprising a choice of fruit, ice cream or flan (crème caramel).

Health

Travellers should use sunscreen to protect against the intense Andalucían sun. Insect repellent is also advised for hikers. Travellers should carry a full supply of prescription medications and an extra pair of prescription eyeglasses. Copies of prescriptions are also a wise precaution. While almost everyone seems to drink bottled water, tap water is safe. Cautious travellers should avoid all public fountains; don't drink from a fountain that is not marked *agua potable*.

For life threatening medical problems, it's best to head directly to the emergency room (*urgencias*) of the hospital. For other situations, there are private clinics and health centres (*centros de salud*), some of which also do emergency care. EU citizens are entitled to free Spanish national health medical care, but must present Form E111, issued by the Post Office in Britain. This care does not cover private treatment or prescription medications. Other travellers should ascertain whether their health insurance remains in effect while travelling, and take steps to ensure adequate coverage.

Maps

The best single road map to Andalucía is the Michelin *Southern Spain,* issued annually and widely available. More manageable inside the automobile is the Michelin map book *Motoring in Southern Spain and Portugal*. Individual city and region maps available at Andalucía Tourist Board offices are usually best for larger scale detail. The best detailed maps for hikers are published by the Centro Nacional de Información Geográfica (CNIG), including the *Mapa Guía* covering national and natural parks. CNIG has outlets in Granada: *Avda Divina*

Useful websites
www.andalucia.com;
www.typicallyspanish.com

**Tourist Offices in
the Americas:**

CANADA
Tourist Office of Spain
*2 Bloor Street West, 34th
floor, Toronto, Ontario M4W
3E2;
tel: 1 (416) 961–3131;
fax: 1 (416) 961–1992;
e-mail:
toronto@tourspain.es;
www.tourspain.toronto.on.es*

UNITED STATES
Tourist Office of Spain
*Water Tower Place, Suite
915 East, 845 North
Michigan Avenue, Chicago, IL
60611;
tel: 1 (312) 642–1992;
fax: 1 (312) 642 9817;
e-mail: chicago@tourspain.es*

Tourist Office of Spain
*8383 Wilshire Boulevard,
Suite 960, Beverly Hills, CA
90211;
tel: 1 (323) 658–7195;
fax: 1 (323) 658–1061;
e-mail:
losangeles@tourspain.es*

Tourist Office of Spain
*1221 Brickell Avenue
Miami, FL 33131;
tel: 1 (305) 358–1992;
fax: 1 (315) 358–8223;
e-mail: miami@tourspain.es*

Tourist Office of Spain
*666 Fifth Avenue, 35th floor,
New York, NY 10103;
tel: 1 (212) 265–8822;
fax: 1 (212) 265–8864;
e-mail:
neuvayork@tourspain.es;
www.okspain.org*

Pastora 7, tel: (95) 829–0411, Málaga: *Ramos Carrión 48 tel: (95)
221–2018* and Sevilla: *Avda San Francisco Javier 9 tel: (95) 464–4256.*

Museums

Most museums keep normal business hours (*see page 20*) with shorter
hours on Sun. Museums in cities often stay open throughout the day.
Schedules shift by a few hours at different seasons and museums
generally close on holidays and, in smaller towns, on Mondays. Most
museums offer free admission to EU residents. Symbols in this book
indicate price level:

no symbol	free
€	cheap
€€	moderate
€€€	expensive

National parks

Parques Nacionales, which include Doñana and the northern section
of the Sierra Nevada, enjoy strict controls to preserve important flora,
fauna or other natural features. By contrast, the **Parques Naturales** –
more than 20 in Andalucía – often include towns, farms, orchards and
other human presences. Visitors are expected to follow common-sense
rules, usually but not always posted. Camp only in designated areas,
stay on trails, pick up litter, do not disturb plants or wildlife.

Opening times

Banks are open Mon–Sat 0830–1400. From Jun to Sept they are closed on Sat. Stores are generally open Mon–Sat 0930–1330 and 1630–2000. Major department stores and supermarkets tend to stay open without a break and are occasionally open on Sun. Pharmacies keep the same hours as stores, but there will always be a *Farmacia de Guardia* open 24 hours. These operate on a rota schedule, details of which are posted outside every pharmacy. Nightlife is just that, with music clubs and discotheques rarely getting started until 2300 and going until the *madrugada,* or early morning.

Packing

Note that Spanish airport security does not permit hand inspection of cameras, film or computers.

In addition, most towns celebrate their local saint's day.

Hitting a holiday will pose inconveniences, since banks, businesses, attractions, shops and many restaurants will be closed. For many visitors, this will be compensated by the chance to observe and even participate in celebrations that bind a community together.

Spaniards go on holiday from mid-July through August and during Semana Santa, an especially pleasant time along the coast, as Spanish holiday-makers enjoy their country before the start of the tourist season.

Depending on the time of year, essentials in Andalucía are sunglasses and sunscreen, a small umbrella and a light jacket or sweater to ward off evening chills. Dressing comfortably and looking like a tourist, right down to comfortable shoes, is acceptable, but be aware that Spaniards are fairly formal and like to dress up. Revealing clothing is considered especially disrespectful in a church.

Postal services/Communications

At full service branch offices of the Spanish Post Office (*oficina de correos*) visitors can send mail and parcels and send or receive money orders. Visitors can also rent post office boxes to receive mail. Many post offices also offer fax services. Hours are usually Mon–Fri 0830–1400, Sat 0900–1300. In larger towns the opening hours may be slightly longer. Postage stamps are also sold in tobacco shops (look for a sign with *Tabacos* in yellow letters). Yellow or red mail boxes are placed throughout cities and towns. Internet cafés are widespread; the respective tourist office can provide you with a list.

Public transport

High speed rail service from Madrid to Sevilla and Córdoba is available on the AVE and from Madrid to Málaga, Cádiz and Huelva on the Talgo 200. There is extensive rail service throughout Andalucía. For information, contact RENFE, *tel: (90) 224–0202; www.renfe.es.* From Apr–Jun and Sept–Dec the Al-Andalus Express, a classic luxury train, offers a five-day touring itinerary; *www.iber-rail.es*

InterRail passes (travellers under 26 resident for 6 months in Europe) and Eurail passes (North American residents) are valid on all RENFE trains, but inter-city express trains carry supplementary charges. The RENFE Tarjeta Turística, available only in Spain, will provide three or ten days' unlimited train travel in a one-month period.

Rail Europe offers an Iberia Flexipass that can be bought in advance by travellers from North America for discount travel for a certain number of days within a specific time period.

For information contact: *www.raileurope.co.uk*

Buses are generally recommended for short-distance travel and short trips out of cities. RENFE-operated buses are replacing trains on many short-haul routes.

Reading

The modern classics of Gerald Brenan, *South from Granada* and *The Face of Spain*, recount the ex-pat life in an Alpujarran village in the 1920s. More recent accounts are the entertaining and autobiographical *Driving Over Lemons* and its sequel, *A Parrot in the Pepper Tree*, by Chris Stewart.

Wildlife Travelling Companion Spain by John Measures includes a field guide to common plants and animals. The Andalucía Tourist

Office publishes a superb *Hiking* guide. English editions are available in tourist offices.

The Routes of al-Andalus, published in Spain by El País/Aguilar, combines a Moorish perspective on the history of Andalucía with useful touring routes.

The best overall guide to Spanish cuisine in English is *The Foods and Wines of Spain* by Penelope Casas.

Safety and security

The Basque terrorist organisation ETA has occasionally targeted tourist resorts on the Spanish Costas, however there is usually advance warning and few casualties. Madrid's horrific train bombing on Mar 11 2004 by Al-Qaeda terrorists led to a new political party, president and the withdrawal of Spanish troops from Iraq. Check your country's foreign affairs department for the up-to-date travel situation in Spain. Overall, it is a safe country with little violent crime, provided normal precautions are taken. Do not publicly discuss travel plans, or money or valuables that you are carrying. Stay in well-lit areas. Do not be ostentatious with banknotes or jewellery. Use a hidden money-belt for valuables, travel documents and spare cash. Be vigilant as regards distractions for pickpockets.

Shopping

For local colour, shoppers can't beat market days and flea markets. Many are listed in the following chapters. Andalucía is rich in handicrafts, including pottery and tiles (Sevilla, Granada, Córdoba, Nijar, Ubeda); leather goods (Ubrique, Córdoba); woven blankets and rugs (Nijar, Grazalema); gold and silver filigree jewellery (Córdoba, Granada); wooden marquetry (Granada); woven straw, raffia or palm goods (Alpujarras, all coastal regions). The best guitar makers are found in Sevilla and Granada.

Sport

Fútbol is Andalucía's most popular sport, with professional teams in Sevilla, Cádiz, Málaga and Almería. Tickets are readily available. Bullfighting is less a sport than a spectacle linked to Andalucían identity. The season begins when the Semana Santa celebrations end on Easter Sunday and concludes on Oct 12, Spain's national day. The schedule tends to follow local *ferias*.

Stores

The large department store chain El Corte Inglés has branches in most large cities and medium-size towns in Andalucía. All branches offer a

Taxes

A 7% Value Added Tax, known as IVA, is added to hotel and restaurant bills. IVA on purchases and car hire is 16%. Non-EU residents are entitled to a reimbursement of the IVA on purchases of more than €90 in one shop if the items will be taken out of the EU within three months. Ask the shop for an invoice to be presented to the customs booth when leaving the last EU country before returning home.

Time

Local time is GMT +1 in winter and GMT +2 in summer.

Tipping

Most restaurants include service in the price, but it is customary to tip 5–10% in bars, restaurants, hotels and taxis.

wide range of Spanish-made goods and the largest branches have excellent gourmet sections.

Telephones

International and domestic calls can be made from public phones using coins or phone cards (*tarjetas telefónicas*), which are sold at post offices and tobacco shops. To place an international call, first dial 00. On hearing a continuous tone, dial the country and city codes and then the phone number. Spain's country code for calling from abroad is '34'.

International standard modular phone jacks are far from standard in Spanish hotels, and substandard central office switching often means that overseas modem connections are unreliable. If you must have e-mail access, check with your Internet service provider for advice.

Toilets

Some cities are experimenting with high-tech coin-operated toilets in high traffic areas, but the best bet is usually a bar, restaurant, museum or other attraction. Some tourist offices and most beaches also have public facilities, which are sometimes free or require a 20-cent coin. Carrying a pack of paper tissues is a good idea. Public toilets are generally called *servicios*, *aseos*, or *Damas* and *Cabelleros*.

Travellers with disabilities

Inquire at Spanish tourist offices for information about accessible accommodation and other useful information. Wheelchair accessibility in Andalucía is limited. Efforts are being made, and all new buildings must have wheelchair access. But Andalucía has few new buildings and many ancient ones, where adaptation is by no means universal.

Driver's guide

Automobile clubs

Members of motoring organisations in their home countries (AA, AAA, RAC, etc) can take advantage of the 24-hour emergency breakdown service of Spain's Real Automóvil Club de España (RACE) by calling the emergency breakdown assistance *tel:* 902 300 505. *www.race.es*

Autoroutes

Over the last few years the Spanish motorway system has undergone great expansion throughout the country, with most major centres connected by *autopistas* (toll motorways or *autovías* (toll-free motorways).

Tolls (*peaje*) must be paid on a number of motorways. A fixed-price toll is payable on some small stretches of motorway, but the usual system is to pick up a ticket when you drive on and pay when you leave, according to the distance travelled. Tolls can be paid by cash or by credit card. Should you wish to avoid the tolls, there are usually signs directing you to a toll-free route, which will be slower but generally more scenic.

There are two toll highways in Andalucía, the A4 between Sevilla and Cádiz and the A7, which runs west of Malaga to Guadiaro (just beyond Estepona). Tolls can be paid in cash or by credit card.

Accidents

Drivers involved in an accident are required to mark the presence of their vehicle by placing two warning triangles, one 50 metres in front of the car and another 50 metres behind, so that they are visible to approaching cars from at least 100metres. If possible you should move your car into a lay-by or on to the hard shoulder and arrange for it to be removed by the rescue services.

Should there be any injuries or damage to vehicles you must attend to the victims, request the assistance of the rescue services and inform the police immediately. You can make your report in English by calling 902 102 112.

Try to have your statement taken by someone who speaks your language. You must carry identification and evidence of insurance with you at all times, and it can also be useful to have a bail bond card and/or insurance for legal costs. If you are not a Spanish resident, assume that you will be judged at fault. On the bright side, minor car-body repairs are relatively inexpensive in Spain.

After an accident make sure you take down the name, address, registration number and insurance details of any other party, preferably on the standard European Accident Statement form which your insurer should be able to provide. The advantage of this form is that it is identical in every language, so both parties understand that they are answering the same questions. If the other driver refuses to co-operate call the police – there are SOS telephone posts situated every 2km or so on motorways and dual carriageways.

Should you witness an accident you must stop, give assistance to any injured persons and call the emergency services. Most highway patrols are carried out by the guardia civil, a constant presence on Spanish roads and recognisable by their olive green uniforms. Each town has its policia local, while the policia nacional deal with serious crimes.

Breakdown

When taking your car to Spain you should take out European breakdown cover. In the event of a breakdown, pull over to the side of the road where you will be visible but out of the way of traffic. Switch on hazard lights and place a warning triangle (required in Spain) at the road's edge. If it is safe to do so, raise the car bonnet and boot. Change a tyre only if you are out of the flow of traffic. If you can find a telephone or have a mobile, dial 091 if you need emergency medical service, reporting the number from which you are calling, your location and

Documents

If you choose to drive your own car in Spain, obtain an International Motor Insurance Certificate (Green Card) and a bail bond. Be sure to carry your vehicle registration documents as well. EU licences (pink or pink and green) are valid in all EU member states, including Spain. The older UK green licence without photo ID is not accepted. Residents of other countries are often told that they may drive with their home country licences, but the Guardia Civil has become quite insistent that you also carry an international driver's licence, available through automobile clubs. Car hire agencies may also require it. Minimum driving age in Spain for most vehicles is 18. It is 14 for scooters and mopeds with an engine displacement of 75cc or less.

Drivers from all non-EU countries except Switzerland must hold a Green Card, the insurance policy covering the cost of assistance in the event of an accident. Insurance to cover legal costs is also a good idea.

emergency needs. Otherwise The RACE operates a 24-hour emergency breakdown service for its members (*tel*: 902 300505). Car hire firms have their own breakdown arrangements.

The towing of a vehicle immobolised by an accident or breakdown may only be carried out by a breakdown vehicle.

Caravans and camper vans (Trailers and RV)

Cars towing caravans are limited to a maximum speed of 80kph and the maximum permitted dimensions of a private vehicle, including a trailer or caravan, are 12m long, 4m high and 2.5m wide. Check that the caravan braking system is correctly adjusted and that all the lights of the caravan or trailer are operating. Make sure, also, that both of the caravan's tyres are of the same size and type and in good order.

When travelling with a caravan avoid overtaking other vehicles if possible and do not overtake more than two vehicles in one stretch. Always keep a safe distance between vehicles. If you need to stop, pull up off the carriageway and onto the hard shoulder. If you can, drive off the road altogether.

Campsites are classified from one to three stars, according to the facilities they offer.

Permission is required from the police and the landowner for off-site camping and camping is forbidden on beaches and in many forest areas in case of fire.

Note, however, that both caravans and camper vans are very difficult to manoeuvre on the narrow streets of Andalucía's towns and villages, so that tenting might be a better camping option.

Driving in Andalucía

The main types of roads in Spain are toll-paying motorways (*autopistas*), toll-free dual carriageways (*autovias*), national carriageways (*carreteras nacionales*, prefaced with N) and regional roads (*carreteras comarcales*, prefaced with C or with the first two letters of the province).

There are two toll motorways in Andalucía, the A4 between Sevilla and Cádiz and the A7 which runs west of Málaga to Guadiaro, past Estepona. The Autopista del Sol, as it is called, by-passes all the main resorts, from Torremolinos to Estepona, and has done much to alleviate the over-congested traffic along the N340 Costa del Sol coastal road. The toll-free Autovía del Mediterraneo, also the A7, runs east from Málaga to beyond Nerja, with ongoing plans for an extension.

There is also an excellent network of dual-carriageway roads linking Sevilla, Córdoba, Granada and other major towns in Andalucia.

Andalucían roads cross extraordinarily beautiful scenery, but drivers need to stay alert. Andalucían drivers behave as if they were veterans of the Grand Prix circuit, indulging in tailgating and daredevil overtaking as a matter of course.

Drinking and driving laws

It is illegal to drink alcoholic beverages in a moving vehicle in Spain. The blood alcohol limit is 0.05% – a level you are likely to exceed after imbibing one glass of wine or the equivalent. Roadside breath tests are conducted on occasion and you are legally required to co-operate. Fines for driving while legally intoxicated are high, and generally not imposed until the morning after you have been introduced to the pleasures of a Spanish jail. It is illegal to use a mobile phone while driving and, again, if caught the fine is considerable.

Essentials

By law, drivers must carry two warning triangles, a spare set of light bulbs and fuses, a spare tyre and a reflective vest for roadside emergencies. Also advisable are a first-aid kit and a spare fanbelt. Drivers who wear glasses are required to carry a spare set. An appropriate country of origin must be displayed on your vehicle.

Petrol = gasolina
Unleaded = sin plomo
Normal = 92 octane
Super = 98 octane
Diesel = gasoleo

Driving rules

Driving is on the right. Be watchful of British and Japanese tourists in the roads around Málaga airport, where driving on the wrong side is the leading cause of accidents. The highways in Andalucía have improved dramatically in the last 15 years, thanks to massive reconstruction for EXPO 92. The major cities are linked by limited-access multilane motorways (*autovías*). Even most smaller towns lie near well-maintained roads.

There are still challenging roads to drive, in particular the twisting mountain roads that cling precariously to the hillsides and often lack barriers on the sides. Narrow village streets pose another serious challenge to driving skills, the difficulties often exacerbated by motor scooters buzzing past.

Spain does not generally permit a right turn on a red light. Vehicles entering a roundabout are expected to cede the right-of-way to vehicles already on the roundabout, although in practice it's usually every driver for him- or herself. Left turns from the roadway are generally forbidden; drivers are expected to use a right-hand turn-off, a *cambio de sentido,* or 'change of direction'.

Fuel

The price of petrol varies continuously and will differ from one supplier to another. Most petrol stations are operated by Spanish companies, including Campsa, Cepsa and Repsol. Self-service stations are beoming more widespread but many still have attendants. Ask for the tank to be filled (lleno) or quote an amount in euros. Credit cards are widely accepted and at some stations it is possible to make an automated payment using your credit card, but be aware that you may sometimes have to pay in cash, in euros. The majority of petrol stations stay open from early in the morning to late evening and many remain open 24 hours on motorways and major highways. But they can be scarce in rural areas, so make sure you are well stocked up.

Fines

Spain has a long history of respect for and deference to authority. Drivers who are stopped by the police are strongly advised not to antagonise the authorities, as a minor traffic violation can escalate through additional citations for such offences as failure to carry a first-aid kit, spare headlight bulbs or a warning triangle. The policía local have jurisdiction of local roads and urban streets and are sometimes somewhat lax about enforcing penalties for certain minor offences. The Guardia Civil traffic police are quite another kettle of fish. They are charged with enforcing traffic law on the main national routes and carriageways and take the task very seriously. It is generally hopeless to contest the fine for a traffic infringement, so apologetic sheepishness is usually the best strategy if stopped. Even if you wish to contest a fine in court, non-residents of Spain must pay on the spot or have their vehicles impounded. If you lack the necessary cash, the officer will accompany you to the nearest bank or automated cash machine.

Watch out for speeding as radar speedtraps are becoming increasingly common. Non-resident offenders are usually expected to pay on-the-spot fines, receiving the dubious privilege of of a 30 per cent discount for doing so.

Right
Jimena de la Frontera

Information

Route numbers have been changing extensively in Andalucía in the last few years, but Michelin's *Andalucía* map and the *Michelin Motoring Atlas – Spain and Portugal* stay fairly up-to-date and show relative road conditions – useful in planning the time it will take for a given drive. The Spanish Ministry of Public Works, Transport and Environment also issues an atlas of all the roads in Spain that is very good if you can find a recently updated edition.

Parking

The most important Spanish term to know is *aviso grúa*, which translates loosely as 'don't even think of parking here because I will have your car towed away and you will pay a pound of flesh to get it back'. Read posted parking regulations carefully to avoid being towed, as parking is prohibited on some streets at certain hours. Parking on a taxi-rank is also a towable offence.

Parking in Andalucían towns can be difficult. In small towns, park on the outskirts (near the bullring is often good) or on the side of the highway and walk into town. In larger towns, be resigned to using car parks. If parking on the street, especially in a blue-lined or yellow-lined zone, purchase a parking permit either from an automated machine nearby or from one of the 'parking assistants'. In many cities the assistants wear hats or badges indicating their official status – many municipalities give the concession to the handicapped. If you do receive a parking ticket – pay up. Spain has an agreement with several countries, including Ireland and the UK, to recover outstanding fines.

Lights

Sidelights and dipped headlights should be used between sunset and sunrise, in poor visibility and in tunnels. Full headlights are prohibited in built-up areas and rear fog lamps should only be used in the event of very poor visibility. Headlights on unmodified right-hand drive vehicles illuminate the wrong side of the road when motoring in Europe. Drivers of vehicles from the UK and Ireland should affix beam benders, available as stick-on accessories from car parts dealers, to their headlights.

Mobile Phones

The use of mobile phones and any other communications apparatus is forbidden at all times when driving unless the vehicle is fitted with a hands-free unit.

Seat belts

Buckle up. Seat belt usage is mandatory. If a vehicle is fitted with rear seat belts, they must also be used. Fines for failure to comply can exceed e90.

TELERUTA

For information on road works, weather and traffic conditions, check the local newspapers, or the recorded information service in Spain (tel: TELERUTA, freephone within Spain 900 123505.

Security

Theft from cars are all too common, especially in Sevilla and the larger cities, with foreign-registered cars a clear target. Do not leave anything visible in a parked car. Break-ins are common in urban areas, beaches and in remote scenic areas. When selecting an overnight car park, look for broken glass on the pavement. If you find it, choose a different car park. Remove any identification indicating that you are driving a rental vehicle, and when it gets dusty and dirty, do not be tempted to wash it. Make sure you remove the keys from inside the car, at petrol stations, for instance, or while you are unloading your luggage on arrival at a hotel or apartment. Don't leave anything of value in the boot. If possible remove or disable any radios or audio equipment when leaving your car. Keep your important documents with you, leaving photocopies, whenever possible, in a safe place. Also keep an eye on anyone nearby who might be watching. Car thieves gravitate to shiny, recent-model vehicles, figuring that tourists are more likely to have something valuable inside.

Speed limits

The following speed limits apply throughout Spain unless otherwise indicated:

Motorways 120 kph
Dual carriageways or with overtaking lanes 100 kph
Other roads 90 kph
Built-up areas 50kph

Cars with caravans in tow are limited to a maximum speed of 80kph on motorways and dual carriageways and 70kph on other roads.

Road signs

Aparcamiento – parking
Calzada deteriorada – bad road
Calzada estrecha – narrow road
Cambio de sentido – change direction
Ceda el paso – give way
Cuidado – drive with care
Cruce peligroso – dangerous
 crossroad
Curva peligrosa – dangerous bend
Despecio – slow
Desvío/desviación – detour
Dirección única – one-way street
Estaciónamiento prohibido –
 no parking
Gasolinera – petrol station
Mantenga su derecha – keep to
 the right

Mantenga su izquierda – keep to
 the left
Obras – roadworks
Peaje – toll
Peligro – danger
Prioridad a la derecha – priority to
 the right
Prioridad a la izquierda – priority to
 the left
Prohibido el paso – road closed
Salida – exit

SPANISH ROAD SIGNS

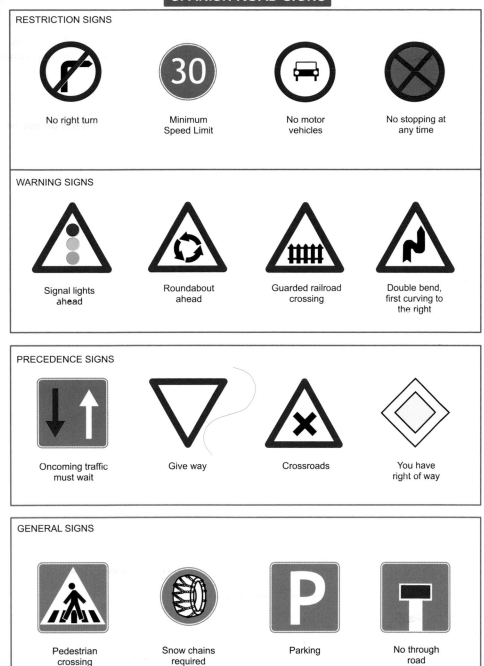

RESTRICTION SIGNS

No right turn

Minimum
Speed Limit

No motor
vehicles

No stopping at
any time

WARNING SIGNS

Signal lights
ahead

Roundabout
ahead

Guarded railroad
crossing

Double bend,
first curving to
the right

PRECEDENCE SIGNS

Oncoming traffic
must wait

Give way

Crossroads

You have
right of way

GENERAL SIGNS

Pedestrian
crossing

Snow chains
required

Parking

No through
road

Thanks to the following website for its kind permission to reproduce the above signs:
www.eurodriveregs.co.uk

Getting to Andalucía

By air

Most major international airlines serve Madrid's Barajas airport or the Málaga airport on the Costa del Sol with their own scheduled flights or through code-sharing arrangements. Spain's national carrier, Iberia, has the most scheduled flights to both airports and best connecting service to Sevilla, Jerez and Almería. Travellers from the UK can also elect to fly into Gibraltar. You can also book your flight online through several companies, including Easyjet and Monarch.

In addition, UK and Ireland travellers can also choose to travel on charter flights, usually run by package holiday firms that sell unfilled seats to 'flights-only' passengers. Charter flights are often less expensive but have the disadvantages of fixed return dates and often inhumane arrival and departure hours.

Most scheduled flights from North America arrive in Madrid, requiring a transfer to a regional flight or some form of land transportation to reach Andalucía. Charter flights are sometimes available to Málaga from New York, Washington, Miami and Toronto. Travellers from South Africa, Australia and New Zealand will generally fly into a European hub city outside Spain before changing airlines to connect to Madrid or Málaga. All European destinations are usually priced at a common fare. Particularly good connections are also available via Argentina.

All Spanish airports have some form of public transport into the city as well as car-hire facilities.

By train

Travellers arriving in Madrid may prefer to make their way overland to Andalucía. The quickest, most comfortable way to travel is on the AVE high-speed trains to Córdoba and Sevilla that depart from Atocha station. The AVE covers the 471km from Madrid to Sevilla in just 2 hours. Less luxurious but swift Talgo 200 trains – conventional electric trains running on improved tracks – serve Cádiz, Huelva and Málaga. The Málaga trip on the Talgo 200 from Madrid's Atocha station takes about 4½ hours.

Reaching other points in Andalucía by train from Madrid means taking the slower standard RENFE service, which also leaves from Atocha station. One line runs to Linares–Baeza north of Jaén, where it divides into branches for Córdoba and Sevilla to the west and Granada to the south. Between Linares–Baeza and Granada, at Moreda, another branch splits off southeast to Almería. Málaga trains pass through

Córdoba. Cádiz and Huelva are reached through Sevilla. At Bobadilla, between Córdoba and Málaga, a branch heads off southwest to Ronda and Algeciras.

For information on the complete schedules and fares of Spanish trains, contact RENFE, *tel: (90) 224–0202; www.renfe.es*

Connections for making the entire journey by train from Britain have improved with the opening of the Channel Tunnel, but remain a test of endurance, requiring 1–2 days to reach Málaga for about the same cost as a direct flight. UK travellers can inquire at Eurostar; *tel: (0870) 518–6186; www.eurostar.com*

By road

Travel from Britain to Andalucía by bus is an arduous journey. Connecting to Andalucía by bus from Madrid can be more interesting, as the roads pass through a range of landscapes, but plan on wasting the better part of a full day in transit. Buses from Madrid depart from Estación Sur de Autobuses, *c/ Méndez Alvaro; tel: (91) 468–4200*. Travellers planning to hire a car should arrange for pick-up in Andalucía, rather than spending the first 7–8 hours after arrival coping with traffic. The main highway to Andalucía from Madrid is the N-IV to Córdoba, Sevilla and Cádiz. At Bailén, additional *autovías* branch toward Jaén, Granada, Almería or Málaga. An alternate route from Madrid is to take the N401, which becomes the N420, and passes through Toledo and Ciudad Real on the way to Córdoba.

By ferry

Some travellers from the UK prefer to reach Spain by ferry so that they can bring their own cars. A ferry service from Great Britain to Spain's north coast operates from Portsmouth to Bilbao. The 34-hour crossing is operated by P&O European Ferries (*tel: (0870) 242–4999; www.poportsmouth.com*). Brittany Ferries (*tel: (0870) 536–0360; www.brittany-ferries.com*) operates a minimum 24-hour crossing from Plymouth to Santander, in northern Spain.

From Bilbao or Santander, the most direct driving route is to head first to Burgos, and then it's a pretty straight 240km to Madrid.

Setting the scene

Places and peoples

Andalucía is where Europe yearns south toward Africa – an elliptical mass of limestone walled off from the rest of Iberia by the low, glacier-rounded hills of the Sierra Morena. Four geological zones wrap across this southernmost region of Spain: the Sierra Morena, the Guadalquivir valley and its associated plains, a band of high mountain ranges and long sandy coasts on both the Atlantic and Mediterranean. Almost the entire 87,000-km² area of Andalucía is supported on limestone bedrock, buckled into jagged, crumbly mountains each time Europe and Africa collided in the eternal bump and grind of plate tectonics. The very softness of the rock makes it subject to erosion by wind and especially by water, which has carved out extensive caves through the Andalucían mountains. These caverns, in turn, have preserved some of the earliest evidence of human incursions into Europe, from the 1.5 million-year-old bone fragments of *Homo erectus* found in Granada to the Neanderthal skulls of 50,000 years ago along the Costa de la Luz or the Palaeolithic cave paintings discovered on the coastal-facing mountains from Cádiz province east to Almería.

Evidence of the earliest cultures are found in archaeological digs: the copper-smelting people who lived near Antequera around 3000 BC and the engineers of dolmen-capped mausoleums built from 2500–1800 BC north of Almería. Practically every Andalucían village big enough to have a ruined castle also boasts a local archaeological museum. If it lacks Palaeolithic paintings, it is nonetheless guaranteed to display at least a few artefacts chronicling the progression of cultures that shaped Andalucía. Only a handful of statues and a few tantalising pieces of gold jewellery crafted from ore extracted along the Río Tinto remain of ancient Tartessos, which flourished southwest of Sevilla around 1000 BC. Actually, the Bible alludes to Tartessian women dancing with castanets, perhaps the culture's most ancient and persistent legacy.

But the Phoenician traders who founded Cádiz around 1100 BC and the Greeks who followed them left more than statues and necklaces. They brought the olive tree and grapevine, establishing the basis for enduring agricultural industries, as well as the potter's wheel, which made possible the creation of urns to ship oil and wine throughout the Mediterranean basin. The Romans were drawn into the Iberian Peninsula in their 3rd century BC war with Carthage. They came, they saw, they conquered. In the process, they transformed Andalucía into a unified, coherent colony fit to stand as a country in its own right.

Under the *Pax Romana*, Andalucía became one of the most productive Roman regions outside Italy, producing wheat and wine from the Guadalquivir valley and plains, olive oil from the mountainsides and the fermented anchovy sauce of *garum* along the coast. By the 1st century BC, the Romans had made Córdoba capital of the province of Baetica, which encompassed Andalucía and some adjacent portions of Extremadura and Castilla-La Mancha. Rome gave Baetica its language, its legal system, Christianity and an infrastructure of roads, bridges and aqueducts, some of which are still in service. Baetica gave Rome three emperors – Theodosius, Hadrian and Trajan – and the philosopher Seneca.

When Germanic invaders swamped the Roman Empire, Baetica wound up, in the 6th century AD, in the hands of the Visigoths who almost immediately assimilated Roman ways. Their legacy lies principally in Gothic churches, most either in ruins or subsumed under later mosques and churches. By the beginning of the 8th century the Visigoths were squabbling among themselves over the royal succession when one of the contenders for the throne made the fatal error of seeking military assistance from the Muslims in Morocco.

In 711, general Tarik ibn Ziyad crossed the Straits of Gibraltar from Tangier with 9000 Berber troops. As they swept through the crumbling kingdom, they were welcomed at every turn by the Celtic slaves and Jews who had suffered under the Visigoths. In 712 Tarik solidified the Moorish hold on the Guadalquivir valley and seized the capital at Córdoba, fated to become the first great Moorish city. Within a few years, the Moors (as Muslims were called in Europe) held most of the Iberian Peninsula and had crossed the Pyrenees, only to be stopped in 732 at Poitiers by Charles Martel, the grandfather of Charlemagne. The Moors called their new lands 'al-Andalus', the name that survives for the heart of the kingdom, Andalucía. Yet the fighting between Moors and Christians never really stopped, as Christian strongholds in northern Spain began the slow, 800-year march of the Reconquest – the crucible in which the Spanish identity was ultimately born.

Many of Andalucía's 'monuments' date from the struggle, as the Moors quickly read the landscape and established hilltop towns to control the mountain passes and river valleys. Over the centuries every high point to the horizon bristled with fortifications, even the sweeping plains of the *campiña* on the south side of the Guadalquivir valley. That legacy remains in the ruined castles and in place names. Throughout the high mountain ranges of southern Andalucía, towns are called 'Alcalá' or fortress or are identified as *de la Frontera*, 'of the frontier'. And the legacy also remains in the string of Mediterranean coastal watchtowers, ever vigilant for Christian invaders and for Norman, Viking and North African pirates.

Below
Baeza

The fall of the Umayyad dynasty in Córdoba in 1031 marked the slow ebb of Moorish dominance in Andalucía, as the region broke up into dozens of independent *taifas* ruled by local strongmen. The second great Moorish city, Sevilla, reunited al-Andalus in 1163, but less than 50 years later, the allied Christian kings of the north breached the Sierra Morena. Led by Fernando III of Castilla, victorious armies marched into Córdoba in 1236 and Sevilla in 1248. Independent Christian armies like the Knights of the Templar seized Moorish hill towns and al-Andalus crumbled. Only the kingdom of Granada, which made a pact with Castilla that included annual tribute payments, managed to hold on to become the last and perhaps greatest of the Moorish cities. But even the glories of the Nasrid kings of Granada could not stop the Holy War of Reconquest launched by Fernando and Isabela in 1482 that resulted in the fall of Granada on 2 January 1492.

Ruler of a New World

The year 1492 was a turning point for Andalucía in more ways than one. In a bid to refill the royal coffers after the Reconquest, Fernando and Isabela gave the go-ahead to Genoese navigator Cristóbal Colón, or Christopher Columbus, for his voyages of discovery. Columbus

Moorish terms

alcazaba fortified enclosure

alcázar fortified palace

caliph prince who represented spiritual and civil power

emir prince or leader

medina town or urban centre

mezquita mosque

mihrab prayer niche of mosque oriented toward Mecca

Morisco Muslim, nominally baptised as Christian, who remained in Spain after the Reconquest

Mozárabe Christian living under Moorish rule

Mudéjar During the Reconquest, a Muslim who was permitted to remain under Christian rule without converting. Also, the architecture built by Moorish craftsmen under Christian rule, and more generally Moorish-inspired architecture

taha district

taifa small Moorish kingdom

recruited his ships and sailors from the Atlantic coast between Huelva and Cádiz, a region that remembers him well with a trail of sites associated with the explorer and re-creations of his vessels. But Columbus spent a lot of time in Sevilla and even Córdoba, as the Río Guadalquivir was navigable by ocean-going vessels in his day. Where today tourist boats set off for a leisurely cruise down the river to Sanlúcar, caravels once set sail to cross the Atlantic.

For three centuries the riches of New World trade flowed into Andalucía, making Cádiz the great treasure port and Sevilla the administrative centre of the American colonies. The fortifications of Cádiz harbour date from this era, as the treasure ships were attractive prey to pirates and foreign navies, and trade wealth funded the swift reconstruction of the city after the 1755 earthquake.

Sevilla flourished as the centre of world commerce and a magnet for bankers, traders and speculators from across Europe. It quickly developed into a sophisticated and cosmopolitan centre, spawning a spurt of artistic creativity. (Murillo and Velázquez were born in Sevilla and Zurbarán did most of his work there.) Many of the noble families that had received their titles as reward for fighting the Moors were awarded New World holdings *in absentia*, entitling them to a percentage of the new wealth. Throughout the 16th–18th centuries they commissioned Renaissance and baroque palaces, churches and convents, bequeathing a monumental architecture that stands cheek by jowl with Moorish fortresses and Gothic churches of the Reconquest.

Passions

Andalucía is a land of deep feeling, where emotion is meant to be expressed. Pleasure is 'enjoyed with the rapture of children', as 19th-century British travel writer Richard Ford observed; courage is celebrated in a frenzy of adoration and the deepest sorrows are bewailed with unremitting grief. This expressive quality of Andalucían character is manifested most explicitly in the region's religious spectacles, its music and dance, and in the bullfight. It is no coincidence that Andalucían *ferias* – complete with flamenco and bullfighting – inevitably follow close on the heels of the local holy days.

The most widespread of Andalucían religious extravaganzas are the processions associated with Semana Santa (Easter Week) in which holy images related to the Passion of Christ, the Crucifixion and the Resurrection are carried around the parish or city. Virtually every church, no matter how poor its parishioners may be, has one or more 'parade floats' for the Christian scenes. These are roughly 2x3m and are usually heavily encrusted in silver decoration, weighing as much as 500kg. During Semana Santa they are hoisted onto the shoulders of 20–30 members of a penitential brotherhood, who shuffle along the parade route in time to droning, modal music, pausing every 10m or so to rest. The parades typically take hours to pass, lasting deep into the night. In large cities like Sevilla and Málaga, there are processions every night; smaller towns may be limited to Good Friday and Easter Sunday morning.

The other typically Andalucían emotive outpouring of faith is the *romería* or pilgrimage. Pilgrims elsewhere may go to grand cathedrals or even to Jerusalem, but the typical Andalucían destination is a remote mountaintop or the depths of a miasmal swamp, where one of the various manifestations of the Virgin Mary appeared as a carved image to a pious peasant, usually about the same time that the Christians retook the area from the Muslims. These statues are often associated with miraculous cures, bountiful harvests and other acts of God. Some *romerías* have grown into major cultural phenomena, annually attracting tens of thousands of believers from across the region. In mid-May, for example, all roads heading west are lined with caravans of automobiles and farm equipment with signs indicating they are heading to El Rocío.

Like the *romería*, the bullfight channels the wilful primitivism of the Andalucían spirit into ritual expression. The spectacle is clearly not for everyone and is controversial even in Spain. But some form of bullfighting in the region predates even the Roman presence. The 'modern' style of fighting the bull on foot, *la lidia*, really emerged in the mid 18th century, with three generations of the Romero family in Ronda establishing many of the basic moves and gestures.

The bullfight has evolved as a ritualised display of courage, skill and grace in the ancient conflict between man and beast. The *corrida* usually consists of three matadors fighting two bulls each in the course of an afternoon. Each fight generally lasts 15–20 minutes and consists

Architectural styles of Andalucía

Baroque Spanish baroque of the 17th and 18th centuries followed classical structural proportions but emphasised extravagant ornament. The term is also applied to the contemporaneous Golden Age of Spanish painters – Velázquez, Murillo, Zurbarán and José Ribera.

Churrigueresque The Churriguera brothers, who drew on Moorish and Plateresque styles for exceedingly ornamental façades on late Baroque architecture, were widely imitated.

Moorish The Muslims brought Near Eastern construction techniques and design motifs that evolved into a unique vernacular style. Among its characteristic elements were the use of brick as a building material, horseshoe arches, elaborate tiles, carved plaster or stucco, and fountains and gardens as essential design elements.

Mudéjar Muslim craftsmen working under Christian rule often adapted Muslim design motifs to Christian themes and building styles. Mudéjar buildings often have intricate wooden ceilings. Late 19th- and early 20th-century Andalucían architects striving for a regional style drew inspiration from the 13th–15th-century Mudéjar buildings in a decorative revival.

Plateresque An early 16th-century style in which façades were decorated with stone carvings and complex ornamentation that resembled the fluid lines and volumetric rendering associated with silversmiths.

Renaissance Spanish Renaissance architecture shares the classic proportions and simple lines of the earlier Italian revival of Roman motifs, but tends to indulge in the Spanish fascination with ornament and dissolves in a generation into full-blown baroque.

of three stages. In the first, matador and bull face each other and horseback picadors lance the bull in its withers to weaken the beast and make him put his head down and horns forward. In the second stage, the matador watches as the *banderilleros* stick short beribboned *banderillas* into the withers to goad the bull. Finally, in the *muleta*, matador and bull are alone in the ring as the matador wears down the beast, ideally completing the fight with a single plunge of the sword and a clean kill. Most of the great matadors – and most of all matadors, for that matter – have been and still are Andalucían. The best matadors used to enjoy the status of folk heroes. Bullfights are now a television staple, and matadors are treated like film and pop stars.

The quintessential expression of passion in Andalucía is the music and dance of flamenco, an art that is central to the regional identity. With influences as ancient as the Moorish guitar, Celtic modal song and Jewish percussion, flamenco could only have arisen in Andalucía. Always part of the folk tradition, it began to coalesce in small villages and urban *barrios* alike in the 18th century. Gypsies were among the first to sing, play and dance flamenco professionally in the 19th century, and the art came to be identified as Gypsy by the rest of the world.

But not in Andalucía. Both traditional and contemporary flamenco is part of every celebration, from the local agricultural fair to impromptu parties on the street. Each region has its special styles – only the *malagüeno* traditionally uses castanets, for example – and some regions emphasise the dancer, others the singer. Most travellers are introduced to flamenco in the frankly commercial performances of nightclub-style *tablaos*. Some of these performers are quite accomplished, and true

Right
The Costa Oriental

Overleaf
Looking from the Costa de la Luz
across to the coast of Africa

aficionados will find themselves seeking out the bars and *peñas* (clubs) where *flamenco puro* and the *canto jondo* ('deep song') are performed with more spontaneous joy and more heartfelt *duende,* or passion.

The edible landscape

In Andalucía, to a large extent, what you see is what you eat and drink: wine from the fields of grapes, olives from the hillsides, cheeses from the herds encountered by the side of the road.

Andalucíans pride themselves on the wines known collectively as 'sherry', which come from Jerez de la Frontera, Sanlúcar de la Barrameda, El Puerto de Santa María and nearby villages where Palomino grapes spring from the chalky soil. The most delicate and distinctive sherries are the *finos,* which need the least ageing, sweetening or blending. A great *fino* has vitality and a freshness like bread from the oven. Softer and darker, *amontillados* are *finos* that lacked youthful brilliance but acquire a dark, rich tang with ageing. Wines that seem heavy or overpowering when young end up becoming *olorosos,* a class of sherries that are, at their best, plump and smooth. So-called 'cream sherry' is a sweetened style of *oloroso.*

Andalucíans drink sherry at every turn – a *fino* with the local green olives as an apertif, *manzanilla* (the *fino* of Sanlúcar) with boiled shrimp or grilled *rape* (known as both angler-fish and monkfish), *amontillado* to ward off the chill of winter, and *oloroso* as an alternative to brandy to cap off the evening. The standard beverage with *tapas* is a *fino* or *manzanilla.* Note that Andalucíans never just order a sherry – they ask for the style or specify the brand.

The most classic accompaniments to sherry are ham and cheese. Andalucía does not make such a fetish of its cheeses as La Mancha, but goats roam the countryside and large herds of sheep are pastured on scrubby hillsides. Almost every little village produces excellent cheese. Ask for *queso* and you will usually get a firm cheese similar in style to the more famous Manchego.

Hams hang above every bar in Andalucía, and Andalucíans can discern nuances in flavour that escape anyone who has not grown up with the same reverence for salt-cured, air-dried hams. *Aficionados* generally agree that the finest hams come from the black pigs of the Sierra Aracena, and that the finest of the fine are produced in Jabugo. Such hams, identified as *jamón ibérico,* can sell for more than €34 per kilo and €6 for a small plate of paper-thin slices. White pigs also produce extraordinary hams, especially in Alpujarra de Granada. Generically identified as *jamón serrano,* the best hams of Trevélez or Portugos can fetch almost as much as the Jabugo hams.

An essential element in all these foods is the ageing process, but along the coast, freshness is everything. Even in some of the largest resorts, early risers can head to the beach to watch fisherman set their nets for the mixture of fish that will be fried and served within hours as what one Spanish gourmet called 'an anthology of the ocean'.

Touring itineraries

The Grand Tour

The longest of the three trips, this itinerary of 'monumental Andalucía' circles the great Moorish cities with a good look at the Renaissance achievements of Jaén province and a tour through the sherry towns and elegant Cádiz.

Begin at Sevilla (*see page 164*), driving east 138km on the N-IV *autovía* through the wheat and sunflower plains around Carmona and Ecija, detailed in 'East of Sevilla' (*see page 180*). The first major capital of Moorish al-Andalus awaits at Córdoba (*see page 188*).

The landscape becomes mountainous and the villages smaller as you follow the 144km route detailed in 'Jaén's high country' (*see page 224*), going the whole distance to the mountain pass where Christian armies began the Reconquest, then passing through Linares for another 6km to Ubeda, the open-air museum of architecture. Drive west 57km through Baeza and into Jaén to enjoy all three cities detailed in 'Renaissance cities' (*see page 212*). The N323 heads directly south 95km from Jaén to Granada, the last of the Moorish capitals (*see page 232*).

From Granada, the A92 heads west 100km to Antequera, detailed in 'North of Málaga' (*see page 72*). The same road continues another 129km west to Arcos de la Frontera, featured in 'White Villages' (*see page 130*), then 35km west to Jerez de la Frontera, central city in 'Sherry country' (*see page 118*). From Jerez it's a quick 36km drive to Cádiz (*see page 98*) on the N-IV. Return to Sevilla by driving 120km north on the A4 toll road.

Mountains and beaches

This itinerary, which circles the mountains and beaches of southwestern Andalucía is a good scenic drive with many opportunities for hiking, windsurfing and other outdoor activities. It is a particularly good route for a second visit – when you feel that you have had enough of big churches and palaces and would like to experience the countryside.

Begin at Málaga (*see page 42*) and drive west on the narrow mountain road of A366 for 97km to Ronda, featured in 'Heart of the Frontera' (*see page 108*). From Ronda, follow the 'White Villages' driving tour (*see page 130*) in reverse for 83km across the Sierra Grazalema to Arcos de la Frontera. From Arcos, the A393 leads 34km south to Medina Sidonia, detailed in 'Heart of the Frontera' (*see page 108*) and another 29km south to Vejer de

la Frontera, a stunning hilltop village featured in 'Costa de la Luz' (*see page 90*).

At Vejer, pick up the suggested driving tour to see the small fishing villages and stunning dune-backed beached on the way to Tarifa, where it might be worth stopping to wind-surf. Continue on to Algeciras on the N340, then detour at San Roque to visit Gibraltar (*see page 82*). Returning to the N340 brings you to the 'Costa del Sol' (*see page 52*) and returns to Málaga with a choice of carrying along the coastal N340 or picking up the AP7 toll road which runs between Guadiaro and Málaga.

The roads less travelled

Travellers who enjoy long vistas and high cliffs above crashing seas and who want to avoid crowds would do well to head east from Málaga rather than west. This circuit takes in the less-populated coast between Málaga and Almería, circles through some of the most dramatically different scenery in all of Andalucía, and traces its way through the scenic valleys of Las Alpujarras.

From Málaga (*see page 42*) take the ring road east around the city and follow the route outlined in 'Costa del Sol Oriental and Axarquía' (*see page 64*). The 110km route to Salobreña includes some wonderful vistas where the mountains come within 1km of the sea and the road follows the seaward ridge. This is the area where the Moorish watchtowers – built to provide an early warning system against pirates or sea-borne invaders – are still most evident. From Salobreña, the N340 continues another 120km east through hothouse agricultural country to reach Almería, detailed in 'Almería and environs' (*see page 266*).

At Almería, follow the route for 'Costa de Almería' (*see page 274*) as far as the directions to the N340. At the N340, follow signs to the A370 to reach the 'Desierto de Tabernas', detailed in 'Almería and environs' (*see page 266*). On the way back toward Almería, turn right onto N324 to follow the suggested tour of 'Las Alpujarras de Almería' (*see page 258*). At Laujar de Andarax, continue west on the C322, turning right after 14km to tour through the High Alpujarras, detailed in 'Las Alpujarras de Granada' (*see page 246*). After passing through Lanjarón, follow the N323 north to Granada to pick up the A329 west, and then the A359 turn in 90km to return 31km to Málaga.

Málaga

Ratings

Gastronomy ●●●●○

Architecture ●●●○○

Entertainment
●●●○○

History ●●●○○

Museums ●●●○○

Beaches ●●○○○

Nature and
wildlife ●●○○○

Shopping and
crafts ●●○○○

Málaga sticks out on the Costa del Sol because it is a vibrant urban centre. While not unfriendly, Malagueños move purposefully down their streets, seemingly more abrupt than their resort-town cousins. The buildings are gracious, the parks are green and glorious, but there is always business to be transacted, even if the beach is only a five-minute walk away. As Andalucía's second largest city and the capital of the Costa del Sol, Málaga does not rely on tourism for its livelihood. Indeed, many travellers to the fabled coast go directly from airport to beach, unaware of Málaga's attractions. But the city has a full complement of historic sites, chic shops, sandy beaches and restaurants to keep visitors busy for a couple of days – especially those who crave the urban bustle and energy as a change of pace from days spent vegetating beneath a beach umbrella.

Getting there and getting around

ⓘ Oficina de Turismo
Casa del Jardinero-Park,
Avda Cervantes 1; tel: (95)
260–4410; closed Sun.
Several information kiosks
are stationed throughout
the city.

Oficina de Turismo
Junta de Andalucía
Pasaje de Chinitas 4;
tel: (95) 221–3445;
fax: (95) 222–9421; e-mail:
otmalaga@andalucia.org;
www.malagaturismo.com.
Provides information for
the entire region.

Arriving and departing: Most international flights to Andalucía land at Málaga's airport (*A340, Torremolinos; tel: (95) 204–8804*). The city centre can be reached by taxi (€€), train (€) or the number 19 bus (€).

Parking: Metered on-street parking is usually limited to a 1-hr maximum. Long-term car parks are found throughout the city.

Buses and trains: Buses leave from Alameda Principal for Pedregalejo Beach (number 11) and Gibralfaro (number 35). Discount passes are available for unlimited travel for one, three or five days on the Málaga commuter train that runs from the city to the beach at Fuengirola, with numerous stops including Torremolinos and Benalmádena.

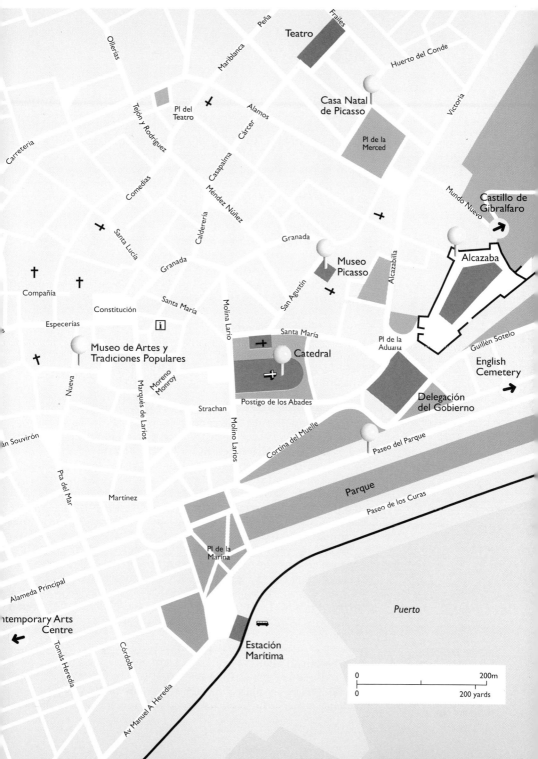

Sights

Alcazaba de Málaga
*Open Tue–Sun
0930–2000.*

Casa Natal de Picasso €
*Pl. Merced 15; open Mon–Sat
1100–1400 and 1700–2000,
Sun 1100–1400.*

Alcazaba**

Confounding the typical Andalucían pattern, the Alcazaba (citadel) does not dominate the highest point of the city, ceding that place of honour to the Gibralfaro. It does, however, occupy a good vantage point for watching the flow of cruise vessels, large tankers and container ships in the Bay of Málaga, and is floodlit at night. The Moors began fortifying the site in the 8th century, with the major building taking place after 1057 when Málaga became an independent *taifa*. The fortification's complex defence system – including three lines of walls, a walled corridor, parapets and watchtowers – made it almost impregnable. Today its military demeanour is softened by a profusion of palm trees and the brilliant blooms of bougainvillaea climbing the walls. The living quarters of the Alcazaba are as remarkable as its defensive structure, comprising one of the most complete groups of Islamic dwellings of the 11th and 12th centuries with their characteristically ornate columns and horseshoe arches. This section of the fortress houses a fascinating archaeological museum with a display that includes Islamic pottery found at the site and throughout the province. The Roman amphitheatre that sits at the foot of the Alcazaba walls near the main entrance is a reminder that Málaga figured as an important port for Baetica. Currently under restoration, there are some explanatory placards in English.

Casa Natal de Picasso**

Málaga's most famous native son was born in this house on one corner of the busy plaza Merced and lived here until the age of three. The house has undergone extensive renovations since Picasso's birth in 1881, but it's still intriguing to look out of the four big first-floor windows of the artist's former bedroom and imagine how his vision was formed by the busy square below. Today the room serves as a gallery and has been remodelled with gleaming wood floors and white walls. The collection includes many photographs of Picasso – from precocious child to famous adult – and a small selection of works on paper and ceramics that are well-suited to the exhibition spaces. The birthplace has not been forgotten by Christine Ruiz-Picasso, benefactress of the Museo Picasso. Her donations include illustrations for the book *Vingt Poèmes de Góngora* (1948) by Luis de Góngora y Argote (1561–1627), called the *padre de la poesía moderna*. The series of animated portraits are among Picasso's most flattering depictions of women.

Castillo de Gibralfaro*

The 14th-century Gibralfaro castle (*open daily 0930–2000*) sits above the Alcazaba, commanding the highest point in the city. Fortified since Phoenician times, the name translates from the Arabic as 'Lighthouse

Cathedral €
*c/ Molina Lario; open
Mon–Sat 1000–1845.
Closed Sunday except for
services.*

Mountain'. History does not record a lighthouse on this spot, but a beacon placed on this prominent peak could have been seen for great distances along the coast and out to sea. From the castle walls, the city and the harbour unfold below. This vantage allows for views into the bullring, and provides the unusual opportunity to look down on the Alcazaba for a bird's-eye view of the maze of defensive walls.

Cathedral✧✧

Málaga's cathedral, built on the site of the city's former main mosque, was begun in the 16th century but never finished. Its profile is easily distinguished on the skyline because only one of two planned towers was ever completed. The money for the second was instead donated to the American patriots to help fund their war for independence and at some point over the years the cathedral was dubbed *La Manquita*, or 'one-armed lady'. Although the cathedral has undergone renovations, plans to build the missing tower do not seem to be on the agenda. Inside, huge columns support a towering, ornate domed ceiling and create a space that reverberates with even the slightest noise. Highlights of the interior include a wooden choir stall, with detailed images of saints carved by Pedro de Mena, and the beautiful Gothic retable in the Capilla de Santa Bárbara, carved by Nicolás Tiller of Sevilla.

Below
Málaga's Alcazaba

English Cemetery
Pas. de Reding (beyond the Plaza de Toros); open Mon–Fri 0900–1700, Sat–Sun 0900–1100.

Museo Picasso €€
c/ San Agustín 8;
tel: (95) 260–2731;
www.museopicassomalaga.org;
open Mon–Sat 0900–2100,
Sun 0900–1400.

Right
Málaga bar commemorating Picasso

English Cemetery*

Málaga's British Protestants were no doubt appalled to find themselves among the 'infidels' to whom the Spaniards denied Christian burial – instead interring bodies upright, up to their necks, in the sand below the tide line. This situation was remedied in 1829 when the English Cemetery was founded by British consul William Mark to serve the growing expatriate population. Mark himself rests securely in a sepulchre in front of the Anglican St George's church in the grounds. Tombstone inscriptions detail military exploits and provide hints about lives lived abroad.

Museo Picasso***

The **Museo Picasso** is located in the 16th-century Buenavista Palace, near the cathedral, formerly the site of the Museo de Bellas Artes (Fine Arts Museum). The artist's daughter-in-law Christine Ruiz-Picasso has donated paintings, sculptures and ceramics valued at more than €85 million. The permanent collection spans Picasso's entire career, from his earliest work to several of his last paintings created shortly before his death in 1973. The works are shown in chronological order taking visitors on a didactic tour of his different 'periods', including Cubism.

The **Museo de Bellas Artes**** is housed in the old customs house (*aduana*) on the Paseo del Parque.

Museo de Artes y Costumbres Populares € c/ Pasillo de Santa Isabel 10; tel: (95) 221–7137; open Mon–Fri 1000–1330 and 1600–1900, Sat 1000–1330.

Contemporáneo de Málaga (Contemporary Arts Centre) € c/ Alemania; open Tue–Sun 1000–2000.

Museo de Bellas Artes € Paseo del Parque; tel: (95) 206–0215; open daily 1100–1400.

Museo de Artes y Costumbres Populares*

The tone of this colourful but earnest museum is set by the building, a 17th-century former inn with an arcaded central patio far simpler than those usually found in contemporaneous noble palacios of the era. The ambitious exhibits attempt to recapture the lifestyle and traditions of the area, including Málaga's role as a major trade port with the American colonies and the region's wine industry. Phoenician traders who founded the city in the 8th century BC are credited with planting the first vineyards that have for centuries produced the eponymous dessert wine. The museum also evokes bygone ways of domestic life with displays of tools and clothing and period rooms, including a country-house kitchen and modest bedroom. An extensive collection of 19th-century earthenware figurines depicts popular activities and folk heroes.

Contemporáneo de Málaga*

Opened in early 2003 in a former warehouse, this modern art gallery has a permanent exhibition of contemporary art, as well as temporary shows dedicated to both up and coming and renowned modern artists.

Paseo del Parque**

This broad swathe of greenery separates the city from the harbour and provides an elegant promenade along marble sidewalks, where ocean breezes calm the city's heat. Málaga gained this extension to the more modest Alameda Principal in the 1890s, when land was reclaimed during the construction of the Cánovas Harbour. The park features a botanical garden, where tall tropical trees provide deep shade and exotic flowers produce a riot of colour. Among the fountains and sculptures along the paseo, El Jazminero by Pimentel depicts the jasmine seller, one of the city's most colourful types.

Accommodation and food

Antigua Casa de Guardia € Alameda Principal 18; tel: (95) 221–4680. This wine bar seems little changed since its founding in 1840. Customers stand at a long wooden bar, watching bartenders draw Málaga dulce or seco from barrels and chalk up the tab on the bar. Even Picasso tossed back a few here.

Hotel Don Curro €€ c/ Sancha de Lara 7; tel: (95) 222–7200; fax: (95) 221–5946; e-mail: reservas@hoteldoncurro.com; www.doncurro.com. Near all the main attractions, the Don Curro dates from 1933 but has been updated without losing its traditional character.

Hotel Los Naranjos €€ Pas. de Sancha 35; tel: (95) 222–4316; fax: (95) 222–5975; e-mail: reserve@hotel-losnaranjos.com; www.hotel-losnaranjos.com. Located in a residential area about 1km from the city

Larios Centro *Avda de la Aurora 25* is a shopping centre with more than 100 stores, a supermarket and a food court. A large El Corte Inglés department store is a few blocks away.

4 Ingletes *c/ Marqués de Larios 3; tel: (95) 221–9914* has a good selection of original prints of modern and historic city scenes.

El Cantor de Jazz *c/ Lazcano 7; no tel.* Just one of several clubs in town where you can enjoy live jazz. The atmosphere here is suitably Chicago-style intimate, if smoky. Thursdays are best.

centre and near Caleta beach, Los Naranjos has 41 rooms and a garage for parking.

Lepanto € *c/ Marqués Larios 7; tel: (95) 222–6221.* A good place for sandwiches and elegant pastries on the city's best shopping street.

Mercado de Atarazanas *c/ Atarazanas 8 and 10* is the city's main produce market. The 19th-century building incorporates a 14th-century Moorish arch.

Parador de Málaga-Gibralfaro €€–€€€ *Castillo de Gibralfaro s/n; tel: (95) 222–1902; www.parador.es.* Located near the Gibralfaro castle, the Parador commands the same grand views of the city and harbour. The restaurant is known for its fried fish.

Restaurante Antonio Martín €€ *Paseo Marítimo s/n; tel: (95) 222–2113.* Elegant fish restaurant looking out on the beach frequented by matadors from the nearby bullring.

Restaurante Chinitas €€ *c/ El Moreno Monroy 4; tel: (95) 221–0972.* Enjoy traditional local cuisine in this century-old building with paintings of local bullfighters lining the walls. Specialities include oxtail and calf sirloin and *solomillo al vino de Málaga* (fillet steak in a wine sauce).

Vista Andalucía *Avenida de los Guindos; tel: (95) 223–1157.* Nightly flamenco shows here – olé!

Teatro Municipal Miguel de Cervantes *c/ Ramos Martín 2; tel: (95) 222–4100.* This historic theatre was inaugurated in 1870. It's worth attending a performance to get a glimpse at the large horseshoe-shaped canvas depicting an allegory of Málaga.

Plaza de Toros de la Malagueta *Paseo de Reding; tel: (95) 221–9482.* Those who do not want to see a bullfight can visit from 0900–1400.

Semana Santa *tel: (95) 260–4410.* Málaga is second only to Sevilla for its Holy Week processions, which occur nightly from Palm Sunday to Good Friday.

Feria de Málaga *tel: (95) 260–4410.* Málaga's main bullfighting season is held during this nine-day August event. One of Andalucía's largest summer festivals, it also includes fireworks, music and dancing.

Tryp Alameda €€ *Avda Aurora s/n; tel: (95) 236–8020; fax: (95) 236–8024; e-mail: alameda@trypnet.com; www.solmelia.com.* This cheerful small hotel designed mainly for business people is located at the Larios Centro shopping centre. It's an inexpensive cab ride to the main tourist sites.

The best *tapas* hopping in Málaga can be found around the historic centre of town. The most famous is **Bar Logueno**, *c/ Marín Garcia*; an L-shaped bar shoehorned into a deceptively small space crammed with a tantalising 75-plus choice of tapas. On nearby c/ Esparteros, **Rincón de Mata** has inexpensive, tasty tapas like *gambas al pil-pil* (spicy fresh prawns), while **Taperia Siglo XXI**, *Plaza de la Merced 12*, is a wonderful old-fashioned bar in the square where Picasso was born, specialising in delicious local cheeses and Serrano ham.

Suggested tour

Total distance: 7km for the main route, with the detour adding an extra 6km.

Time: A casual day.

Route: This walking tour begins at the **CASTILLO DE GIBRALFARO** ❶, the highest spot in the city, easily reached by bus or inexpensive cab ride. From here, it's all downhill. After exploring the fortification and getting an overview of the city and the harbour, stroll through the walled garden path to the **ALCAZABA** ❷.

Leaving the Alcazaba, note the Roman amphitheatre still under excavation. Follow c/ Alcazabilla to Pl. María Guerrero, which leads to Pl. de la Merced. Eateries, language schools and other establishments bear the name of the plaza's most famous former resident, Pablo Picasso. The **CASA NATAL DE PICASSO** ❸ sits on the north corner. Having had a taster, head next for the city's most famous new museum. Cross the plaza and head down c/ Granada, turning left onto c/ Agustín. The Museo Picasso is on your left. After perusing the museum, carry on down this street and turn right on c/ Santa Maria and left onto c/ Molina Lario.

Here you will find the **CATHEDRAL** ❹, easily identified by its missing tower. The smaller **Palacio Episcopal*** in front almost steals the scene with one of the city's most beautiful façades. With an impressive staircase and beautiful patio, the interior is well suited for its current use as an exhibition centre.

Follow c/ Salinas for the short walk from ecclesiastical Málaga to commercial Málaga; c/ Marqués de Larios is the city's best street for shopping and window shopping. At Pl. Constitución, double back on Larios, taking a left on to c/ Moreno Monroy if it is time for *tapas*.

El Jardín Botánico La Concepción €

4km north from city centre; tel: (95) 225–2148. The garden opens at 1000. Last guided tours begin at 1830 (Apr 1–Jun 20), 1930 (Jun 21–Sept 10), 1730 (Sept 11–Oct 20), 1630 (Oct 21–Dec 10), 1600 (Dec 11–Mar 31). Bus #2 goes to La Concepción (#61 at weekends), though the stop is a short walk from the entrance to the garden. By car, take the N331 north out of the city and turn at km166, following signs to the park.

Continue along Larios to **Alameda Principal**◆, which flows into the more stately and elegant **PASEO DEL PARQUE** ❺. Azulejo-covered benches dot the park and provide shady rest spots. Most are inscribed with poems and quotes singing the praises of Málaga, the *ciudad angélica*. Stalls of booksellers also line the promenade.

The park is so diverting that it's easy to overlook the delightful architecture on its north side. The former gardener's cottage now houses the tourist office, but the most spectacular building is the early 20th-century **Ayuntamiento**◆◆, which looks for all the world like an Art Nouveau confection transplanted from Budapest or even Paris. Cross the street to the grand entrance topped by classical statues and step inside to see the stained-glass windows on the staircase. This has to be one of the most enchanting places in the world to queue up to pay a parking fine.

The **Fuente Genovesa**◆ signals the end of the park. This Italian Renaissance fountain of the Three Graces was captured by pirates while being transported to Spain. Upon recovery, Carlos V ignored the original purchaser and deeded the fountain to the city. At the fountain, turn right on to Paseo de la Farola, with a lighthouse visible at the far end. Another statue by Pimentel captures **El Cenachero**◆ or 'fish seller' at work. Avda Vélez on the left leads to the Paseo Marítimo and the **Playa de la Malagueta**◆, Málaga's in-town sandy beach.

Detour: Continue along Paseo Marítimo for 2–3km to **Pedregalejo Beach**◆◆, the old fishing quarters that contains many of the city's best casual fish restaurants. Málaga is known for its *fritura malagueña*, a combination of fried fish, anchovies and squid. The best and freshest fish is nearest to the source. Retrace the walking route to Playa de la Malagueta or take a bus to return to the city centre.

From Playa de la Malagueta take c/ Keromnes to Paseo de Reding, which passes the **Plaza de Toros**◆. The **ENGLISH CEMETERY** ❻ is about 150m east of the bullring. Continue on Paseo de Reding to complete the circuit back to the Fuente Genovesa and the start of the Paseo del Parque.

Also worth exploring

The transplanted English gardening impulse has created the striking **Jardín Botánico la Concepción** amid parched hills. The gardens were begun in the 1850s by Amalia Heredia Livermore, the granddaughter of the British consul, and her husband Jorge Loring Oyarzábal, the Marqués de Casa Loring. The city now owns the 50-hectare estate, ranked among Europe's finest tropical gardens. The well-established perennials are known as 'the garden with the hundred shades of green', but other colours provide seasonal accents: golden and copper leaves in autumn, yellow mimosa in winter, wisteria in spring, and blue water lilies in summer.

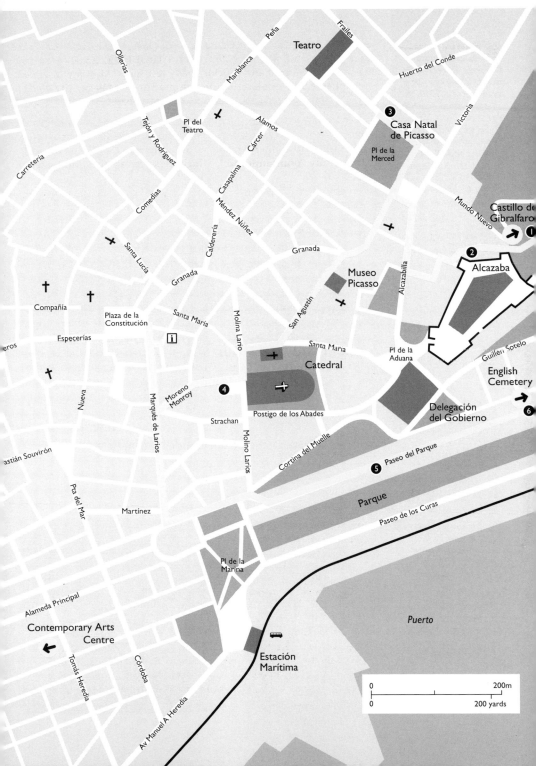

Ollerías

Peña

Frailes

Teatro

Mariblanca

Huerto del Conde

Carretería

Tejón y Rodríguez

Pl del Teatro

Álamos

Cárcel

Victoria

3 Casa Natal de Picasso

Pl de la Merced

Comedias

Casapalma

Méndez Núñez

Mundo Nuevo

Castillo de Gibralfaro 1

Santa Lucía

Caldereria

Granada

2 Alcazaba

Compañía

Granada

Santa María

San Agustín

Museo Picasso

Alcazabilla

Plaza de la Constitución

Especerías

Molina Lario

Santa María

Pl de la Aduana

Guillén Sotelo

English Cemetery

eros

i

Catedral

6

Nueva

Moreno Monroy

4

Santa María

Delegación del Gobierno

Marqués de Larios

Strachan

Postigo de los Abades

Molino Larios

Cortina del Muelle

astián Souvirón

Pta del Mar

Martínez

5 Paseo del Parque

Parque

Paseo de los Curas

Alameda Principal

Pl de la Marina

Contemporary Arts Centre

Puerto

Tomás Heredia

Córdoba

Estación Marítima

Av Manuel A Heredia

| 0 | | 200m |
| 0 | | 200 yards |

The Costa del Sol

Ratings

Beaches ●●●●●

Shopping and crafts ●●●●●

Entertainment ●●●●○

Gastronomy ●●●●○

Nature and wildlife ●●●○○

Architecture ●●○○○

History ●●○○○

Museums ●●○○○

The 85km stretch of Mediterranean coast west of Málaga to Estepona is Spain's famed Costa del Sol. With 325 sunny days per year, the region has striking vistas where mountains tower just inland from the sea, and a nearly continuous strand of clean beaches, including 15 with EU Blue Flags. While Costa del Sol has some of Spain's densest development, it is not just a concrete jungle. It offers high-density resorts on the east end in Torremolinos, Benalmádena and Fuengirola, a luxurious middle belt centred on Marbella, and a contemplative western segment anchored by Estepona. The towns follow a similar pattern: delightful beaches flanked by a fishing fleet and a yacht marina, the core of an old town, or *casco antiguo*, and a modern commercial centre. Extensive hotel renovations and improved roads, landscaping, seafront promenades and litter control have given this venerable resort area new legs.

BENALMÁDENA❖❖

ℹ **Oficina de Turismo** *c/ Antonio Machado 14; tel: (95) 244–2494; fax: (95) 244–0678; www.benalmadena.com*

♧ **Casino de Benalmádena** *Hotel Torrequebrada, Carretera. Bacuibak 340; tel: (95) 244–6000. Formal dress, also piano bar and floor show.*

A nearly seamless westward extension of Torremolinos, **Benalmádena Costa**❖ is a densely packed area of high-rise hotels and flats. Its 9km of beaches include a small nudist beach, Playa Las Yucas, and a popular **casino**❖. About 1km inland from the beaches is souvenir-central, the shopping area of **Arroyo de Miel**❖. The whitewashed **Benalmádena Pueblo**❖❖ in the hill provides something of a respite.

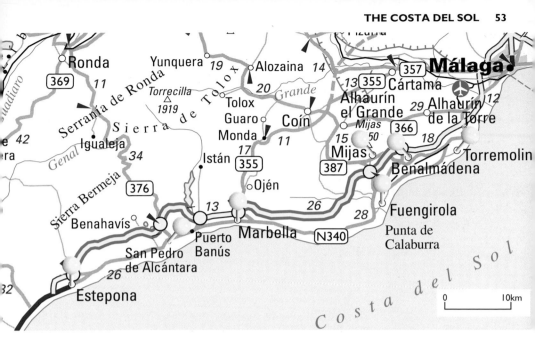

Accommodation and food in Benalmádena

Hotel Triton €€ *Avda Antonio Machado 29; tel: (95) 244–3240; www.besthotels.es*. Set in beautiful gardens near a golf course at a quiet remove from the beach.

The best casual dining is found at *chiringuitos* (snack bars) on the beaches and in *marisquerías* (seafood bars) along the *paseo*.

ESTEPONA✦✦✦

ⓘ Oficina de Turismo
Avda San Lorenzo; tel: (95) 280–0913; fax: (95) 280–2260; e-mail: estepona@vnet.es; www.infoestepona.com

↻ Follow signs from N340 to 'centro', avoiding the exit for 'zona polígono'.

Ⓟ The scarce on-street parking is free. A large underground car park serves the main beach on Avda España.

Graceful and low-rise, with the coast's largest fishing fleet, Estepona evokes the Costa del Sol before the tourism boom. Despite a glut of construction near the yacht harbour, the town stands back 100m or more from its broad beach, **Playa Rada✦✦**, and seaside *paseo*. The *casco antiguo*✦✦ is full of shops offering attractive merchandise, rather than souvenirs and superb small restaurants. Some set their tables beneath orange trees on squares arranged around bubbling fountains. Prevailing breezes make Estepona the most temperate spot on the Costa del Sol – cooler in the summer, warmer in the winter. To escape the wind, locals favour **Playa Cristo✦✦** in a sheltered cove about 4km west from town.

Estepona has undergone considerable development, partly as a result of the expressway and new toll road. On the edges of town there are now luxury resort developments and the port is fast becoming a contender with Puerto Banús with more choice of sophisticated

A city bus runs hourly along c/ España with a stop at Playa Cristo.

The Wed market is on *Avda Juan Carlos I* and the Sun market in *Puerto de Estepona*, both 0900–1400.

Selwo Wildlife Park € *Carretera C-N340 Km 162.5; tel: (90) 219–0482; www.selwo.es; open daily 1000–1900.*

restaurants and nightlife. Just east of town at Selwo Wildlife Park, more than 2000 animals from the five continents live in semi-wild conditions, primarily viewed from safari-style vehicles.

Accommodation and food in Estepona

Costa Natura €–€€ *N340 km151; tel: (95) 280–8065; fax: (95) 280–8074; e-mail: info@costanaturaholidays.com; www.costanatura holidays.com.* Situated on the coast, this small-scale group of white bungalows is the Costa del Sol's oldest nudist/naturist resort.

Las Duñas Beach Hotel & Spa €€€ *N340 km163, east of town; tel: (95) 279–4345; fax: (95) 279–5554; e-mail: lasdunas@las-dunas.com; www.las-dunas.com.* One of the most luxurious properties west of Marbella, complete with beauty and medical spa and garden estate leading to private beach.

Hotel Aguamarina € *Avda San Lorenzo 32; tel: (95) 280–6155; fax: (95) 280–4598; www.hotelaguamarina.com.* Total remake of a solidly constructed 1970s hotel opened in Feb 1999 offers very pleasant rooms. Centrally located for the old town and beach.

Marisquería/Freiduría El Gavilán del Mar €–€€ *Pl. Doctor Arce 1; tel: (95) 280–2856.* Restaurant with superb wine list dominates one of the old town's most pleasant squares.

Parque Tropical € *N340 km162, east of town; tel: (95) 279–3618.* Camping with amenities; access to beach via pedestrian overpass above highway.

For a taste of delicious fried fish and seafood, head along to the *freidurias* on c/ Terraza in the centre of town.

Cafetería Churrería Veracruz € *corner of c/ Huerto; no tel.* Join local policemen from the station next door for early morning *churros* and chocolate.

Mercado Abastos *c/ Raphael, Pl. Flores* is worth visiting to purchase the superb goat cheeses from Estepona's own breed of goat.

FUENGIROLA❖

Oficina de Turismo *Avda Jesús Santos Rein 6; tel: (95) 246–7457; fax: (95) 246–5100; www.fuengirola.org*

Highly favoured by northern Europeans who winter in its high-rise apartment blocks, Fuengirola's density dwarfs even Torremolinos, with the beachfront an almost unbroken sequence of tall buildings. **Paseo Marítimo**❖❖ is the longest on Costa del Sol, and features the greatest concentration of dance clubs and party bars – all of which seem ghostly until close to sundown. The town is dominated by Sohail Castle, recently renovated and now a regular venue for concerts and theatrical productions. Remnants of the old town remain,

Above
Fuengirola

Fuengirola Zoo €
c/ Camilo José Cela; tel:
(95) 266–6301; open daily
from 1000 until dusk.

however, with atmospheric tapas bars and cafés to the west of the **Plaza Constitución***, behind the main post office and around the attractive pedestrian square, Plaza Yates. Beachfront **marisquerías** are the best bet for seafood. From 6 to 12 Oct, the **Feria Fuengirola** (tel: (95) 246–7457) honours the Virgen del Rosario, and is the last of the big international equestrian fairs of the year.

Las Piramides €€ c/ Miguel Marquez 43; tel: (95) 247–0600; fax: (95) 258–3297; www.hotellaspiramides.com is located at the quieter end of the paseo. This hotel is comfortable and convenient for the beach and also offers live entertainment nightly.

MARBELLA✧✧✧

Oficina de Turismo
Glorieta Fontanilla; tel:
(95) 277–1442 and Pl.
Naranjos; tel: (95)
282–3550; fax: (95)
277–1442; e-mail:
turismomarbella@ctv.es;
www.marbella.es

Museo del Grabado Contemporáneo € c/
Hospital Bazán; tel: (95)
282–5035; open Mon
0930–1400, Tue–Sat
1000–1400, 1730–2030.

Museo Bonsai € Arroya
Represa; tel: (95)
286–2926; open daily
1000–1330 and
1600–1900.

Perhaps only in Marbella could a modest rental car cross paths with a Bentley, a Rolls Royce, a BMW and a sleek Rover sedan in less than three blocks. If Torremolinos launched mass-market tourism on the Costa del Sol, Marbella established the area as a destination for the international jet set, beginning in the 1950s. Twice a day the west side of town echoes with the amplified call to prayer from the shining white mosque built by Saudi King Fahd, and many of Marbella's estates belong to Gulf oil millionaires.

The pedestrianised *casco antiguo*✧✧✧ is partially walled and set back from the ocean. Its centre is the lively **Plaza Naranjos✧✧**. Shops quietly hawk fine jewellery, haute couture and impulse luxury items, but it's as much fun simply to wander the narrow streets, coming across such delights as the little chapel of **San Juan de Dios***, as to charge, charge, charge. A 16th-century convent hospital houses the excellent **Museo del Grabado Contemporáneo✧✧**, with a permanent collection that includes prints by Picasso, Miró and Dalí. Latin American art and sculpture is on show at the light and airy **Museu Ralli***, just outside the centre. The **Museo Bonsai***, just above the *casco antiguo*, has a charming collection of miniature trees.

Casino Marbella *Andalucía Palace Hotel, Urb. Nueva Andalucía, N340 km174; tel: (95) 281–4000; fax: (95) 281–2844; www.casinomarbella.com.* Formal attire, and shows of flamenco and *sevillana* dancing.

Nightlife centres on *Pl. Puente de Ronda, c/ Pantaleón and Pl. Africa.* Activity is minimal before midnight.

Boutique Donna Piu *c/ Benábola 87, Puerto Banús.* Fashion with an Italian cut.

Don Miguel *Avda Ricardo Soriano 5, Marbella.* Brand-name fashion for men and women.

El Corte Inglés *N340 km179, Puerto Banús.* Marbella's branch of the definitively Spanish department store favours the high end of the market.

Museo Ralli €* *CN–340, km 176; tel: (95) 285–7923; open Tue–Sat 1000–1400.*

The fine old **Alameda**** serves as a garden-square for Marbella's downtown. The marble-paved pedestrian **Avenida Atlántica*** connects it to the pleasant **Paseo Marítimo****, really the golden promenade of the entire Costa del Sol. The best combination of fine sand and amenities in central Marbella is at **Playa de Venus****, east of the yacht marina, where the 400 slips hold some vessels as big as a small Spanish village.

'Marbella' is a name to conjure with in these parts, so surrounding municipalities have readily allied themselves with the resort to the point where seemingly separate communities, like the chic port-resort of **Puerto Banús**** and the sprawling luxury developments of **Nueva Andalucía***, lie within Marbella's bounds. Even **San Pedro de Alcántara*** has recently been swallowed in Marbella's tidal wave.

The so-called 'Golden Mile' of Marbella consists of the 5km stretch west of the main town toward Puerto Banús, where the **Marbella Club****, brainchild of the Prince of Liechtenstein, pioneered the jet-set scene in the late 1940s and early 1950s. Its 'partner' in that process, the exclusive **Los Monteros**** on the east side of town, has undergone a €1 million renovation. Indeed, all the luxury properties of Marbella have been spruced up of late, restoring some of the glamour of its movie-star heyday.

Accommodation and food in Marbella

La Hacienda €€€ *Urb. Hacienda Las Chapas, N340 km193; tel: (95) 282–1267; closed Mon–Tue.* Easily Marbella's top gourmet restaurant; reserve far ahead.

Hostal Pilar € *c/ Peral; tel: (95) 282–9936.* British-run friendly place with pool table, roof terrace and slap-up breakfast.

Hotel El Fuerte €€–€€€ *Avda El Fuerte s/n; tel: (95) 286–1500; fax: (95) 282–4411; e-mail: fuerte@fuertehoteles.com; www.fuertehoteles.com.* Handsome hotel on garden-like grounds; a short walk to beach and *casco antiguo.*

Hotel Puente Romano €€€ *N340 km177; tel: (95) 282–0900; fax: (95) 286–6164; e-mail: reservas@puenteromano.com; www.puenteromano.com.* The standard of luxury for Marbella since the 1980s. Stunning grounds, spacious rooms with private patios in bungalow village.

Marbella Club Hotel €€€ *N340 km178; tel: (95) 282–2211; fax: (95) 282–9884; e-mail: hotel@marbellaclub.com; www.marbellaclub.com.* This formal central hotel and compound of private villas is beautifully set amid vast gardens. A pioneer of jet-set tourism the hotel was completely renovated in 1999.

Marbella Patio €€ *Virgen de los Dolores 4; tel: (95) 277–5429.* In the *casco antiguo* with patio and terrace dining. The ovens are the feature here, with superb roasted fish, suckling pig and lamb. *Closed Sun.*

Above
A typical street in the village of Mijas

Taberna del Alabardero €€–€€€ *Carretera de Ronda, Km 167; tel: (95) 281-2794; fax: (95) 281-8630; e-mail: taberna.alabardero@teleline.es.* Facing the luxury yachts in the marina. Come here to enjoy serious gourmet treatment of classic Andalucían cuisine lightened for contemporary cosmopolitan taste.

MIJAS ❖❖

ⓘ **Mijas Tourist Office** *Pl. Virgen de la Pena; tel: (95) 248-5900 ext 244; fax: (95) 248-5199; e-mail: turismo@mijas.es; www.mijas.es*

🏇 **Hippodrome** € *La Cala de Mijas; tel: (95) 259-2700; www.hipodromocostadelsol.com*

The beautiful village of Mijas, a mountain 'white town' 8km inland from Fuengirola, suffers from its proximity to the beach resorts. It has become a very popular bus tour destination to see a 'typical' village with its truly atypical, if endearing, *burro* taxis. Views from the **mirador**❖❖ are spectacular, and the tiny **Ermita de la Virgen de la Peña**❖❖ – shrine to an image kept hidden from the Moors between 865 and 1586 – is delightfully intimate. A small rectangular bullring stands north of the centre, much hyped in tourism literature as one of 'Spain's most beautiful'. The assessment is a stretch, and the lack of facilities dictates that only matadors in training ever fight here. Between the village and the sea, a large racecourse, the Hippodrome, makes Mijas a winter base for horse races in Europe.

Accommodation and food in Mijas

Hotel Byblos €€€ *Urb Mijas Golf; tel: (95) 247–3050; fax: (95) 247–6783; e-mail: byblos@spa.es; www.hotel-byblos.com.* Luxurious hotel set amidst a golf course on the Mijas road, with excellent restaurant serving traditional, yet innovative cuisine.

Hotel Mijas €€ *c/ Obispo Juan Alonso 4; tel: (95) 248–5800; fax: (95) 248–5825; e-mail: mijasres@hotasa.es; www.hotasa.es.* Striking, comfortable hotel amid beautiful gardens perched on the hillside of lower Mijas. Great lawn bowls.

Restaurante La Alcababa €€ *Plaza de la Constitución; tel: (95) 259–0253.* Enjoy spectacular views of the coast from this glass-fronted restaurant where the menu is more Spanish than most, with a fabulous *ajo blanco* (almond and garlic soup) and good choice of salads and seafood. *Closed Mon.*

SAN PEDRO DE ALCANTARA*

ⓘ Oficina de Turismo *Avenida Principal; tel: (95) 278–5252; e-mail: turismosanpedro@marbella web.com; www.vidauna.com, and at Arco San Pedro, tel: (95) 278–1360, west of town, across the N340. The Arco San Pedro office arranges free guided visits to the archaeological sites on Tue, Thur and Sat at 1200. Bring your car.*

Now part of the Marbella municipality, San Pedro is the 'bargain' offer 10km west of the 'Golden Mile'. The town sits about 2km from the beach, which is only now being developed with luxury flats. The main sites are on the beach west of the promenade. Ruins of the 6th-century basilica at **Vega del Mar**, one of the premier Visigothic sites in Iberia, can be found in a grove of tall eucalyptus trees 150m down the beach. The **Roman bathhouses*** of Las Bóvedas are 400m west of the basilica and almost on the beach by a watchtower. The octagonal baths date from the third century. To get to both sites, take the beach road off the N340 from the San Pedro roundabout.

⬤ Thur morning flea market in the city's fairgrounds.

Accommodation and food in San Pedro de Alcántara

El Cortijo Blanco €–€€ *N340 km172; tel: (95) 278–0900; fax: (95) 278–0916; www.hoteltur.com.* Andalucían-style hotel adjacent to the highway and close to the beach. Good rates for the area.

Alfredos € *Av Andalucía; tel: (95) 278–6165.* Popular local restaurant, specialising in Andalucían meat and fish dishes. *Closed Wed.*

TORREMOLINOS**

Depending on one's point of view, Torremolinos got the credit – or the blame – for the development of the Costa del Sol as a tourist area.

ℹ **Oficina de Turismo**
Plaza Blas Infante 1,
tel: (95) 237–9512;
fax: (95) 237–9551;
www.ayto-torremolinos.org;
open daily 0900–1400,
1700–2000, winter hours
are 0930–1400. Other
offices are located in Pl. Lido
at Bajondillo Beach; tel: (95)
237–1909 and Pl.
Independenia; tel: (95)
237–4231.

🌙 Nightlife is centred
around Avda Palma
de Mallorca.

Crocodile Park c/ Cuba
14; tel: (95) 205–1782.
Next to Aquapark with
more than 300 crocodiles,
plus museum, film show,
gift shop, mini zoo and
'croc nursery'.

Romería de San Miguel
tel: (95) 237–9512. This
celebration on 29 Sept
honouring the town's
patron saint is said to be
one of the best in
Andalucía with a
pilgrimage, giant *paella* and
sampling of local wines.

In the 1930s, Englishman George Langworthy started the phenomenon by opening his estate to foreign visitors who shared his love of the low-key fishing village. The real tourism boom began in the 1950s with the building of the first big hotels. And despite subsequent development along the Costa del Sol, Torremolinos still has the largest number and greatest concentration of hotels. These concrete high-rises may not be for everyone, and their cavernous capacity guarantees crowds during the height of the season, but 'Torrie' does offer, for many, an affordable holiday.

In the last few years, the town has been spruced up for its visitors. **Calle San Miguel✷✷**, the main pedestrian street, has been repaved with marble. It heads past shops and restaurants and down a flight of steps to **Bajondillo Beach✷✷**, one of the most popular. Torremolinos' 7-km **Paseo Marítimo✷✷✷** has also been upgraded with more benches and graceful palm trees, permitting a continuous walk along the town's six beaches and to the adjoining Benalmádena port.

One of the most popular destinations along the promenade is **La Carihuela✷✷**, an old district where the erstwhile fishermen now all seem to operate fish restaurants. These are some of the city's best and many of the colourful establishments sport terraces looking out onto the beach.

Accommodation and food in Torremolinos

The hotel **La Barracuda** €€ *Av Espana 1; tel: (92) 238–5400; fax: (95) 238–9121; www.hotellabarracuda.com* is ideally situated a few minutes' stroll from the Playamar Beach, and offers all the amenities you would expect from a quality hotel, including a pool, tennis court and reliably good restaurant.

Hotel Isabel €–€€ *Pas. Marítimo 97; tel: (95) 238–1744; fax: (95) 238–1198; e-mail: reservas@hotelisabel.net; www.hotelisabel.net.* Six-storey, 40-room hotel with pool sits across the street from Playa del Lido.

Miami €€ *c/ Aladino 14; tel: (95) 238–5255; www.residencia-miami.com.* Tastefully renovated Andalucían villa with pretty gardens and a pool. A short stroll to the beach and to La Carihuela restaurants.

Parador de Málaga (Parador del Golf) €€€ *airport road off N340; tel: (95) 238–1255; fax: (95) 238–8963; www.parador.es.* Beautiful grounds near the ocean and 10km from Málaga centre make for a peaceful retreat. The only distraction is the noise from planes landing and taking off at the airport, only 3km away. The 18-hole golf course is open to non-residents (€€€ green fees).

Restaurante La Jabega €€ *c/ Mar 11; tel: (95) 238–6375.* This excellent fish restaurant in Carihuela has a pretty dining room and terrace looking out at the beach.

Suggested tour

Tivoli World €€
*Arroyo de la Miel; tel:
(95) 256–6017; open daily
1000–1800.*

Total distance: 145km, 160km with detour.

Time: 8 hours. Allow an extra 1½ hours for the detour.

Links: Connects to heart of the Frontera (*pages 108–17*) by taking the Ronda road from San Pedro de Alcántara.

Route: From **TORREMOLINOS ❶** head west on the N340 bypass road, which was completed in 1992. With pedestrian overpasses, breakdown lanes and acceleration lanes, it immediately improved road safety on the Costa del Sol. Follow west to the roundabout for **BENALMADENA ❷**, turning right on the beach road and continuing slowly into **FUENGIROLA ❸**.

Detour: Head east 1km from Benalmádena Costa on the N340, taking the turn-off for **Arroyo de la Miel**. In the village, turn left at the lights and follow signs for 'Tivoli World', passing the amusement park continuing on to Benalmádena Pueblo. Follow signs to **MIJAS ❹**, on a very narrow, very winding mountain road. Return by following signs to Fuengirola on another twisting and scenic road. The drive is only 8km each way.

Depending on traffic density, continue west on the beach road from Fuengirola or on the high-speed, AP7 toll road that begins around km200, watching for turn-offs to places of interest. This stretch of the N340 has long vistas down to the ocean, but watch the traffic, not the scenery, as it is still a dangerous highway. Take the 'centro' turn-off for **MARBELLA ❺**, drive through the triumphal arch erected by the controversial former (late) mayor Jesús Gil and duck into the Avda Atlántica underground car park near the *casco antiguo*.

The pedestrian exit from the car park comes out on the marble-paved plaza of Avda Atlántica. Walk directly uphill to the beautiful **Alameda**, cross the main street, and continue two blocks uphill into the *casco antiguo*. Return, this time following the marble plaza down to the sea and walking in each direction on the **Paseo Marítimo** for a sense of Marbella's pampered ambience.

After exiting the car park, follow the beach road west. This is the 'old' N340, and it passes the glories of the 5km 'Golden Mile' between Marbella and Puerto Banús. Among the exquisite homes that gave the area its sobriquet is *Mar Mar,* the estate of King Fahd of Saudi Arabia, complete with a mosque. Pull into the marina area at **Puerto Banús** for a look at the coast's most glamorous yachts. There is a choice of two exits.

After passing **SAN PEDRO DE ALCANTARA ❻**, traffic thins out a bit en route to **ESTEPONA ❼**.

Return to Torremolinos on the Estepona–Málaga toll road for a safe and swift trip.

Also worth exploring

Just beyond Estepona at Manilva, a turn-off heads into the Sierra Bermeja hills to the white village of **Casares**, a town that changed hands many times between Christians and Moors. Noted for its olive oil and goat cheese, Casares is worth visiting simply for the scenic vistas from the roads leading to and from it.

Costa del Golf

The name began as a joke, but the Costa del Sol now proudly trumpets itself as the 'Costa del Golf', with 37 18-hole and 13 9-hole courses. Most are open to non-members with presentation of a handicap certificate and payment of green fees (€–€€). The largest concentration of courses is found in Estepona (four) and Marbella (eight). For a complete guide to the courses, pick up the *Andalucía Golf Guide* available at tourist offices. *Sun Golf* is a free glossy magazine, published monthly and available from hotels and golf clubs.

Costa del Sol Oriental and Axarquía

Ratings

Beaches	●●●○○
Gastronomy	●●●○○
History	●●●○○
Nature and wildlife	●●●○○
Shopping and crafts	●●●○○
Architecture	●●○○○
Entertainment	●●○○○
Museums	●●○○○

Beaches and mountains soon converge east of Málaga, where the Axarquía hill country meets the ocean with spectacular results. The villages of the eastern Costa del Sol typically perch on the south-facing shelf of the mountain range, parked high above their beaches. Yet despite the presence of several beach communities within easy reach for weekend holidaymakers from Málaga, this parched countryside remains primarily agricultural, thanks to deep-well irrigation. Large sugar cane plantations alternate with hectares of fruits and vegetables grown under plastic to retain the precious moisture. Further east, the high mountain ranges of the Sierra Almijara run all the way to the sea, and the highway winds along the edges of dramatic cliffs dotted with a succession of watchtowers. Mountains as high as 2000m loom just inland, seeming to push this coastal strip into the sea, while tiny switchbacks zigzag to the beaches below.

ALMUNECAR***

ⓘ Oficina de Turismo *Avda Europa s/n; tel: (95) 863–1125; fax: (95) 863–5007; e-mail: ofitur@almunecar.info; www.almunecar.info.* The neo-Mudéjar building is one of the town's most delightful sites.

ⓜ Museo Arqueológico (Cueva de los Siete Palacios) *Pl. Eras del Castillo; open Tue–Sat 1030–1330, 1600–1800, Sun 1030–1330.*

Founded in the 8th century BC as *Sexi*, Almuñécar was a major producer of *garum marsala* (fermented fish paste) for Phoenicia and then Rome. Ruins hint at Almuñécar's rich history. The fine **Museo Arqueológico**** in the Cueva de los Siete Palacios has Phoenician, Roman and Moorish objects. On the northwest side of town, the Phoenician necropolis of **Tumbas Fenicias Puente de Noy*** dates from the first millennium BC. The two-level Roman aqueduct, **Acueducto de la Carrera***, about 1km out of town along the Río Seco, was built to last: it supplied the city with water until just a few years ago. In the middle of town, on the north end of the delightful **Parque el Majuelo**** just a few blocks from the beach, are the remains of a Roman-era fish-curing factory, the **Factoría de Salazones Romana***. The *monumentos* don't end with the ancient world. The **Castillo de San Miguel*** sits on a headland above Parque el Majuelo. Much

🏛 **Castillo de San Miguel** € *Open Mon–Fri 1000–1400 and 1600–1900, Sat 1000–1400.*

Parque Ornitológico Loro Sexi € *off Pl. Abderraman; open daily 1000–1400 and 1700–1900.*

🍴 Small stalls in Parque El Majuelo are given over to artisans making leather, ceramics, fabric, raffia and other crafts.

renovated by medieval Christian kings and modern restorers, it occupies the site of a Moorish *alcazaba* (citadel), built over a Roman fort. No wonder successive occupiers favoured the location. The walls have commanding coastal views.

Fishermen and sunbathers share Almuñécar's gravel beaches with equanimity. Best of the five beaches is **Playa de San Cristóbal**∗∗, which has the liveliest café life, best *chiringuitos* (snack bars) and the better hotels. Near the east end, **Parque Ornitológico Loro-Sexi**∗ houses 120 species of tropical and subtropical birds in large outdoor cages.

Accommodation and food in Almuñécar

La Bodega del Jamón *Avda Europa 17; tel: (95) 863–0587.* Local hams and cheeses, sweets and wines are the specialities of this high-quality gourmet shop with generous free samples. *Closed Sun.*

Hotel Carmen € *Avda Europa 19; tel: (95) 863–1413; fax: (95) 863–4889; e-mail: h_carmen@teleline.es; www.hotelcarmenalmunecar.com.* Fifty-room hotel with friendly proprietors near Parque El Majuelo.

Hotel Helios €–€€ *Paseo de las Flores; tel: (95) 863–4459; fax: (95) 863–4469; www.heliosalmunecar.com.* Unusually attractive high-rise hotel across from Playa de San Cristóbal attracts bus groups.

Restaurante Boto's €€ *Playa de San Cristóbal; tel: (95) 863–4657.* Situated right on the beach with big windows to enjoy the view, this restaurant specialises in fresh fish and *paella*.

Churrerías line Playa de San Cristóbal. *Tapas* **bars** concentrate around Plaza de la Constitución.

La Cueva del Tesoro✦✦

La Cueva del Tesoro € *east of the village of La Cala del Moral off N340A; tel: (95) 240-6160; open daily 1000–1400 and 1600–2000.*

The limestone karst of eastern Andalucía is riddled with caves hollowed out by dripping water. According to legend, fleeing Muslim emirs took sanctuary in these caves and left behind some of their gold, hence the name 'Treasure Cave'. With their fantastic stalactites and swirling columns of limestone checked with reflective flakes of mica, these caves could have inspired architect Antonio Gaudi. Most striking of all in this labyrinth of seven well-lit chambers is the constant sound of dripping and running water. The chamber with Neolithic wall paintings is closed to public viewing, as the paintings have grown very faint.

Nerja✦✦✦

Oficina de Turismo *c/ Puerta del Mar 2, Balcón de Europa; tel: (95) 252–1531; fax: (95) 252–6287; e-mail: turismo@nerja.org; www.nerja.org*

Cuevas de Nerja €€ *Off N340 3 km east of town; tel: (95) 252–9520; fax: (95) 252–6287; open Mon–Fri 1000–1400, 1730–2030, Sat 1000–1300. During July a performing arts festival is held in the caves.*

El Colono €€€ *c/ Granada 6; tel: (95) 252–1826 presents a flamenco show with dinner on Wed and Fri. No credit cards.*

Pub El Burro Blanco € *c/ Gloria 3 presents flamenco nightly in a more casual atmosphere.*

An earthquake destroyed much of Nerja in 1884. The rebuilt community combines a modern grace and love of open space to balance the usual twisting streets of an old town that splashes uphill from the beaches like the froth of a large wave. The heart of town is the **Balcón de Europa**✦✦, a natural belvedere transformed into a marble-paved, tree-lined square surrounded by restaurants, hotels and bars. Nerja has perhaps the best **up-market shopping**✦✦ along the Costa del Sol east of Marbella. The best of the beaches is **Playa Burriana**✦ on the eastern side of town below the *parador*, although it is sometimes beset by strong winds and heavy surf.

Just 3km east of town off the N340 are the **Cuevas de Nerja**✦✦, an enormous cavern created by water dripping through the limestone about 5 million years ago. Nearly half the parking area around the caves is dedicated to tour buses. The world's largest known stalactite (63m) lies within. Neolithic rock paintings about 17,000 years old have been found in the caves, but are no longer on view.

Accommodation and food in Nerja

Hotel Balcón de Europa €€–€€€ *Pas. Balcón de Europa 1; tel: (95) 252–0800; fax: (95) 252–4490; e-mail: balconeuropa@spa.es; www.hotel-balconeuropa.com.* Refurbished 105-room hotel holds a key corner of the Balcón de Europa area right in the midst of the action.

Hotel Paraiso del Mar €€ *c/ Carabeo 22; tel: (95) 252–1621; fax: (95) 252–2309; www.hotelparaisodelmar.com.* Up-market, attractive hotel with views over the sweeping Playa de Burriana.

Parador de Nerja €€–€€€ *c/ Almuñécar 8; tel: (95) 252–0050; fax: (95) 252–1997; www.parador.es.* A severe exterior hides an enchanting interior with a central courtyard and pool, a long stairway down to the beach and great views of the ocean and mountains.

Don Comer € *c/ Granada; tel: (95) 252–6006; closed Wed.* Stylish spot for sandwiches and snacks at a slight remove from the crowds around the Balcón de Europa.

Restaurante Miguel €€ *corner c/ Almirante and c/ Pintada; tel: (95) 252–2996.* Where Nerjans go for steak, veal and fish on special occasions.

Right
Nerja

SALOBRENA ✧✧

Oficina de Turismo
*Pl. de Goya s/n; tel:
(95) 861–0314; open
Mon–Sun 1000–1330,
1700–2000.*

A bus (€) runs from
the tourist office to
the Castillo Arabe.

Castillo Arabe €
*Open daily 1000–1400
and 1600–1700.*

Salobreña emerges as an apparition from the distance: a 13th-century hilltop Moorish castle, **Castillo Arabe**✧✧, flanked by a Cubist jumble of white houses tumbling down the slopes. Tourists, including the Granada emirs, have been coming here for seven centuries. The town's main plaza, once the mosque, is dominated by the 16th-century **Iglesia de Nuestra Señora del Rosario**✧. The town stands about 2km steeply uphill from the beaches, and has so far escaped coastal real-estate developers. As a result, Salobreña moves with the steady daily pace of an agricultural centre, in this case a sugar-cane capital. The main harvest occurs between March and June, and fields are burned immediately after cutting to return nutrients to the soil. Market days in Salobreña are on Tue and Fri at the Mercado Nuevo between Avda García Lorca and Fábrica Nueva. And in the town's old quarters the **Zoco de Artesanía**✧ on Pl. Antiguo Mercado contains studios for artisans working in ceramics, glass, metal and wood.

Accommodation and food in Salobreña

Hotel Salobreña € *N340 km341; tel: (95) 861–0261; fax: (95) 861–0101; e-mail: info@hotelsalobrena.com; www.hotelsalobrena.com.* The town centre has no hotels; this one stands on a high bluff a few km west of town.

Restaurante El Peñón € *Pas. Marítimo; tel: (95) 861–0538.* Restaurant at Playa del Peñón specialising in *zarzuela*, grilled fish and fish cooked in salt.

Restaurante Pesetas € *c/ Bóveda s/n; tel: (95) 861–0182; closed Wed.* Located near the Iglesia de Nuestra Señora del Rosario in the old quarter; the terrace has attractive views of surrounding buildings.

Below
Torre del Mar

TORRE DEL MAR❖

ⓘ Oficina de Turismo
Avda Andalucía 52; tel:
(95) 254–1104; e-mail:
turismovelez@msn.com;
www.ayto.velezmalaga.es;
open Mon–Fri 0800–1500,
1800–2100, Sat
1030–1330, 1700–2000.

The Thur market is
held on Avda Duque
Ahumada.

Rancho del Arte *Avda*
Duque Ahumada 26–28
sells ceramics from
throughout Spain with
especially good *cazuelas*
and garden pottery.

Torre del Mar is a beach centre backed by holiday flats. Its brown-sand beaches are long and clean, and the seaside marble walkway has an unusual elegance. A lively nightlife rocks the bars and discos on each side of the central park that divides the Paseo Poniente (west) from the Paseo Levante (east). The east end of the promenade continues about 1km past Torre with sweeping coastal views to the erstwhile fishing community of **Caleta de Vélez**❖.

Accommodation and food in Torre del Mar

Camping Naturista Almanat € *N340A; tel: (95) 255–6271; e-mail: almanat@arrakis.es*. Naturist camping area west of town.

Hotel Las Yucas € *Avda Andaluciá s/n; tel: (95) 254–0901; fax: (95) 254–2272*. One of several hotels in town has 38 well-maintained rooms and a casual cafeteria.

Restaurants on the east end of the seaside promenade in Caleta de Vélez, including **El Huerto de la Tara** *no tel,* specialise in sardines grilled over wood fires (*espada*).

VELEZ-MALAGA❖❖

ⓐ Follow signs to the
Ayuntamiento on Pl.
Carmelitas in the city
centre for a map.

The Thur market is
held on c/ Magallanes.

Vélez-Málaga, 4km inland from Torre del Mar, has a romantic history first as the centre of Moorish resistance, then a bandit stronghold and finally a guerrilla holdout against Franco's Guardia Civil. Today it's a prosperous agricultural centre where sun-dried red grapes are used for the powerful Málaga red wines – the locals drink them mixed 50-50 with carbonated water. At the highest point of the town stands a restored **Muslim castle**❖ with commanding views of the coast below. The town has a flair for the arts: its streets are named after poets and painters, it has an active programme of theatre and music, and there are many good bookstores. The **Teatro del Carmen**❖ (*Pl. Carmen; tel: (95) 250–7106*) presents a series of adventurous performing arts events, and the Holy Week celebrations (*tel: (95) 254–1104*), with 24 processions, are of the best in the Axarquía.

Accommodation and food in Vélez-Málaga

Hotel Residencia Dila € *Avda Vivar Téllez 3; tel: (95) 250–3900; fax: (95) 250–3908; e-mail: hoteldila@hoteldila.com; www.hoteldila.com*. Small hotel off the town centre has 18 rooms with private bath.

Restaurante El Rubio € *c/ Alcalde Juan Barranquero 14; tel: (95) 250–1213; closed Sun*. A cross-section of locals favour this bright restaurant and bar for its *cocina casera*, or 'home cooking'.

Suggested tour

Total distance: 110km, 120km with detour.

Time: 3 hours.

Links: Links to Málaga (*see pages 42–51*) on the west, and to Almería (*see pages 258–73*) on the east.

Below
Almuñécar

Route: Leave **Málaga** on the N340, taking the E15/N340A turn-off at **Cala del Moral**. Drive through the town, watching on the east end for a left turn to **CUEVA DEL TESORO ❶**. The land soon rises and becomes very arid, but irrigated terraces support groves of olive and citrus trees. There are striking views of the coast and beaches on one side of the road, while on the other, the distant but immense Sierra Nevada is visible behind the closer, lower ranges of the Axarquía. Drive into **TORRE DEL MAR ❷** and follow the Paseo Marítimo east, curving back to the N340.

Detour: The road up to **VELEZ-MALAGA ❸** goes across several roundabouts and past an unattractive strip-mall development, but the tower of the city and its white jumble on the hill beckons.

Double back to the N340 and drive through the pleasant little seaside village of **Torrox**, which marks a transition on the coast from sand to stone beaches. This windy area is great for surfing and windsurfing. The road continues to **NERJA ❹**, with its lookout position on cliffs above the sea.

East of Nerja the coast becomes wilder, the bluffs higher, and the

nearby mountain ranges break directly into the sea. A steady succession of **Moorish watchtowers** begins just east of Nerja. At km296, a scenic turn-off to **Torre del Maro** supplies amazing views, including three additional towers on the points ahead. Several aqueducts – some Roman, some Moorish – also lie along the route. The 20th-century Maro aqueduct was built to supply water for sugar cane processing. The next tower, **Torre del Miel**, is marked with a sign announcing *Paisaje Pintoresco* (picturesque landscape), something of an understatement. These vertiginous turn-offs continue until km302.

Further east, the N340 twists and climbs through parched, nearly lifeless landscape where the mountains really do meet the Mediterranean. The drylands bloom, however, beneath a sea of plastic that retains irrigation moisture, and the beaches of **ALMUNECAR** ❺ and **SALOBRENA** ❻ lie cupped between cliff and sea.

Also worth exploring

The pretty Arabic village of **Frigiliana⁺⁺**, perched 6km up in the hills behind Nerja, is a mass of narrow, cobbled streets shared by donkeys and motor scooters. In a mansion built of stones recovered from a Moorish fortress, **Artesanía de Frigiliana** (*Pl. Ingenio 4*) features ceramics, pottery and basketry as well as the local oil, figs, almonds, raisins, wine and honey.

North of Málaga

Ratings

Nature and wildlife	●●●●●
Architecture	●●●○○
History	●●●○○
Outdoor activities	●●●○○
Entertainment	●●○○○
Gastronomy	●●○○○
Museums	●●○○○
Shopping and crafts	●○○○○

Northwest of Málaga, the Río Guadalhorce valley and the ancient crossroads city of Antequera provide striking contrast both to the nearby Costa del Sol and to the inland cities of Andalucía. Along the river valley, long stretches of limestone bedrock lie exposed to the strange shaping powers of wind and water, resulting in an often other-worldly landscape and some excellent opportunities for hiking, caving and rock climbing. The *de facto* capital of the region, Antequera, is a handsome city that rises on a bluff amid long vistas of agricultural countryside. The city is rich with ecclesiastical architecture and has a stylish grace. Few travellers set their sights on this region, yet precisely because it lies half-way between Granada and Sevilla, close to Málaga and not far from Córdoba, the district makes a splendid stopover for a few days of slow-paced respite from the urban centres.

ALORA✶

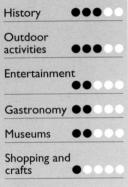

🛈 **Oficina de Turismo**
Avda Constitución 102;
tel: (95) 249–8380;
www.ayto-alora.org; open
Mon–Sat 1000–1400.

🌙 **Hostal Durán €** *c/*
La Parra 9; tel/fax: (95)
249–6642. Modest lodging
with private baths.

An ancient town dating back to the Tartessians, Alora commands a vast bowl along the Río Guadalhorce where lemons, oranges, almonds and green olives flourish. Local promoters have good reason to call it the 'valley of the sun': the hills north of town tend to block rain clouds coming from the north and west, yet the runoff from the mountains keeps the land well irrigated. As a result, the valley has been a hot property since the time of the Phoenicians, who built a castle here around 300 BC which the Romans expanded and the Visigoths sacked in the 5th century. The existing ruins are yet another Andalucían *castillo árabe*, complete with horseshoe gate and *mirador* that commands panoramic views; this explains why Alora was not reconquered by the Christians until 1484. The castle keep has become the town graveyard. The location at the base of the hills has made Alora something of a

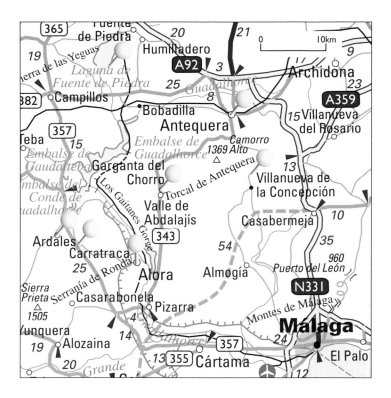

Flamenco Singing Festival *tel: (95) 249–8380.* Early Jun, emphasises *malagueña jondo.*

Romería de La Virgen de las Flores *tel: (95) 249–8380.* First Sun after 8 Sept, traditional *verdiales* are sung.

refuge from authorities in Málaga, leading to an anarchist tradition that gave birth both to the *malagueña jondo* style of flamenco and to some of the most extreme left-wing organisations of the Civil War period. Even today Alora has a strongly left-wing local government.

On market day, Monday, farmers bring in their fruits and vegetables and local artisans sell basketry, saddles and the castanets that traditionally accompany the *verdiales*, a local musical tradition with Tartessian roots.

ANTEQUERA❖❖❖

ℹ Oficina de Turismo *Pl. San Sebastían 7; tel: (95) 270–2505; www.aytoantequera.com; open summer Mon–Sat 1000–1400, 1700–2000; winter Mon–Sat 1000–1330, 1600–1900; Sun 1000–1330.*

The Romans gave Antequera its name, which means 'ancient city' in deference to settlements that predated them by a couple of millennia. The name entered the popular Spanish lexicon following the Christian reconquest in 1410, when the town was the first to fall in the long assault on the kingdom of Granada. After laying siege for five months, Prince Fernando of Castille (later Fernando I El Católico) launched a surprise night attack with the cry, 'Let us go and may the sun rise for Antequera'. The town fell quickly, perhaps because the Spanish made

🔵 Sun morning flea market is held on Avda de la Estación.

ℹ️ **Plaza de Toros** *Jct. Paseo Real and Avda Andalucía; tel: (95) 270-2676.* **Museo Taurino €** *Open Sat–Sun 1000–1300 and 1800–2000. Free.*

🔵 **Semana Santa** *tel: (95) 270–2505.* Holy Week celebrations are considered among the most festive in Spain.

Feria de Primavera (late May–early Jun) and **Real Feria de Agosto** (late Aug) *tel: (95) 270–2505.* Both feature bullfights and flamenco.

their first use of gunpowder. Ever since, the prince's celebrated battle-cry has been used to characterise any bold and decisive action in the face of danger.

Fernando deported the entire Moorish population, and the Christians who moved into Antequera began a building spurt that lasted for the next two centuries. The compact historic district sits on the edge of a smart and prosperous commercial centre that serves the entire valley. At the hub is the **Plaza de San Sebastián***, dominated by the Renaissance **Colegiata de San Sebastián***. From the plaza, c/ Encarnación leads to **Plaza de las Descalzas***, where nuns in the 18th-century Carmelite convent sell sweets from a *retorno*.

Heading uphill towards the Alcazaba, the broad streets narrow into the **Barrio del Coso Viejo***, the Arabic quarter. The **Museo Municipal de Antequera*** (*€ Pl. Coso Viejo; open Tue–Fri 1000–1330, Sat–Sun 1100–1330*), former ducal Palacio de Nájera, attempts to interpret the history and culture of the entire region, but is worth visiting mostly to see just one item: the first-century Roman bronze, called *El Efebo de Antequera*, discovered on a nearby farm in 1955. Two millennia after it was cast, the statue of a youth caught in mid-gesture retains a striking immediacy.

The 16th-century **Arco de los Gigantes*** makes for a ceremonial entry to the flattened hill that holds the Alcazaba. It is also the Antequera's best photo opportunity, with the city and the belltower of San Sebastián framed through the arch. Less interpreted and restored than some, but fronted by attractive gardens, the **Alcazaba**** provides panoramic views of the town and countryside from its towers: the **Torre Papabellotas*** has housed the town bells since 1582, while the 13th-century **Torre del Homenaje***, the oldest tower of this Moorish fortress, was the first to fall to Christians during the Reconquest of Granada.

Sharing the city heights with the Alcazaba is the **Real Colegiata de Santa María la Mayor**** (*Pl. Santa María; open Mon–Fri 1030–1400, 1630–1830, Sat 1030–1400*), a strikingly restrained and simple church interior distinguished by a row of four large columns and arches on each side and a wooden Mudéjar ceiling. Even at the height of the Inquisition, the *colegiata* was the centre of a humanistic movement that profoundly affected Baroque literature, producing, among others, the poet Pedro Espinosa. The church now serves as a concert hall.

The **Iglesia de Nuestra Señora del Carmen**** (*Pl. Carmen; open Mon–Sat 1000–1400 and 1600–1900, Sun 1000–1400*) is the stylistic opposite of the Renaissance-inspired Colegiata. Sitting below the Alcazaba, the church is nominally a Mudéjar building, but actually defies categorisation. The astonishing carved 18th-century baroque altarpiece stretches from the floor to the domed ceiling, and virtually every square centimetre of the interior seems covered in ornate paintings, carved angels and saints, and gilt-encrusted side altars.

Much earlier and far more mysterious, the prehistoric **dolmens** of **Menga**, **Viera** and **El Romeral**** (*open Wed–Sat 0900–1800, Sun and*

Tue 0900–1530) lie on the northern edge of town. Follow c/ Encarnación, which becomes c/ Carrera to Pl. Santiago, taking a right turn on to c/ Belén, through the **Puerta de Granada*** and past a scenic viewpoint. Continue in the direction of Málaga and Granada. The Menga and Viera caves date from 2500–2400 BC. Romeral, which has a false dome vault behind the massive table of stone, dates from 1800 BC. These huge blocks of stone were Neolithic tombs, probably for chieftains buried with their weapons and treasures. Beware of claims that they are sited for astronomical observation, as the position of the sun in the sky has changed dramatically since they were constructed.

Accommodation and food in Antequera

Hostal-Restaurante Manzanito € *Pl. San Sebastían; tel: (95) 284–1023.* Across the plaza from Colegiata San Sebastián, Manzanito has smart renovated rooms and a terrace restaurant (€) serving local cuisine.

Parador de Antequera €€€ *Pas. García del Olmo s/n; tel: (95) 284–0901; fax: (95) 284–1312; www.parador.es.* Modern-style *parador* sitting above the bullring at the edge of town.

El Angclote Restaurante €€ *Plaza Coso Viejo; tel: (95) 270–3465; closed Mon.* Restaurant in restored building on Pl. Coso Viejo serves Antequeran cooking including a regional *gazpacho* and a white garlic soup.

Below
Antequera

La Espuela €–€€ c/de San Augustin 2; tel: (95) 270–3031. In the walls of the bullring, this modern bar-restaurant specialises in such local delicacies as *patas de cerdo* – pigs' feet stewed with chickpeas – and, of course, *rabo de toro* (braised bull's tail).

ARDALES*

Hostal-Restaurante El Cruce € *Carretera Alora–Campillos s/n (north side of bridge); tel: (95) 245–9012.* Good country meals and seven bargain-priced modest double rooms with bath.

This enormous reservoir dominates the landscape for miles around and has plenty to offer, including local archaeology, caves, and a couple of good restaurants and bars. The reservoir is noted for its carp fishing and you can hire a pedalo here in the summer. **Cueva de Doña Trinidad***, which has faint Palaeolithic wall paintings. The **Museo Municipal*** € (*Pl. Constitución 1; open Tue–Sat 1000–1400*) has photographs, however, and holds the keys, should you wish to visit when access is restored.

CARRATRACA*

Balneario de Carratraca € *Jct. MA441 and MA442 in village centre; tel/fax: (95) 245–8020. Open Jun–Sept 0800–1300 and 1700–1900.*

Carratraca was famous 2000 years ago, first among the Greeks and then among the Romans for its sulphurous spa waters, which perfume the air with the acrid tinge of burnt matches during the high spa season. After enjoying great popularity from the 1820s to about 1920, with a number of famous visitors – Byron, Alexandre Dumas and Rilke among them – the *balneario* (spa) lapsed into inactivity during the Civil War, reopening in the prosperous mid-1990s.

Accommodation and food in Carratraca

El Trillo € *Carretera Alora-Carratraca (MA441) km16; tel: (95) 245–8199.* El Trillo looks like an unpromising roadside bar from the outside, but opens into a good country restaurant (€–€€). Four double rooms with shared baths are upstairs and five self-catering bungalows overlook a lovely valley.

GARGANTA DEL CHORRO***

Oficina de Turismo *at Camping El Chorro; tel: (95) 249–8380.*

Southwest of Antequera and northwest of Alora, El Chorro Gorge is the top rock-climbing destination in Andalucía. The Río Guadalhorce has cut rocky labyrinths with 300m vertical cliffs in the soft limestone. The main defile is an extremely narrow cut crossed by the one-time trail called **El Camino del Rey***; King Alfonso XIII is said to have walked it to dedicate a railroad tunnel in the 1920s. It is now officially closed and, when asked about it, local authorities simply shake their heads and mutter *muy peligroso,* or 'very dangerous'. The drop-offs from the trail are truly stomach-wrenching, but many foolhardy hikers are not deterred.

Accommodation in Garganta del Chorro

Apartamentos Garganta del Chorro € *at El Chorro train station; tel: (95) 249–5119; www.lagarganta.com.* This converted flour mill has a pool, good restaurant (€) and 32 self-contained apartments.

Finca La Campana € *Garganta del Chorro; tel: (95) 211–2019; www.el-chorro.com.* Set in beautiful countryside with a choice of rooms, bungalows and facilities for camping.

Pensión-Restaurante Estación El Chorro € *at El Chorro train station; tel: (95) 249–5004.* Fine small bar-cafetería also has two clean and simple double rooms with bath – a real step up from the dormitory-style lodgings for hikers elsewhere in the village.

Laguna de Fuente de Piedra*

❶ Laguna de Fuente de Piedra Centro de Interpretación *Cerro del Palo; tel: (95) 211–1050; fax: (95) 211–1715; open Tue–Sun 0900–1400 and 1600–1900.*

Bring powerful binoculars or a long camera lens to Laguna de Fuente de Piedra, the only significant inland breeding ground of the greater flamingo in Europe. The broad, very shallow and saline lake is perfect habitat for brine shrimp, and hence for flamingos in the spring and summer. The birds build nests – truncated muddy cones – on which they lay their eggs in late April to early May. By the end of August the young are ready to join their parents for the flight back to Africa. Many other waders and several species of duck frequent the lake during the rest of the year. The visitor centre rents binoculars and has a good audio-visual presentation about the lake ecology. Because the lake is a wildlife sanctuary, a high fence surrounds its marshy edges, preventing a close look at the creatures inside.

Accommodation in Fuente de Piedra

Camping La Laguna € *c/ Camino Rábita; tel: (95) 273–5294.* Campsite has a swimming pool and bungalow apartments for longer stays.

Hostal La Laguna € *A92 km132; tel: (95) 273–6014.* Modest lodgings at a rest area along the main highway.

Torcal de Antequera**

This natural area is a geology lesson in the round: 12km² of serrated, pillared, twisted, water-etched and wind-blown limestone. The bedrock extrudes above the surface here, and aeons of natural weathering have created fantastic shapes which humans seem destined to interpret in their own cultural terms. The map available in the visitor centre identifies some of the most famous rock formations – the

Left
Torcal de Antequera

ⓘ Centro de Visitantes Parque Natural Torcal de Antequera tel: (95) 203–1389; open daily 1000–1700. Call in advance to book a guided tour of the area.

Oficina de Turismo, c/ Plaza San Sebastían 7, Antequera; e-mail: turismo@aytoantequera; www.aytoantequera.com; open summer Mon–Sat 1000–1300, 1700–2000; winter Mon–Sat 1000–1330, 1600–1900; Sun 1000–1330.

Needles, the Camel, the Sphinx, the Screw, the Binoculars, the Jar – and provides a sketchy outline of a 45-min walking tour. The stones are blazed in different colours to delineate the paths.

While most visitors never see past the rocks, this weird landscape has other, more organic attractions. The area supports a substantial herd of ibex, most noticeable during the autumn mating season when males fight by clashing horns. Throughout the warm months, several species of lizard can be observed skittering across the rocks. Soil in the rock fissures supports a number of wildflowers and shrubs such as the common hawthorn. During the winter the hawthorn turns grey-green, its bare branches covered with lichens. In spring, bursting green leaves are followed by extremely fragrant white flowers. The great grey shrike builds its nest in the branches of this thorny shrub, using the spines to impale its prey.

Suggested tour

Total distance: 177km, 183km with detour.

Time: One long day.

Links: This tour connects with Málaga (see pages 42–51) and the Costa del Sol (see pages 52–63) in the south.

Route: Leave **ANTEQUERA ❶** by the A343, following signs towards Alora. Continue for 12km and take the well-marked turning for Estación de Gobantes. After another 2km, turn right through the tiny village of **Valle de Abdalajís**✦ and follow the rough twisting mountainside road 10km through the village of **Huma**✦ to **EL CHORRO ❷**. Drive 800m past the entrance to Camping El Chorro, park and walk up the boulder-strewn road for a high overview of the Garganta del Chorro. To continue, drive over the bridge and turn right towards **Bobastro**✦. Turn into one of several side roads for a better look at the narrow cut of the defile, and an attractive little hermitage near the gorge itself.

Detour: At Bobastro, turn off at the sign to **Iglesia Mozárabe** then wind 2km to *mesas* above El Chorro Gorge, where the renegade bandit Omar ibn Hafsun kept the Córdoban emirate at bay from 880 until 917. A Muslim convert to Christianity, he commissioned a rare Mozarabic church here, where he was buried after being posthumously crucified by the Córdoban army.

Back on the road, the MA444 winds up for about 3km into Parque de Ardales at Bobastro, then proceeds another 3km through swirling, rounded sandstone formations. At the road's terminus, a right turn goes 800m to a picnic area.

Instead, turn left on to the MA442 and proceed 6km to **ARDALES ❸**. After seeing the local museum, go back across the bridge and

turn right for 7km to **CARRATRACA** ❹, taking the turn-off for the town. In front of the spa, take the MA441 towards Alora. This 17km road follows the ridges and rises into a regional pine forest where hiking is permitted. On the far side of the wooded hills, the road descends through groves of olives with roadside thickets of wild artichokes and other thistles favoured by finches. When the lemon groves begin, the road has arrived in the Valley of the Sun: **ALORA** ❺.

At Alora, follow signs toward Málaga for 6km through **Pizarra**✷ on the A343, then 12.5km to Estación Cártama. Cross the bridge to **Cártama**✷, a white town overlooked by a handsome church, and take the A357 to Málaga. At Málaga (*see pages 42–51*), follow the Ronda de Málaga towards Mótril, picking up the N331 north towards Antequera. After 44km take the km139 exit and drive 8km west to **Villanueva de la Concepción**✷. At Villanueva, follow the C3310 north 4km to **TORCAL** ❻. Continue north 8km on the C3310 to link up with the A343 just 3km south of Antequera, following the road back to the city.

Gibraltar

Ratings

History	●●●●
Museums	●●●
Nature and wildlife	●●●
Shopping and crafts	●●●
Entertainment	●●
Architecture	●
Beaches	●
Gastronomy	●

The Rock of Gibraltar towers on the southern coast of Spain, rising like a colossus from the sea. This gigantic chunk of limestone – tumbled end over end by geological forces, whipped by winds and honeycombed by dripping water – long ago assumed mythical significance. The ancients paired it with Morocco's Jebel Musa mountain, terming the two the Pillars of Hercules that marked the end of the known world. Just 5km long, 2km wide and 450m high, the rock is connected tangentially to Spain by a narrow isthmus, making it easy for both sides to control border crossings. Political insecurity sometimes makes Gibraltar seem more British than Britain, and it is a handy spot for expats to buy English-language books and familiar comestibles. Even travellers immersed in the experience of Andalucía should consider spending a day visiting this cultural and geological anomaly, where cool breezes evoke more northerly climes.

Getting there and getting around

Tourist Office
Duke of Kent House, Cathedral Square; tel: 74950; e-mail: tourism@gibraltar.gi; www.gibraltar.gov.gi; open Mon–Fri 0900–1700. There is also a smaller office – really just a desk – at the border crossing.

Gibraltar Taxi Association
19 Waterport Wharf; tel: 70052.

Arriving and departing: The international border is at the southern end of Avda 20 de Abril in the Spanish town of La Línea de la Concepción, approached from the Costa del Sol by the A383 off the N340, or from Algeciras via the A351. A passport or EU identity card is necessary to enter Gibraltar. A sign at passport control reads: 'Gibraltar regrets the inconvenience caused to you due to frontier restrictions imposed by Spanish authorities contrary to your European Union rights to free movement'. British control is a sore point for Spain, and Spanish border guards often cause long delays for vehicles re-entering Spain. Park in La Línea either on the street or in more secure underground car parks. Driving is on the right in Gibraltar.

Getting around: A cable car (€€) from the south end of Main St ascends to the summit of the Rock, operating *daily 1000–1800*. Ticket includes entry to the Nature Reserve, Apes' Den and St Michael's Cave.

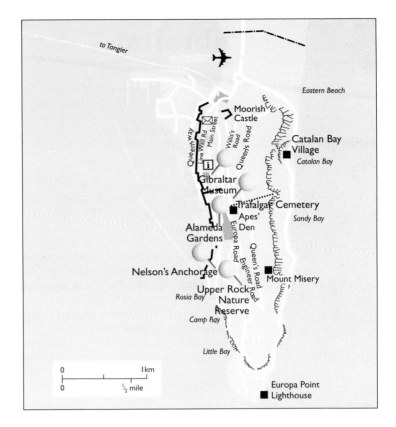

The best way to tour the Rock is to take the cable car to the summit, walk down to St Michael's Cave and Apes' Den and then take the return cable car from the midway stop at Apes' Den. This involves about an hour's walk on a fairly steep downhill grade.

Those who fear heights or prefer not to walk can purchase **taxi tours** (€€) from many licensed operators on Main St. Long traffic delays at popular spots along the route are the chief drawback of taxi tours.

Communications: Telephone numbers within Gibraltar are five digits, as given in this chapter. Calling from outside the district requires different prefix codes depending on the origin of the call. From the UK, Gibraltar uses a regional code of 350. From Spain, it uses a regional code of 9567.

Currency: Gibraltar Government notes are the legal tender, but UK coins and notes are accepted, as well as euros for everything except coin-operated vending machines and parking meters.

Sights

Alameda Botanical Gardens Entry on Europa Rd; open daily 0800–sunset.

Gibraltar Museum € Bomb House Lane; open Mon–Fri 1000–1800, Sat 1000–1400.

Alameda Botanical Gardens*

British gardening talent took root in Gibraltar's subtropical climate, especially in the Alameda Botanical Gardens centred on Grand Parade. First planted in 1816, the gardens have been restored and upgraded. They feature Mediterranean pines and olives as well as a collection of cacti and other succulent plants from around the world. The Dell, a peaceful area that resembles a sunken Italian garden, has fountains, ponds and waterfalls.

Gibraltar Museum***

The museum attempts to condense a long history, as Gibraltar was one of the first places in Europe inhabited by both *Homo Neanderthal* and *Homo Sapiens*. The skull of a woman, later dated as 100,000 years old, was found on the north face of Gibraltar in 1848. Its significance did not emerge until *Homo Neanderthal* was later named after similar skeletal remains found in Germany. The original skull now resides in the Natural History Museum in London, and the Gibraltar Museum exhibits a casting.

Unlike most of the Andalucían coast, Gibraltar was never settled by the Phoenicians or the Romans. In 711, the Rock became a stepping-stone for Islamic conquest and was lightly fortified by Moorish forces until 1068, when the first major fortress was built. The museum complex contains Moorish baths, considered among the best preserved in Europe.

Nelson's Anchorage € (or free with ticket to Upper Rock Nature Reserve); *Rosia Rd; open Mon–Sat 0930–1700.*

Upper Rock Nature Reserve €€ *Open daily 0930–1900.* Drivers or intrepid hikers who pay at the gate gain entry to Nelson's Anchorage, Apes' Den, O'Hara's Battery, St Michael's Cave, Military Heritage Centre, Great Siege Tunnels and other sites, most of which have military associations.

Gibraltar Crystal *Grand Casemates; tel: 50136; www.gibraltarcrystal.com* Creates handblown glass, including a handsome set of stemware called 'The Trafalgar Range' in honour of the famous battle.

There's karaoke on Wed and Sat at the Market Tavern, *1 Waterport; tel: 50800.* Tue is quiz night at **The Cannon Bar** *27 Cannon Lane; tel: 77288.*

The vagaries of politics delivered Gibraltar to Britain. A joint British and Dutch force seized the Rock in 1704 in the name of Charles V of Austria, pretender to the Spanish throne. The 1713 Treaty of Utrecht gave the Rock to Great Britain, but Spanish forces continued attacking the fortress. The Great Siege Room holds weapons and artefacts from the trying 1779–83 siege.

British attachment to the Rock is perhaps most evident in the detailed model created by officers of the Royal Engineers in the 1860s. This evocative time capsule now fills a large gallery and is surrounded by present-day views that demonstrate Gibraltar's changes in the ensuing years.

Nelson's Anchorage*

Located just off Rosia Rd with distant views of Rosia Bay and across the Straits of Gibraltar, this is the spot where HMS *Victory* brought Nelson's body ashore after the Battle of Trafalgar – in a rum barrel, legend says. Adjacent is the Napier Battery, site of the best preserved of the 100-ton Victorian 'super guns', of which only four were cast in 1870.

Trafalgar Cemetery**

This park-like cemetery sits just outside the city walls on Prince Edward's Rd. From 1708 to 1835 it served as a burial ground for His Majesty's forces and members of their families. It was named in memory of the casualties in the great Trafalgar victory of 21 Oct, 1805, but casualties of other naval actions along the coast are also buried here. A moving ceremony of remembrance is held on Trafalgar Day.

Upper Rock Nature Reserve***

'Nature Reserve' may seem a bit of an overstatement for the Upper Rock, but it has distant views and many walking paths. Because Gibraltar lies on the migratory flyway between Europe and Africa, the Upper Rock is an excellent vantage to spy migrating flocks of raptors, storks and songbirds.

Most local flora and fauna are modest, such as the Barbary partridge and such rock-clinging indigenous plants as chickweed, thyme and candytuft. The Rock Apes – actually Barbary macaques – get most of the attention. These tailless monkeys were probably introduced from North Africa in the 18th century, as the species is found fully wild in Morocco and Algeria. The Gibraltar macaques are the only semi-wild monkeys in Europe. Legend maintains that the British will keep Gibraltar only as long as the apes remain, which led Winston Churchill to increase their numbers. More recently, contraception has been introduced to curb breeding. Mothers with their young often congregate at **Apes' Den**.**

Perhaps because humans ignore the admonishments not to feed them, the apes gather near visitor attractions, including the midpoint and summit cable-car stations. They are also often sighted at the **Great Siege Tunnels***; these gun emplacements carved out of the rock are only a small example of the honeycomb of tunnels and galleries that pierce the limestone.

Also within the reserve is **St Michael's Cave**♦♦, a natural cavern inhabited during Neolithic times and now used for performing arts presentations. The cave has an upper hall with five connecting passages and drops between 12m and 45m to a smaller hall, which leads to more chambers that reach as far as 62m below the entrance. The stalactites and stalagmites are most impressive. During World War II, Allied landings in North Africa were staged from Gibraltar, and the cave was prepared as an emergency hospital but never used.

Accommodation and food

Bristol Hotel €€ *10 Cathedral Sq; tel: 76800; e-mail: bristhtl@gibnet.gi; www.gibraltar.gi/bristolhotel.* The 60 bedrooms in this centrally located hotel were recently refurbished. Some have views of the Bay of Gibraltar. Guests enjoy a small swimming pool and tropical garden. Rates include parking.

Cannon Hotel € *9 Cannon Lane; tel: 51711; e-mail: cannon@gibnet.gi; www.cannonhotel.gi.* This 18-room hotel with small patio opened in 1995 a block off Main St. The price includes English breakfast. Use of credit cards incurs a 5 per cent surcharge.

Maharaja €€ *5 Tucker's Lane; tel: 75233.* Excellent Indian restaurant tucked down a side street and dishing up suitably spicy Indian classic dishes, as well as *chicken tikka* and *kebabs*.

Queen's Hotel €€€ *1 Boyd St; tel: 74000 or 41682; e-mail: queenshotel@gibnynex.gi; www.queenshotel.gi.* Built in the international concrete block with stucco style, this large hotel is more welcoming inside than out. Offers options of rooms with shared or private baths and adjoining rooms for families. Rates include parking and English breakfast.

The Star Bar €€ *12 Parliament Lane; tel: 75924.* This snug tavern claims to be the oldest in Gibraltar and has a traditional Sunday lunch.

Waterfront Restaurant, Bar and Café €€ *Queensway Quay; tel: 40849.* A good place at the marina to have a quiet meal away from the crowds on Main St and check out the pleasure craft.

Suggested tour

Total distance: 6km.

Time: 4 hours, 7 hours with detour.

Route: The border crossing is enlivened by walking through the Gibraltar Airport runway area. But the walk doesn't really begin until

Nimo (tel: 73719) and *Dolphin World (tel: 81000)* offer dolphin watching cruises among others. Call for schedules.

the end of Main St at Casemates Square, which was once the site of public executions. Gibraltar Crystal is at the north end of the square, housed in a former army barracks.

Main St is a duty-free riot of shops hawking cigarettes, tobacco, liquor, Spanish and English porcelain, electronic gadgets and perfumes. Despite the free-for-all, there is also a distinctly British feel, owing to the presence of Marks & Spencer and the ready availability of fish and chips, English breakfasts and ice cream cones with a Cadbury Flake. Bear right on to Bomb House Lane to the **GIBRALTAR MUSEUM ❶**.

Detour: Continue down Bomb House Lane to Cathedral Square and down a flight of steps. Turn left at Queensway to reach Queensway Quay Marina. This pleasant spot dotted with cafés is also the departure point for several dolphin-watching cruises. The gregarious common, striped and bottle-nosed dolphins breed in the Bay of Gibraltar and

allow boats to get quite close. Pilot whales, killer whales (orcas) and sperm whales are also sometimes spotted during autumn and spring migrations.

Return to Main St. The beautiful courtyard of the **Governor's Residence**, about half-way along the street, is not open to the public. But Changing of the Guard takes place several times daily on weekdays outside the residence and is carried out by Gibraltar's native-born Regiment, formed in the 1970s.

Stop at **King's Chapel** next door, where regimental pomp augments religious circumstance through memorial plaques on the walls, retired regimental flags above the altar and a Moroccan carved-rosette ceiling. Church attendance is no longer compulsory, but Army officers retain the right to order men to services.

Take a left fork on to **Trafalgar Rd** to reach the cable car station. **TRAFALGAR CEMETERY ❷** is on the left, outside Prince Edward's Gate. It's best to take the cable car to the summit, the only place to buy a T-shirt to prove you made it. Enjoy the view, grab a bite to eat and walk downhill to other sites, probably past curious Rock apes. Follow clearly marked signs to **St Michael's Cave** and then to **Apes' Den**. Walkers and vehicles share the narrow roads, so remain alert.

En route to Apes' Den, notice part of the water catchment system that supplied Gibraltar's drinking water before the advent of desalinisation.

Bus Route 2 runs between the Alameda Botanical Gardens and Catalan Bay.

A massive sand dune was covered by sheets of corrugated iron at the beginning of the century. Rain falling on the iron was conveyed into the Rock where reservoirs holding up to 16 million gallons had been excavated. Water is still stored inside the Rock, though the main source of the water supply is now distillation plants at sea level.

Apes' Den is aptly named since apes do congregate here, including the youngest with their mothers. At this point, the intermediate cable-car station picks up passengers for the return journey. Next to the base station, the **ALAMEDA BOTANICAL GARDENS** ❸ make a soothing contrast to the rough limestone of the Upper Rock.

Also worth exploring

Despite the presence of a large, modern hotel, the fishing village at **Catalan Bay** on the eastern side of Gibraltar offers a low-key escape from the crowds. The village was settled by Genoese ship repairmen who followed the British fleet, and their descendants still fish in traditional Italian boats. The beach is tiny, but the village has many pubs for unwinding.

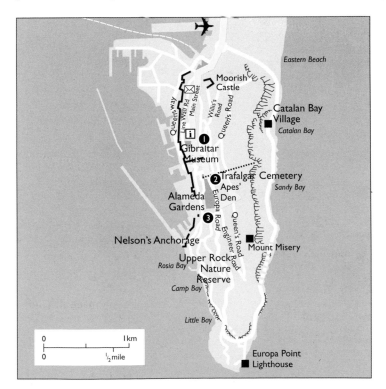

The Costa de la Luz

Ratings

Beaches ●●●●●

Gastronomy ●●●●○

Nature and wildlife ●●●●○

History ●●●○○

Entertainment ●●○○○

Shopping and crafts ●●○○○

Architecture ●○○○○

Museums ●○○○○

Although the entire Atlantic coast of Andalucía goes under the name of the 'Costa de la Luz', the name (Coast of Light) best fits the high dunes and windy shoals of the 90km coastline between Cádiz and Tarifa, Europe's southernmost point (only 8km from Africa).

Cooler and windier than the nearby Costa del Sol, the Costa de la Luz is far less built-up and its clean, white-sand bathing beaches are some of the finest in the world. Although domestic Spanish tourism is making some inroads, the landscape remains for the most part starkly untamed and windblown, and the towns retain their character as fishing villages. From April through July, brawny deep-water fishermen set their giant nets on the shoals to trap migrating tuna fish and throughout the year in-shore fishermen in small boats line the tidal flats to net small fry on the outgoing tide.

ALGECIRAS*

ℹ️ **Turismo** c/ Juan de la Cierva; tel: (95) 657–2636; e-mail: www.andalucia.org; open Mon–Fri 0900–1400.

🚢 **Buquebus €€€** Estación Marítima de Algeciras; tel: (95) 666–6909; www.buquebus.com. The hydrofoil service between Algeciras and Ceuta operates up to a dozen crossings daily, weather permitting.

The main reason to go to Algeciras is to catch a ferry to **Tangier** in Morocco or to **Ceuta***, a Spanish colony on the Moroccan coast. The port district has a wonderful border-town quality, full of cheap hotels, currency traders and the usual hustlers selling dubious tickets on the streets. The best way to make a crossing is simply to drive to the port, park in the garage, buy a ticket and go over as a pedestrian. Rates for exchanging euros for dirham are better on the Morocco side.

Tour offices for 100km in every direction sell package tours (€€€) via hydrofoil to Tangier and Tétuan. The Tangier boat takes an hour to cross the straits. When winds are too strong for hydrofoils to operate, passengers are shifted to a large but slower ferry. The less-frequent **Tétuan** tour reaches Ceuta in 35 minutes, followed by a bus trip to Tétuan. Packages include guided sightseeing, shopping time and lunch.

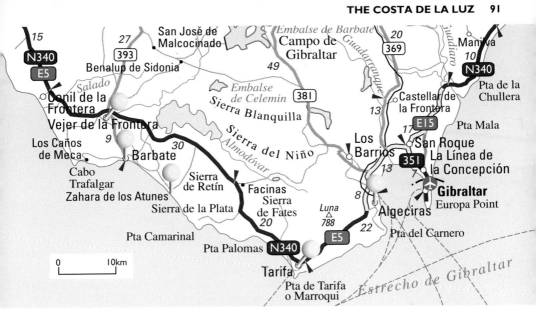

Transmediterránea
€€€ *Estación*
Marítima de Algeciras; tel:
(90) 245–4645;
www.transmediterranea.es
Large ferries take 2hrs to
Tangier, 1½hrs to Ceuta.

Accommodation in Algeciras

Hotel Reina Cristina €€–€€€ *Pas. de la Conferencia s/n; tel: (95) 660–2622; fax: (95) 660–3323; www.reinacristina.com*. If an overnight stay is necessary, this 18th-century grand hotel in British colonial style takes some of the sting out of Algeciras. Its park-like grounds are delightful – just don't look beyond to the industrial port.

BARBATE❖❖

Oficina de Turismo
c/ Vázquez Mella;
tel: (95) 643–3962.

**Fiestas de la
Virgen del Carmen**
*tel: (95) 643–3962. At the
end of the tuna fishing
season, 15–19 Jul, the
fishing boats engage in a
nocturnal thanksgiving
procession.*

Barbate is one of the busiest fishing ports in Spain. The main catch is tuna fish, netted in large deep-sea gear called *mandragues*. The chief tuna runs occur in the spring, as the fish pass from the Atlantic into the Mediterranean to breed, then again in late June and early July when they return to the Atlantic. Like all cannery towns, on a hot July day Barbate is best observed from upwind. Nonetheless, it has long sandy beaches and becomes a busy resort from July to September.

Barbate and surrounding towns prepare tuna in hundreds of ways, although roasted under sliced onions is most traditional. Other local specialities are *caballa con fideos* (mackerel with noodles), *guiso de morrillo* (fish stew) and *ortigas de mar* (sea nettles). Barbate and neighbouring Zahara produce most of Spain's *mojama*, somewhat leathery salted and dried strips of tuna, which is a popular sandwich filling or *tapas* in these parts.

On the west side of Barbate, en route to its daughter village of **Los Caños de Meca**❖❖, is the **Parque Natural del Acantilado y Pinar de Barbate**❖❖. Features of the park are the 100m-high white sandstone cliffs of Barbate and Spain's largest forest of umbrella pines, which spreads back from the cliffs. The forest supplies much of the country's pinenut production, while the cliffs are home to a huge breeding colony of cattle egrets as well as many kestrels and peregrine falcons.

The village of Los Caños has a deserved Bohemian reputation. Camping is still the preferred lodging and nude swimmers routinely cavort in the surf around the headland on the east end of the main beach. A small road on the west end of town leads to a lighthouse atop **Cabo de Trafalgar***, where Nelson destroyed Spain as a nautical power in the decisive battle just offshore. The main sails now seen along the cape are windsurfers.

Accommodation and food in and around Barbate

Camping Caños de Meca € *tel: (95) 643–7120; fax: (95) 643–7137; e-mail: info@canos-de-meca.com; www.camping-canos-de-meca.com.* Easily the best, most family-oriented camping in Los Caños.

Restaurante Torres €–€€ *Avda Ruíz de Alda 1; tel: (95) 643–0985; closed Mon.* Excellent formal restaurant near the Barbate lighthouse serves tuna at least 20 different ways.

TARIFA**

ℹ️ **Oficina de Turismo** *Pas. de la Alameda s/n; tel: (95) 668–0993; e-mail: turismo.tarifa@teleline.es; open Mon–Fri 1000–1400, 1700–1900, Sat–Sun 1000–1400 (summer).*

🏰 **Castillo de Guzmán** **€** *Open Tue–Sun 1000–1330 and 1700–2000.*

🐴 Two hotels on Playa de los Lances west of Tarifa – Hotel Dos Mares *tel: (956) 668–4035* and Hurricane Hotel *tel: (95) 668–4919* – rent horses for rides along the beach and organise wind-and-kite surfing classes (**€€€**).

The Berber warrior Tarif ibn Malluk landed here in 711 to launch his conquest of the Iberian Peninsula, and the town takes its name from him. With its key position controlling the straits between Europe and Africa, Tarifa was a pirates' nest in the 10th century. These entrepreneurs of the high seas demanded protection money from every ship wishing to pass between the Atlantic and Mediterranean – the possible origin of the term 'tariff'.

The hills of Africa rise dreamlike from Tarifa's sea mist, best viewed at sunset from roadside overlooks east of town. Another good spot is from the parapets and towers of **Castillo de Guzmán**** in the old town. The castle, which dates from 960, is named after Guzmán El Bueno, who became a Spanish folk hero during the *Reconquista* when he refused to surrender his Tarifa garrison to save the life of his kidnapped son.

Tarifa has turned the curse of its strong winds into a blessing. The *Levante* blows from the east, the *Poniente* from the west, and windsurfers and kitesurfers from all over the world come to ride them both. The best beaches are between Tarifa and Punta Paloma, about 10km northwest. One of the most popular is **Playa El Porro*** on Ensenada de Valdevaqueros, the bay formed by Punta Paloma. El Porro enjoys stiff *Levante* winds but has fewer dangerous rocks than beaches closer to town. The area at the mouth of the Río Jara, about 3km west of Tarifa, is also popular.

The main street of the new town, c/ Batalla del Salgado, is lined with shops selling and renting windsurfing boards, kitesurfing gear and other accessories. **Club Mistral** at the Hurricane Hotel on Playa de los Lances *(tel: (95) 668–9098)* and the Bic Sport Center *(tel: (63) 034–2258)* also rent Mistral and North Sail boards (€€€) and offer classes at all levels. The Kite School *(tel: (95) 668–1668; www.kitesurfingtarifa.com)* offers kite surfing classes and has a workshop for equipment repairs. Two windsurfing competitions, the **World Speed Cup** and the **World Cup Formula** *(tel: (95) 668–0993)* are held in July and July–Aug respectively.

The Straits of Gibraltar are superb feeding grounds for cetaceans, and daily trips to spot whales and dolphins are run by several operators including **Firmm** *(tel: (95) 662–7008)* which also runs a research centre, and **Turmares** *(tel: (95) 668–0741; www.turmares.com)* which runs excursions on a glass-bottom boat. You can also take a day trip to Tangier via highspeed catamaran with **FRS** *(tel: (95) 668–1830; fax: (95) 668–4835; www.frs.es)*.

Accommodation and food in Tarifa

Camping Paloma € *N340, 10km west of Tarifa; tel: (95) 668–4203; www.campingpaloma.com.* About 400m from the Playa Valdevaqueros, with striking views of Africa. Good modern facilities.

Camping Torre de la Peña € *N340, 4km west of Tarifa; tel: (95) 668–4903; fax: (95) 668–1473; e-mail: info@campingtp.com; www.campingtp.com.* One of the better modern campsites, with good restaurants and bars. Some pitches are across the busy N340 from the beach.

Continental Café € *Pas. de la Alameda s/n; tel: (95) 668–4776.* Good café near the Castillo Guzmán has a bargain *menú del día* at midday.

Hotel Dos Mares €€ *N340, Km 78; tel: (95) 668–4035; fax: (95) 668–1078; e-mail: dosmares@cherrytel.com; www.dosmareshotel.com.* A well-established resort, Dos Mares offers a huge range of facilities, from windsurfing and kitesurfing to horse riding, tennis and football. Recommended.

Hurricane Hotel €€ *N340, 7km west of Tarifa; tel: (95) 668–4919; info@hotelhurricane.com; www.hotelhurricane.com.* Surf bums may stay at campgrounds, but the Hurricane is an idyllic getaway hotel set in subtropical gardens leading to an excellent windsurfing beach. Masseur and fitness instructor on staff. The restaurant (€€), open to non-residents, uses the property's own fresh garden produce.

The main covered **market**, open Mon–Sat, occupies a Mudéjar revival building on c/ Colón.

VEJER DE LA FRONTERA**

This walled white town perched at the edge of a cliff high above rolling green pastures looks like the quintessential unassailable Moorish redoubt – precisely as its builders intended. The blocky, whitewashed labyrinth of its streets bears out the impression. Visitors come to Vejer to see the town hanging on a precipice high above some of Spain's leading bull-breeding farms, or *ganaderías*. Vejer was once famous for garbing its women in long black cloaks that covered everything but their eyes. How times change! Teenage girls hanging out in **Plaza de España*** – also known as *plaza de pescaítos* for the fish-motif tiled fountain in the middle – are likely now to be baring their midriffs to show off new rings in their navels. A truly pagan quality seizes the town at Easter, celebrated by turning a bull loose in the streets for foolish young men to taunt as everyone else celebrates with bacchanalian fervour.

The old walled town, where some streets are so steep that they have handrails, was declared a National Artistic Site in 1976. The **Castillo****
(€ *open daily 1100–1400 and 1800–2200*), in the old town, dates from Moorish times but was extensively rebuilt in the 15th century. It has a small museum where the bygone modesty of Vejer may be contemplated by observing the black cloak of *las cobijadas* on a

ℹ Oficina de Turismo
  c/ Marqués de
Tamarón 10;
tel: (95) 645–0191;
fax: (95) 645–1620;
www.aytovejer.org/prov

⛰ Fiesta del Toro Embolado tel: (95) 645–0191. Easter Sunday fiesta of music and drink while bull runs free in cordoned-off area of the old town.

mannequin. The **Iglesia del Divino Salvador**♦ (open 1100–1300 and 1930–2100), a 16th-century church built over a mosque, demonstrates the effect of slow construction: its altar end is Mudéjar, while the nave is pure Gothic.

Accommodation and food in Vejer de la Frontera

Camping Vejer € N340 km39.5; tel: (95) 645–0098; e-mail: info@campingvejer; www.campingvejer.com

Hotel Convento de San Francisco €–€€ Plazuela s/n; tel: (95) 645–1001; fax: (95) 645–1004; e-mail: convento-san-francisco@tugasa.com; www.tugasa.com. Small hotel in village centre provides quiet rooms.

La Posada € c/ Los Remedios 21; tel: (95) 645–0258. Small rooms with baths above handsome restaurant with windows opening on to town's lower park.

Mesón Judería €€ c/ Judería 5; tel: (95) 644–7657. While not strictly vegetarian, this restaurant emphasises fresh fruits and vegetables. Closed Wed.

ZAHARA DE LOS ATUNES♦♦

Plonked down smack in the middle of a 10km sand beach, Zahara de Los Atunes is a genuine fishing village in the wrenching process of becoming a summer resort. Parts of the village are virtually abandoned, with strong winds blowing rubbish down deserted alleyways, while other sectors are clearly prosperous and well groomed. The ancient **Almadabra**♦, once a combination fish market and fishermen's lodging, is crumbling to dust. Historically, Zahara was famous for its tough guys: Cervantes wrote that no one deserved the name pícaro (low-life scoundrel) until he had spent at least two seasons catching tuna in Zahara. The broad west-facing beach is spectacular but subject to intense winds.

Accommodation and food in Zahara de los Atunes

Camping Bahía de la Plata € Carretera de Atlanterra; tel: (95) 643–9040; www.campingbahiadelaplata.com. Near the beach at the southern edge of town.

Hotel Almadraba € c/ María Luisa 15; tel: (95) 643–9332. Away from the beach near the Mercado Abastos, the modest rooms upstairs are of less interest than the fabulous fish dishes served at the bar (€–€€). This is where the successful fishermen go to dine.

Hotel Gran Sol €€ *Avda de la Playa; tel: (95) 643–9301; fax: (95) 643–9197; e-mail: hotelgransol@infonegocio.com; www.gransolhotel.com.* On the beach, facing the walls of the Almadabra. One of the village's plushest lodgings.

Hotel Pozo del Duque €–€€ *Carretera Atlanterra 32; tel: (95) 643–9097; www.pozodelduque.com.* Small hotel on the beach caters to families and windsurfers.

Suggested tour

Total distance: 170km, 191km with detour.

Time: One–two days.

Links: This route links to four other routes: Cádiz (*see pages 98–107*) to the north, Gibraltar (*see pages 82–9*) to the south, the Heart of the Frontera (*see pages 108–17*) via the A393 between Vejer de la Frontera and Medina Sidonia or via the A369 between Algeciras and Jimena de la Frontera, and to the Costa del Sol route (*see pages 52–63*) via the N340 between Algeciras and Estepona.

Route: This route is the best way to reach the Costa del Sol from Cádiz; few drivers treat it as a circuit. Take the N-IV from Cádiz, turning south on the N340 after 17km. The 28km drive to **VEJER DE LA FRONTERA** ❶ is slow and rather dull, passing inland of several fabulous beaches where either up-market development or a grimy backpack and bedroll crowd have all but spoiled the natural beauty. The situation takes a turn for the better at Vejer, which lies 1km up a steep road, commanding the heights to the horizon. On the south side of the village, the A393 snakes back down the hill to the coast for 10km to **BARBATE** ❷.

Just west of Barbate's long town beach, turn right towards 'Cabo de Trafalgar' for the scenic 12km drive along the CA2223 through the spectacular upland pine forest of **Parque Natural del Acantilado y Pinar de Barbate**. After 3km watch for a left turn signed 'Torre Arabe', where woodland trails lead to the ruins of a Moorish coastal watchtower and stunning clifftop views. Just below this cliff is the principal breeding ground in Spain for the cattle egret.

The road winds through the up-beat village of **Los Caños de Meca**. Fans of nude sunbathing should head to the eastern end of the beach. The rest of the beach is less crowded, nicely sheltered from the wind and far more decorous. At the west end of town a left turn leads across a sand-drifted road to the lighthouse on Cabo de Trafalgar, where the bay below is filled with hardcore windsurfers. After 3km, turn right on to the CA2141 to return 16km to Vejer to resume travelling south on the N340. Take the right-hand turn in 20km on to the CA2221 for **ZAHARA DE LOS ATUNES** ❸, 10km away. Backtrack to the N340 and continue south.

🛈 Conjunto Arqueológico de Baelo Claudia € *Open summer Tue–Sat 1000–1330, 1630–2000, rest of year 1000–1430, 1600–1730; free with EU passport.*

Detour: About 10km south of the junction of the N340 and CA2221, a small sign indicates the road for Bolonia. This narrow, twisting road ascends fierce, serrated limestone hills up over the sharp peaks to the small village and the striking Roman-era ruins of **Baelo Claudia**✦✦. This well-excavated archaeological site tells the tale of a community once famous throughout the Mediterranean for its *garum marsala* paste of fermented anchovies. Descending into the village, there are spectacular views of cattle grazing on green hillsides that sweep down to white-sand beaches separated by high limestone headlands.

The N340 continues 14km to **TARIFA** ❹, with the hills of North Africa visible like a mirage in the distant haze. Leaving town on the east side of Tarifa, the N340 twists and winds as it climbs about 400m above sea level along a series of ridges where gigantic propellers are mounted on pylons. These windfarms buzz with the eerie sound of a giant hive of baritone bees as they pump out electricity into the grid of wires above them. Shortly after the largest windfarm, in 10km, the **Mirador Estrecho**✦✦ is on the right-hand side of the road. This spot offers the clearest and least obstructed view of Africa's distant hills. Their chalky serrations with vibrant greenery were perhaps the inspiration for Ernest Hemingway's title, *The Green Hills of Africa*. In another 11km the N340 enters the large port city of Algeciras – the main port for boat trips to the tantalising shore of Morocco, just across the straits.

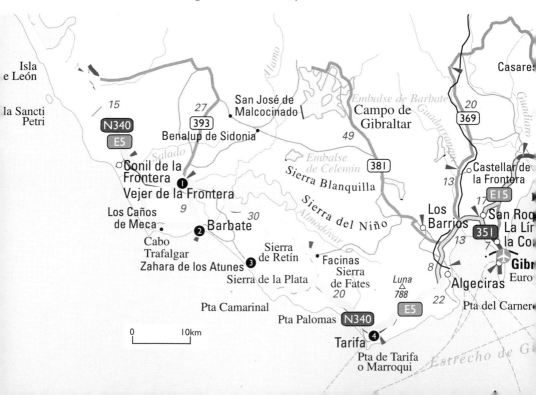

Cádiz

Ratings

Museums	●●●●○
Beaches	●●●○○
Entertainment	●●●○○
Gastronomy	●●●○○
History	●●●○○
Nature and wildlife	●●●○○
Architecture	●●○○○
Shopping and crafts	●●○○○

Reaching back to the origins of European civilisation, Cádiz was founded as the Phoenician port of *Gadir* 3100 years ago, when Rome was still seven wolf-haunted hills. Residents still call themselves *gaditanos*. Its commanding position at the tip of a peninsula guarding the Atlantic coast has made the city a prize for every power since. But Cádiz has worn the yokes of its conquerors lightly, and the 1755 earthquake obliterated most of their traces. Cádiz has no *alcazaba* or mosque, only post-Renaissance fortresses built to protect fortunes extracted from the Americas. A sophisticated 18th-century city that wears its age well, Cádiz basks in seaside light that illuminates even the narrow streets. The city has an intense intellectual history and an enviable legacy of music and poetry. Yet for all its achievements, it is finally an atmospheric and welcoming place, easy to wander, easy to like.

Sights

Turismo c/ Pl. de San Juan de Dios 11; tel: (95) 624–1001; fax: (95) 624–1005; e-mail: otcadiz@andalucia.org; www.cadizayto.es; open Mon–Fri 0900–1400, 1700–2000. A small kiosk is located in Pl. San Juan de Dios.

Patronato Provincial de Turismo Pl. de San Antonio 3; tel: (95) 680–7061. Useful websites for the whole province include: www.infocadiz.com; www.fjate.com

Barrio de la Viña✣
The streets are narrow and the houses small and low-rise in this erstwhile fishermen's quarter. While there are few shops or other sites of intrinsic interest, the neighbourhood is a fascinating place to explore and one of the best areas of the city for seafood. Most of the casual *freidurías* and *tapas* bars are found on Pl. Tío Tiza, which is set up with tables in the summer. A plaque in the plaza notes that it is named after Antonio Rodríguez Martínez, author of 'the most famous *tangos gaditanos*', the classic flamenco of Cádiz.

Catedral Nueva✣
The rough sandstone blocks of the base of Cádiz cathedral have more in common with the city's stalwart defensive walls than with its other, more baroque, houses of worship. The main architectural entrance of

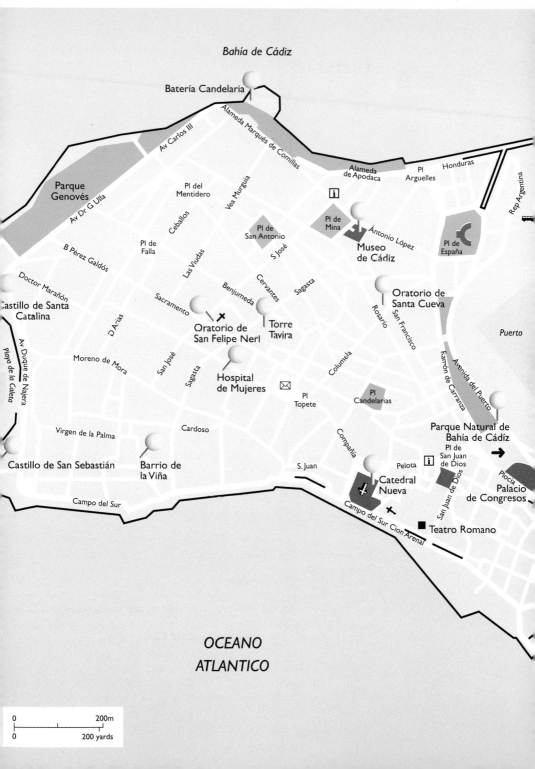

Bahía de Cádiz

Batería Candelaria

Alameda Marqués de Comillas

Av Carlos III

Alameda
de Apodaca

Pl
Arguelles

Honduras

Rep Argentina

Parque
Genovés

Av Dr G Ulla

Pl del
Mentidero

Vea Murguía

i

Pl de
Mina

Ántonio López

Ceballos

Pl de
San Antonio

S José

Museo
de Cádiz

Pl de
España

B Pérez Galdós

Pl de
Falla

Las Viudas

Cervantes

Sagasta

Oratorio de
Santa Cueva

Doctor Marañón

Sacramento

Benjumeda

Rosario

San Francisco

Puerto

Castillo de Santa
Catalina

D A-rias

Oratorio de
San Felipe Nerl

Torre
Tavira

Av Duque de Najera

Moreno de Mora

San José

Sagasta

Hospital
de Mujeres

Columela

playa de la Caleta

Pl
Topete

Pl
Candelarias

Avenida del Puerto

Ramón de Carranza

Virgen de la Palma

Cardoso

Parque Natural de
Bahía de Cádiz

Castillo de San Sebastián

Barrio de
la Viña

S. Juan

Compañía

Pelota

Pl de
San Juan
de Dios

i

Plocia

Campo del Sur

Catedral
Nueva

San Juan de Dios

Palacio
de Congresos

Campo del Sur Clon Arenal

Teatro Romano

*OCEANO
ATLANTICO*

0   200m

0   200 yards

Follow Avda de Andalucía through the modern city to Puerta de Tierra, the 17th-century gate that makes a graceful transition to the old city.

Boats making the 20-minute run across the bay to El Puerto de Santa María depart from Estación Marítima near Pl. de España at 1000, 1200, 1400 and 1830 with additional trips during the summer. €.

Catedral Nueva and Museo € *Pl. Catedral; open Tue–Fri 1000–1245, 1630–1845, Sat 1000–1245.*

Museo de Cádiz € *Pl. de Mina s/n; tel: (95) 621–2281; open Tue 1430–2000, Wed–Sat 0900–2000, Sun 0930–1400.*

the cathedral, up a steep flight of steps, fronts on a pleasant plaza with lively cafés, but visitors must enter via a side door to the museum, as the cathedral is locked except during services. Begun in 1722 and completed in 1853, the cathedral is considered 'new' because it replaced an older building destroyed by fire in 1596. Of main interest in the cathedral itself are the carved choir stalls topped with busts of saints and musicians. They predate the new cathedral, having originally been installed in a Carthusian church in Sevilla. The cathedral museum gives pride of place to a towering silver monstrance said to be adorned with a million jewels – certainly too many to count. The crypt beneath the cathedral contains the tombs of Cádiz native Manuel de Falla, one of Spain's most important 20th-century composers, and of poet José María Pemán.

Museo de Cádiz+++

One of Andalucía's best museums, combining archaeology and fine arts, has transformed a handsome mansion on Pl. de Mina into a state-of-the-art facility worthy of its superb collections. The early 19th-century neoclassical building has been imaginatively renovated to create light and airy galleries that accentuate the contemporary and ancient collections with equal success.

As the oldest continuously inhabited city in Europe, founded around 1100 BC as a Phoenician trade port, it is only fitting that Cádiz should have a museum displaying one of the finest collections of Phoenician artefacts anywhere in the Mediterranean. Indeed, the discovery in 1887 of a 5th-century BC carved sarcophagus of a Phoenician man was the impetus for founding the museum. Amazingly, his female counterpart was discovered a century later and they now lie side by side as the centrepiece of the Phoenician collection. With the eclipse of Phoenicia and its daughter city, Carthage, Rome ruled Cádiz as a strategic stronghold; it was here that Julius Caesar held his first public office. The Roman era in Cádiz is represented by a collection of statuary effectively illuminated by natural light, and by other objects that range from coins and mosaics to vessels used for trade.

The museum's visual art collection is equally strong and quite extraordinary for a regional museum. An entire gallery is devoted to works by Zurbarán, whose combination of strong form and lush colour seems entirely appropriate for a city that is simultaneously formal and sensual – perhaps more appropriate here than in many of the churches where the paintings first hung. Among the featured works is a series of portraits of saints from the Carthusian monastery at Jerez, hung as they had been in the church. This is one of only three intact sets in Spain. Zurbarán modelled the faces of the saints on the likenesses of monks he met in Carthusian monasteries throughout Spain, which perhaps explains their expressiveness. Also of note are several paintings by Murillo, including his last work *Los Desposorios de*

Santa Catalina (The Mystic Marriage of Santa Catalina). Murillo fell from a scaffold to his death while working on this painting, which was completed by a student.

The museum also displays contemporary art and the work of Gaditano artists. It's worth seeking out the ethnographic collection, reached by a stairway off one of the side galleries upstairs. As a city with a strong liberal, sometimes progressive, history and a long-standing mistrust of centralised power, Cádiz has a tradition of satirical marionette theatre. The ethnographic collection, which is often closed, includes a substantial collection of antique 'Tía Norica' marionettes, many displayed with their theatrical sets.

Below
The Catedral Nueva

Above
The seafront fortifications of Cádiz

Parque Natural de Bahía de Cádiz**

Although poorly marked, this natural park is evident all along the coastline in and around Cádiz. It encompasses the estuaries and shoals of the city proper, of adjacent San Fernando and Puerto Real and of the coast south of the Cádiz peninsula toward the beach community of Chiclana de la Frontera. No visitor centres exist, but it is usually feasible to pull off the beachside highway, park one's car and whip out binoculars for a better look at the birds. The parklands cover virtually all the estuaries, marshes, streams, seasonal lakes and salt pans of the Bay of Cádiz, although salt pans licensed for commercial salt extraction and regions engaged in fish farming are closed to visitors. The vegetation, even in the dry summer, is a halophytic mixture of reeds, bulrushes, salt cedars and saltwort. The clean, shallow waters teem with invertebrates and small fish, attracting such wading birds as flamingos, avocets, egrets, herons and storks in great numbers. From Apr to Nov, the endangered chameleon can also be found (on close inspection) prowling the shrubs and trees of the park for blowflies, grasshoppers and mantis. Best access to the salt marshes and mudflats are from the N-IV and A4 north of Cádiz and the N340 and C346 south and southeast of the city.

Religious art and architecture**

Three of the city's religious sites merit a visit even by those with no special interest in religious architecture or history, because they contain remarkable works of art. Their locations within the heart of the old city also make them central points of departure for exploring the surrounding districts.

Oratorio de Santa Cueva € c/ Rosario 10; tel: (95) 622–2262; open Tue–Fri 1000–1300, 1700–2000, Sat–Sun 1000–1300.

Oratorio de San Felipe Neri € c/ Santa Inés; tel: (95) 621–1612; open Mon–Sat 1000–1330.

Hospital de Mujeres € c/ Hospital de Mujeres 26; tel: (95) 622–3647; open Mon–Sat 1000–1330.

Castillo de Santa Catalina Playa Caleta; tel: (95) 622–6333; open Mon–Sun 1030–2000.

Sandwiched between other buildings at c/ Rosario 10, one of the main streets, the Baroque **Oratorio de Santa Cueva*** of the Iglesia del Rosario is notable for its trio of Goya frescoes; these include the unusual *Last Supper* where Christ and the disciples sit eastern-style on the floor.

In 1812, refugees from other parts of Spain still occupied by Napoleon issued a Declaration of Independence on the square at the junction of c/ Sacramento and c/ San José. In this same spot the 1812 Cortes met and framed Spain's first liberal constitution, which was not implemented until much later. Nonetheless, the radicals of Cádiz electrified intellectuals throughout Europe as the continent sought to throw off Napoleon's yoke. The **Oratorio de San Felipe Neri****, where the Cortes met, is covered with plaques sent from other countries to voice their support for Spanish independence. The oval nave of the oratory is lit from a pale blue dome, itself illuminated by a row of windows around the base. An immense *Inmaculada* by Murillo crowns the main altarpiece.

Finally, the **Hospital de Mujeres***, an 18th-century women's hospital, is one of the city's best baroque buildings with two beautiful patios. The hospital's chapel has a typically charged El Greco of *San Francisco in Ecstasy*.

Seafront promenades and fortifications***

Cádiz is sometimes nicknamed 'Tacita de Plata' or 'Little Cup of Silver'. While the endearment suffers in translation, in Spanish it evokes the city as a knob of land surrounded by shimmering water and only connected to the mainland by a stem. The seaside promenades reinforce that image of Cádiz as both a strategic guard over the Atlantic coast and a twinkling, Atlantis-like metropolis afloat in the ocean. The promenades are perfect spots for gazing out to sea, fishing or simply enjoying the ocean breezes that help to keep Cádiz fresh and cool.

With the views of the Atlantic Ocean beyond, the **Parque Genovés**** is a classic example of 19th-century park practices, where the trees are sculpted in the Renaissance manner to fit an artful pattern but also bear labels with their scientific names in a nod to the rise of scientific humanism and its penchant for description. An outdoor theatre in the park is often a venue for summer musical and theatrical performances. The adjoining **Alameda Marqués de Comillas**** was also laid out in the 19th century, but in a rather more practical, less fussy design that ultimately proves more welcoming.

The silent remains of the **Batería Candelaria***, **Castillo de Santa Catalina**** and **Castillo de San Sebastián*** are arrayed strategically around the knob of Cádiz from the northwest to the southwest, leaving the shallow, sandy shores of the north and south exposed but hardly vulnerable. The fortifications bear mute witness to the turbulent military history of the area. In 1587 Sir Francis Drake 'singed the King of Spain's beard' by attacking the harbour and thereby delaying the

Torre Tavira € c/ *Marqués Real Tesoro 10; tel: (95) 621–2910; open daily 1000–2000 in summer, 1000–1800 in winter.*

Solves *Pl. del Palillero 4* is one of the nicer gift shops, offering a wide range of craft items, including fine saddlery, religious carvings and exquisite luggage and wallets.

Peña Flamenca Juanito Villar *Puerta Caleta s/n; tel: (95) 622–5290.* Although Cádiz is the birthplace of a distinct flamenco style, it has not participated as extensively in the flamenco revival as other parts of Andalucía. This casual bar near the beach, however, offers flamenco performances at weekends during the summer.

Spanish Armada. Less than a decade later, Anglo-Dutch attackers burned much of the city, and the first of these 'modern' fortifications, the Castillo de Santa Catalina, was built in response. Candelaria and San Sebastián are later fortresses, but they failed to prevent the blockade of Cádiz harbour in the Napoleonic Wars, nor could they aid the Spanish fleet when it was decimated in the Battle of Trafalgar off Los Caños de Meca. Empty of its guns, Candelaria forms the western end of the Alameda. Santa Catalina is open for tours at regular hours. San Sebastián is theoretically closed to visitors, although one would not know it by the numbers of people swarming along the causeway.

Between Castillo de Santa Catalina and Castillo de San Sebastián is the in-city beach **Playa de la Caleta**✦, popular with teenagers, families and people with dogs. An elegant promenade lined with palm trees continues along the rocky shore of Campo del Sur before resuming as the brown-sand beach of **Playa de Santa María del Mar**✦ east of the old city walls.

Torre Tavira✦✦

During the 18th century, when Cádiz dominated over 75 per cent of trade with the Americas, more than 150 watchtowers throughout the city surveyed the harbour and followed the comings and goings of ships. This survivor, the highest lookout of its day, still offers commanding views of the city and enables visitors to visualise the location of Cádiz as a tethered bauble on the sea. The tower's sweeping views have been put to a unique use, with the installation of a rotating *camera obscura* that projects moving images of the town onto the walls of a viewing chamber.

Accommodation and food in Cádiz

Hostal Bahía € *c/ Plocia 5; tel: (95) 625–9061.* All the rooms in this small but cheerful and economical *hostal*, off Pl. San Juan de Dios, have private baths.

Hotel de Francia y París € *Pl. San Francisco 6; tel: (95) 621–2318; fax: (95) 622–2431; www.hotelfrancia.com.* A very pleasant hotel that also offers the option of air-conditioned suites with separate fax/modem lines.

Parador Hotel Atlántico €€ *Avda Duque de Nájera 9; tel: (95) 622–6905; fax: (95) 621–4582; e-mail: cadiz@parador.es; www.parador.es.* Next to the Parque Genovés and looking out over the broad Atlantic, this *parador* is perfectly situated to enjoy the old city. Renovations have returned it to the high standards of the *parador* system.

Achuri € *c/ Plocia 15; tel: (95) 625–3613.* Another superb seafood restaurant, deservedly popular with locals. Book ahead. *Closed Sun–Wed for dinner.*

La Caleta € *Pl. San Juan de Dios 1; tel: (95) 627–2781.* Unpretentious restaurant on one of the city's prettiest squares. Plenty of *tapas* and

Carnaval *tel: (95) 624–1001.*

raciones choice, as well as an economical daily menu with an emphasis on seafood.

La Catedral €–€€ *Pl. de la Catedral; tel: (95) 625–2184.* Prime position, opposite the cathedral, specialising in seafood dishes, as well as a good range of *tapas*, including excellent *tortilla*.

Freiduría Las Flores € *Pl. Flores; no tel.* There's a steady stream of customers for the takeaway shrimp from this *freiduría* in the Pl. del los Flores.

Restaurante El Faro €€€ *c/ San Felix 15; tel: (95) 621–1068.* This elegant fish restaurant in the Barrio de la Viña is one of the best known in the city. The *menú del día* (€€) is a good way to sample their style, alternatively try the *tapas* in the bar.

Cádiz's **Central produce market** is on Pl. Libertad.

Suggested tour

Total distance: about 5km.

Time: 4 hours.

Route: This walking tour begins and ends on the city's seafront promenades that outline the tip of the peninsula. In between, it delves into the heart of the 18th-century city, forging a path along the narrow old streets. Be watchful for bicycles and darting motor scooters – narrow as they are, most of these streets are *not* reserved for pedestrians.

Carnaval

In the 10 days of February leading up to Ash Wednesday, Cádiz sheds its decorum for the non-stop drunken party of Carnaval, with four categories of costumed musicians competing for prizes as they rove the streets singing satirical songs. Getting a room is hopeless; the best bet is to come in on the afternoon train from Sevilla, party all night and take the pre-dawn train back. The biggest parties are at the two weekends.

The route begins at **PARQUE GENOVES ❶**, where a bevy of sleek and contented cats doze beneath the manicured trees and hang out at cafés hoping for the handouts that they invariably receive. **BATERIA CANDELARIA ❷**, the defensive fortress enclosure at the northwest corner of the city, marks the transition to another leafy enclave, **Alameda Marqués de Comillas.** Its benches and fountains are gaudily decorated with *azulejo* tiles, and the heady scent of Seville oranges perfumes the area.

Leave the greenery and ocean views to follow Avda Calderón Barca to Pl. de Mina, where the **MUSEO DE CADIZ ❸** sits on the northeast corner.

The streets of Cádiz are designed to mitigate the warm climate. The four-to five-storey buildings that line either side keep the streets in deep shade, even at midday, and allow them to remain cool. Yet interior Cádiz is hardly claustrophobic, as the streets are punctuated by frequent plazas that serve as bright and sunny oases. From Pl. de Mina, follow c/ Tinte, which becomes c/ Rosario when it passes Pl. San Francisco, past the Iglesia del Rosario and **Oratorio de la Santa Cueva.** Take the next right on to c/ Columela.

Detour: Serious shoppers may want to turn right from c/ Columela on to c/ José del Toro, which becomes c/ Ancha (literally, 'wide street', all 5m of it). This pedestrian zone is lined with shops and antique dealers. The 19th-century mansion at No 28 is open for tours on Sat mornings. C/ Ancha leads into Pl. de San Antonio, one of the city's larger and most attractive squares. Backtrack on c/ Ancha to c/ Columela.

C/ Columela leads to Pl. Palillero – which is lined with a wide variety of shops selling clothing, shoes and gift items – and continues to Pl. Flores, one of the city's most colourful squares. Flores is anchored by an imposing neo-Mudéjar style post office and is full of friendly vendors selling flowers, of course, as well as olives and tiny shrimps wrapped in paper cones, known as *paquetes de camarones*. Try the dried and salted tuna called *mojama* and *burgaillos* (snails).

To the left of the post office, Pl. Flores flows into the **MERCADO CENTRAL** ❹, while c/ Compañía leads to **PL. CATEDRAL** ❺. From here it is a short walk to **PL. SAN JUAN DE DIOS** ❻, site of the medieval fortified area of the city. Only three 13th-century gates remain and the plaza now has a lively restaurant and café scene, watched over by the impressive neoclassical Ayuntamiento (city hall), built around 1800.

Walk back to Pl. Catedral and along c/ Arquitecto Acero by the side of the Cathedral to Campo del Sur. The city opens up again into a broad oceanside *paseo*, where fishermen often perch on the sea walls. Look back for the best view of the cathedral's yellow-tiled dome framed by lower buildings and the sky.

Detour: C/ de Capuchinos, a right turn off Campo del Sur, is a good place to enter the labyrinthine streets of the **BARRIO DE LA VINA** ❼. After wandering through the quarter, find a straight street with a view of bright sky at the end to lead back to the seaside.

Campo del Sur, lined with palm trees, leads to Playa de la Caleta, which is defined by **CASTILLO DE SAN SEBASTIAN** ❽ at one end and **CASTILLO DE SANTA CATALINA** ❾ at the other. A causeway along the beach leads out to Castillo de San Sebastián, which is believed to be on the site of the ancient Phoenician harbour where a temple to the Phoenician god Kronos once stood. This ancient redoubt, redolent of the three-millennium history of Cádiz, is an excellent vantage to view the graceful, modern city.

Also worth exploring

Bus No. 1 from Pl. España serves Playa de la Victoria.

Playa de la Victoria✶✶ is the beach preferred by locals. Located in the newer part of the city, it's longer, cleaner and less-crowded than Playa de la Caleta. Playa de la Victoria is about a 30-minute walk from the old town along Avda Fernández Ladera.

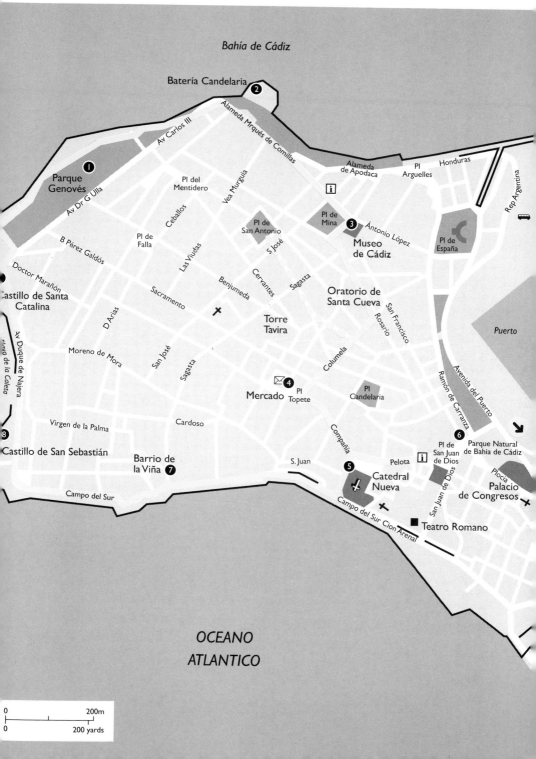

Bahía de Cádiz

Batería Candelaria ②

Alameda Mrqués de Comillas

Av Carlos III

Alameda
de Apodaca

Pl
Arguelles

Honduras

Rep Argentina

Parque
Genovés ①

Pl del
Mentidero

ℹ

Av Dr G Ulla

Ceballos

Vea Murguía

Pl de
San Antonio

Pl de
Mina

③ Antonio López

Pl de
España

Pl de
Falla

S José

Museo
de Cádiz

B Pérez Galdós

Las Viudas

Cervantes

Sagasta

Oratorio de
Santa Cueva

Puerto

Doctor Marañón

Sacramento

Benjumeda

San Francisco

Castillo de Santa
Catalina

D Arias

✝

Rosario

Torre
Tavira

Columela

Avenida del Puerto

Av Duque de Nájera

Moreno de Mora

San José

Sagasta

Mercado

✉ ④ Pl
Topete

Pl
Candelaria

Ramón de Carranza

Virgen de la Palma

Cardoso

Compañía

Pl de
San Juan
de Dios

ℹ

Parque Natural
de Bahía de Cádiz ⑥

Castillo de San Sebastián

Barrio de
la Viña ⑦

S. Juan

⑤

Pelota

Plocia

Campo del Sur

↓✝

Catedral
Nueva

San Juan de Dios

Palacio
de Congresos ✝

Campo del Sur Cion Arenal

■ Teatro Romano

OCEANO
ATLANTICO

0 ————————— 200m

0 ————————— 200 yards

Heart of the Frontera

Ratings

Museums	●●●●
Outdoor activities	●●●●
Architecture	●●●
Gastronomy	●●●
History	●●●
Nature and wildlife	●●●
Entertainment	●●
Shopping and crafts	●●

Asurprising wildness still permeates the mountainous country between the Straits of Gibraltar and the Sierra Grazalema, where Christians and Arabs fought for supremacy over hundreds of years and Robin Hood-like bandits preyed on caravans of riches passing from the coast to the inland cities. The villages of the Frontera were heavily fortified and armed to the teeth, and they still resemble fortresses with towns rather than towns with fortresses. The grandest of them all is Ronda, queen of the mountains for more than 2000 years and a dramatic small city that deserves several days to see it thoroughly. The passage westward across the mountains is slow, as road workers have faced a monumental task to repair the devastating damage of late-1990s floods. Patient travellers are rewarded with beautiful mountain landscapes and sleepy mountain villages that function as starting points in the natural park filled with cork oaks.

ALCALA DE LOS GAZULES*

ⓘ Oficina de Turismo
Pas. Playa s/n; tel: (95) 641–3228. Summer only.

☾ Pensión Restaurante Pizarro € *Pas. Playa 9; tel: (95) 642–0103.*
Comfortable, if modest, rooms and restaurant with a good *menú del día* (€).

Alcalá flourished under Rome and acquired its current name when the Moorish king of Granada presented it to the Knights of Gazules for their service. A single tower of a ruined Moorish *alcázar** stands at the top of the hill near Pl. San Jorge, the rest of the fortress having been blown up in the Peninsular War by the French. Many white houses, interspersed with Gothic and Mudéjar churches, tumble down the hill, and there are a few Roman ruins: **La Salada***, a fountain on c/ Santos, and the remains of a **bridge*** over Río Barbate.

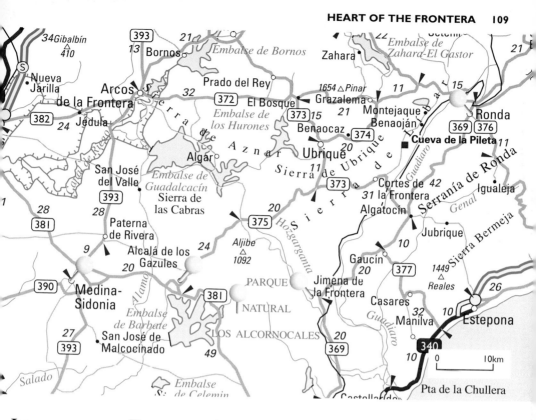

JIMENA DE LA FRONTERA✤

Oficina de Turismo
c/ Sevilla 61; tel: (95) 664–0254; fax: (95) 664–0569.

Camping Los Alcornocales €
Aptdo Correos 7; tel: (95) 664–0060; fax: (95) 664–1290. Camping compound built to harmonise with natural surroundings has a friendly bar and good restaurant (€).

Although human settlement near Jimena dates from the Bronze Age, the town rose to its greatest significance as an important bastion on the frontier between the Moors and Castille. The ruins of an 8th-century Moorish **castillo✤** still stand above the city. The **casco antiguo✤** has a more Moorish flavour than many mountain towns. Locals call the pool behind the castle **El Baño de la Reina Mora✤** but, rather than a 'queen's bath', it is thought to be part of a Moorish temple. In the 18th century Carlos III ordered an artillery factory built to supply some of the cannon balls used in the siege of Gibraltar. The remains of the 650m **canal✤** that controlled the flow of water to power the foundry bellows can be seen on the west side of town. A footpath leaves the bridge by the canal to the **Laja Alta caves✤** in the natural park, where schematic paintings from approximately 100 BC have been found. Because they depict several kinds of boats, archaeologists speculate that they represent either Phoenician sailors or pirates along the coast. Before setting out, ask at the tourist office if the caves are open.

Also ask about the **Feria de Mayo**, an agricultural and livestock fair that takes place in May and features horse-training competitions in addition to the usual music and dance.

MEDINA-SIDONIA✣✣

Oficina de Turismo
*Pl. Iglesia Mayor s/n; tel:
(95) 641–2404;
www.medinasidonia.com;
open Tue–Sun 1000–1400,
1700–1900, and closes one
hour earlier in winter.*

**Iglesia de Santa
María la Mayor la
Coronada €** *Pl. Iglesia
Mayor; open daily
1030–1400 and
1600–2030.*

Ferrochan, S.L. *Pl.
Iglesia Mayor s/n. Up-
market shop specialises in
objects from ironworking
artisans.*

Medina-Sidonia occupies a strategic crossroads between mountains and coast. Following its reconquest in 1264, Alfonso X bestowed the title Duque de Medina-Sidonia on the family of Guzmán El Bueno for his role in taking the town. It later became a powerful ducal seat, and one of the dukes became the admiral who led the Armada against England. Long-ago power is hardly evident in this rural backwater, outstripped by nearby Jerez de la Frontera. **Plaza España**, the town centre, is anchored by a handsome Renaissance *ayuntamiento* (town hall). The Mudéjar-revival main market stands just off the plaza, as does the **Convento de San Cristóbal✣**, where the nuns operate an extensive bakery.

Arco de Belén✣, one of three surviving Moorish gates, leads uphill to the medieval centre and the ruins of the ancient walls. The large plaza at the top, the former site of the mosque, is dominated by the **Iglesia de Santa María la Mayor la Coronada✣✣**. Constructed at the end of the 15th and beginning of the 16th century, it embodies the transition from squat, decoration-encrusted Gothic to the classical proportions of Renaissance architecture. The 15m-high carved wooden retable (1533–84) depicts scenes from the life of Christ. The church attributes a painted wood carving of an anguished *Cristo del Perdón* to the great Pedro Roldán, although some scholars argue it is the work of his daughter Luisa. Climbing the 130 steps to the belfry provides panoramic views of the town and of the Moorish castle further up in the hills.

Below
The bullring at Ronda

Accommodation and food in Medina Sidonia

Casa de Huéspedes Napoleón € *c/ San Juan 21; tel: (95) 641–0183.* Young *toreros* training at local bull ranches often stay in these modest lodgings, and their pictures grace the entrance lobby.

Mesón Machín € *Pl. Iglesia Mayor 9; tel: (95) 641–0850.* The casual bar, attractive formal dining room, and terrace with great views of the city, offer a variety of dining options, including an economical *menú del día. Closed Mon.*

Restaurante-Bar Cádiz €–€€ *Pl. España 13; tel: (95) 641–0250.* Regional specialities range from partridge or hare to homemade sausages.

Parque Natural Los Alcornocales❖❖

ⓘ Centro de Visitantes Parque Natural Los Alcornocales *N340, Km 96; tel: (95) 667–9161; summer hours Thur, Fri and holidays 1000–1400 and 1800–2000; winter hours Thur, Fri 1600–1800.*

A geological extension of the Sierra Grazalema, this mountainous park contains one of the largest stands of Mediterranean forest in Europe, of which the signature species is the *alcornoque,* or cork oak. The trees are stripped of their outer bark every 30 years, exposing the bright red cambium beneath. Southern reaches of the park are also rich in the 'strawberry tree' *arbutus,* myrtle, miniature palms and heather, while poplar, rhododendron, gall oak and wild olive mix with the cork oaks on the steeper uplands. An excellent park for birdwatchers, especially fans of raptors, Alcornocales is also home to red and fallow deer, foxes and badgers. **La Sauceda Recreativa-Ambiental** (*€ C3331, La Sauceda. Information: Avda Democracia s/n, Cortes de la Frontera; tel: (95) 215–4345*) is a starting point for long mountain hikes in the park, including an ascent of El Aljibe peak. The centre also has camp pitches and cabins and can arrange luggage transport to far ends of trails. The surrounding woods are filled with cuckoos.

Ronda❖❖❖

ⓘ Oficina de Turismo de la Junta de Andalucía *Pl. España 9; tel: (95) 287–1272; e-mail: otronda@andalucia.org; www.serraniaronda.org.* Provides information for the entire region.

Pliny the Elder called Ronda 'the glorious' two thousand years ago, and the description still holds. The white city crouches on a limestone shelf cleft by a precipitous gorge called El Tajo, cut by the Río Guadalevin. *La Ciudad,* the old town, follows the classic Moorish model of a hen-scratch street plan compressed between fortified walls and vertiginous cliffs. *El Mercadillo,* of more or less 'modern' origin, is laid out on a grid on the northwest side of El Tajo. It is the classic juxtaposition of old and new, with all the hotels, most restaurants and the bulk of the shopping district in the Mercadillo, and the majority of the 'monuments' in the Ciudad. Three bridges run between the past and present: a low **Puente Arabe❖** in the green valley west of the gorge, the 1616 **Puente Viejo❖** at the western

P Municipal parking lots are off Virgen de la Paz next to the bullring, and at Pl. Socorro and Pl. Merced.

Picadero 'La Granja' *office at Pl. España 3; tel: (95) 287–5956 offers 3-hr to 2-day horse-riding tours.*

The main pedestrianised shopping street is c/ Espinel.

Tienda los Arcos *c/ Tenorio 3 offers handsome hand-painted ceramics trimmed in brass that are a step up from the usual work produced for tourists.*

entrance to the gorge, and the 1793 **Puente Nuevo••** at the top of the gorge, 120m above the river. The lip of Ronda's cliff is lined, to a great extent, with walkways and *miradors* that open onto the emptiness of air and the wide country below. **Los Jardines de Cuenca••** run along the edge of the gorge on the Mercadillo side between the 'old' and 'new' bridges, their stepped terraces providing a gentler view of the Tajo.

At the foot of the gardens, the Puente Viejo crosses the river and ascends into the old town through the Puerta de Felipe V, built in 1742 to replace an Arab gate. Just above the gate, the chief Moorish remains of Ronda are visible. The **Baños Arabes•** *(tel: (95) 287–3889; open Tue 0900–1330, 1600–1800, Wed–Sat 0930–1530)*, which can be reached from stairs by the bridge, are superb 13th-century examples of public architecture, with their barrel vaults, horseshoe arches and brick columns. Stretching along the edge of the city in the distance are the remains of the Arabic fortifications, including the *Alcázar•*, largely destroyed in the 1485 siege by nearly 30,000 Christian troops.

Going up c/ Santo Domingo, two structures give some insight into life within Ronda. On the left, the **Palacio del Marqués de Salvatierra••** *(closed for refurbishment; enquire at the tourist office for opening dates)* offers a glimpse of a home occupied by the same family since 1485. The palacio is built on a series of Arabic houses dug into the rock, with many 18th-century embellishments. Across the street, the **Casa del Rey Moro•** (House of the Moorish King € *Cuesta de Santo Domingo 17; open daily 1000–1900*) has lovely gardens opening on to the gorge and an

Boutique Rural
cl Armiñán 26 and
Tienda Marquéz *cl de la Bola* offer local foodstuffs including cheeses, wines and olive oil.

underground stairway that goes all the way down to the river. The house is *not* open for tours.

The **Palacio de Mondragón***** (*€ Pl. Mondragón s/n; open Mon–Fri 1000–1900, Sat–Sun 1000–1500*) functions as Ronda's city museum, but its best parts are the courtyards that remain almost unchanged since the days of Fernando and Isabela, who lodged here when they visited Ronda. In some ways the palacio embodies Ronda's charm, for a Moorish heart beats in its ostensibly Christian body. The tile work, carved ceilings, fountains and gardens of the palacio show a love of light, sound and pattern as alien to the reconquest mindset as a *mihrab* or the Koran itself.

If Sevilla's bullring is the St Peter's of bullfighting, then Ronda's **Plaza de Toros**** is Notre-Dame. An austere and formal style of bullfighting was perfected here by the legendary Pedro Romero, who killed more than 5000 bulls over six decades before his death from natural causes in 1839. Of the three major bullfighting museums (Sevilla and Córdoba have the others) Ronda's **Museo Taurino***** (*€ Pl. Teniente Arce; tel: (95) 287–4132; open daily 1000–2000*) has the greatest sense of immediacy, with its extensive collection of costumes, photographs and memorabilia. The embroidered *trajes de luces* (or 'suits of lights') emphasise just how small many matadors are. Ronda revived the *Corrida Goyesca* bullfight in period costume in 1954, and all the trappings – ancient and modern – are preserved here.

Banditry was another tradition of the Ronda *cordillera*, especially in the 19th and early 20th centuries, as folk hero desperadoes raided the riches going from the coast up to the capital. The **Museo del**

Below
Ronda

Fiesta de Pedro Romero tel: (95) 287–1272. This Sept festival is known for the 'Corridas Goyescas' with 19th-century costumes that could come straight from a Goya painting.

Festival Flamenco de lo Rancio tel: (95) 287–1272. Aug flamenco festival honours the masters.

Bandolero* (€ c/ Armiñán 65; open daily 1000–2000 in summer, 1015–1800 in winter) treats the subject seriously, evoking both the desperate conditions that fostered banditry and praising the Guardia Civil, formed in 1844 to put a stop to the outlaws. The last of the bandits were rounded up in the 1920s.

Accommodation and food in Ronda

Hotel La Española €€ c/ José Aparicio 5; tel: (95) 287–1051; e-mail: laespanola@ronda.net; www.ronda.net/usuar/laespanola. Traditional hotel between the Puente Nuevo and the bullring; also has a restaurant (€€) with rooftop terrace.

Hotel-Restaurante Don Miguel €–€€ c/ Villanueva 8; tel: (95) 287–7722; fax: (95) 287–8377; e-mail: info@dmiguel.com; www.dmiguel.com. Small hotel, situated above the gorge. Some rooms have views of the gorge and bridge, as does the very good restaurant (€€–€€€).

Hotel-Restaurante Hermanos Macías € c/ Pedro Romero 3; tel: (95) 287–4238; fax: (95) 287–8675. Located halfway between the bullring and Pl. Socorro, this 24-room hotel also has a restaurant (€–€€) and lively tapas bar.

Bodega El Picadero € c/ Nueva 21; tel: (95) 287–2113; closed Thur. Simple and honest food in small, friendly bar-restaurant with flamenco memorabilia in one room and bullfighting in the other.

Parador de Ronda €€ Pl. España s/n; tel: (95) 287–7500; fax: (95) 287–8188; e-mail: ronda@parador.es; www.parador.es. Stylish modern parador with excellent restaurant (€€€) that sits behind the façade of the former ayuntamiento (town hall) at the edge of the gorge. Guided hikes, horse rides, balloon ascents and other activities can be arranged by the parador, which also provides free mountain bikes to guests.

Restaurante Pedro Romero €€€ c/ Virgen de la Paz 18; tel: (95) 287–1110 across from the bullring is filled with bullfighting memorabilia, and features such local specialities as whole baked pheasant, pork steak in a Ronda wine sauce and stewed hare.

Restaurante Tragabuches €€€ c/ José Aparicio 1; tel: (95) 287–8641; tel: (95) 219–0291; closed Mon and Sun evening. Extremely stylish restaurant; the award-winning chef is dedicated to serving 'creative Andalucían cuisine'.

C/ José Aparicio between Pl. España and the Plaza de Toros has several restaurants with a good choice of tapas and economical combination dishes. Pedestrianised Pl. Socorro is lined with tapas bars and cafés frequented by locals as well as tourists. Nuns at the **Convento de Carmelitas Descalzas** (Pl. Merced) sell a variety of sweets and pastries, including delicious mantecadas.

Opposite
Ronda's Palacio de Mondragón

Cueva de la Pileta
€ *tel: (95) 216–7343;
open 1000–1300,
1600–1800.* Tours limited
to 25 people.

**Camping Cabañas
Jimera de Libar** €
*Carretera Jimera–Cortes
km1; tel: (95) 218–0102.*
Camping, cabins and
restaurant (€) are well
situated for hikers.

El Quejigo *A369,
south side of Algatocín.*
This roadside shop carries
Frontera craft products
that range from woven
baskets to fine cheeses to
even finer wines, including
polished Arcos reds.

Suggested tour

Total distance: 161km.

Time: One day.

Links: This tour connects the routes to The White Villages (*see page 130*) at Ronda, and to Sherry country (*see page 118*) and Costa de la Luz (*see page 90*) at Medina Sidonia.

Route: Leave **RONDA** ❶ on the A376 towards Sevilla, turning left in 3km to Benoaján, a 15km drive on a winding mountain road. After passing through the village, watch carefully for a 270-degree left turn toward Cortes de la Frontera. After 3km the road, MA561, comes to a right-hand turn-off to the **Cueva de la Pileta❖❖**, one of the few privately owned caves with Palaeolithic paintings of animals and fish on the walls. The tour lasts about one hour. Be warned: cavern ceilings are covered with bats.

Continue southbound on the MA561, turning left in 4km to Jimera de Líbar on the semi-paved MA508. This area is prime hiking country, with many mountain walking paths emanating from Jimera.

The narrow MA561 winds over the ridges for 5km to join the A369 for a scenic 24km drive along a mountain chain, with views of the broad valley and hillside villages on the erstwhile mountain highway between Algeciras and Ronda.

The road begins to descend as it passes the dramatic little village of **Benarraba⁺**, sitting far down in the valley, and continues to **Gaucín⁺**, where a ruined Moorish castle tops the headland of a limestone ridge. The landscape opens up here into broad green valleys and meadows as the A369 continues 23km to **JIMENA DE LA FRONTERA ❷**.

Turn right onto the C3331 towards Ubrique, entering the highlands of the **PARQUE NATURAL LOS ALCORNOCALES ❸**, passing 30km through dense cork oak stands en route to **La Sauceda⁺⁺**, a prime mountain hiking base. In 2km, the C3331 ends. Turn left on to the A375, badly damaged in 1997 floods, for a slow 22km drive along the Río Barbate to **ALCALA DE LOS GAZULES ❹**.

At Alcalá, the C440 (also marked A381) proceeds 19km through rolling farmland to **MEDINA-SIDONIA ❺**. This stretch is lined with bull-breeding farms where men on horseback tend the *toros bravos*.

Also worth exploring

The village of **Setenil de las Bodegas**, 17km north of Ronda, has cave-like streets and houses built into rock overhangs carved out by the Río Trejo.

Sherry Country

Ratings

Gastronomy	●●●●●
Beaches	●●●
Entertainment	●●●
Nature and wildlife	●●●
Architecture	●●
History	●●
Museums	●●
Shopping and crafts	●

This corner of Andalucía between the mouth of the Río Guadalquivir and the Bahía de Cádiz has been famous for wine since the Phoenicians first planted grapes here 3000 years ago. The weather is warm, the rainfall scant, and the chalky *albarizo* soil crusts over to trap moisture in the root zone. The barrel-fermented wines often develop a yeasty crust (*flor*) that imparts a distinctive flavour. British merchants began trading for wine on this coast in the 1300s and came to dominate first the trade in sherry (an English corruption of the Moorish place name, Xerez) and later, after 1830, its manufacture. The area is unusually prosperous for Andalucía, but otherwise provides a synopsis of the entire region, with a taste of Roman and Moorish heritages, several handsome churches, good flamenco and bullfighting, and a full complement of the sybaritic pleasures for which southern Spain has become famous.

JEREZ DE LA FRONTERA❖❖❖

❶ Oficina de Turismo
c/ Larga 39; tel: (95) 633–1150; fax: (95) 633–1731; e-mail: turismo2@aytojerez.es; www.webjerez.com

Just over 20km northwest of El Puerto and northeast of Sanlúcar, Jerez is the capital of sherry production and the largest and most prosperous of the wine-producing cities. A sprawling industrial community surrounded by rolling countryside of palomino and Pedro Ximénez grapes planted in chalky soil, Jerez is medieval at its heart – half Moorish, half Christian. Its large gypsy community found in the *barrios* of Santiago and San Miguel originated the *bulería*, one of the fastest and most festive forms of flamenco.

The **Old Quarter**❖❖❖ west of c/ Larga retains sections of the city fortifications from the Moorish period, and the **Alcázar**❖❖❖ (€–€€ *Alameda Vieja; tel: (95) 631–9798; open daily summer 1000–2000, Sun 1000–1500, winter 1000–1800*), south of Pl. del Arenal, is one of the most comprehensible in Spain. Small compared to the *alcazares* of Seville and Granada, it contains all the same features: fortified walls, baths, gardens,

towers and a small mosque and *mihrab*. The Islamic places of worship were long ago converted to Christian churches, but have been restored to their Islamic austerity. The serenity of the site is powerful, even subduing tour-bus hordes. An additional charge is made to view the camera obscura in the Palacio de Villavicencio. Almost adjacent to the Alcázar, the **Catedral de San Salvador⁺⁺** is a weighty 18th-century structure that bridges Gothic, baroque and neo-classical styles with impressive success. It is, of course, built on the site of the main mosque of Xerez. The sacristy contains an exquisite Zurbarán portrait of the Virgin as a child, *The Sleeping Girl*. During the Fiestas de Otoño, the first grapes of the sherry harvest are crushed on the ample steps of the cathedral.

The busiest and most interesting part of Jerez for casual visitors is the modernised section of the Old Quarter between Pl. Asunción and the Iglesia de San Miguel. The **Cabildo Municipal⁺** on Asunción, constructed in 1575, marries the two gaudy styles of Mudéjar and Plateresque, and has statues of Hercules and Julius Caesar, references to Andalucía's claims as heir to both Greek and Roman traditions. The **Plaza Arenal⁺⁺** is surrounded by a number of excellent *tapas* bars, which continue up the small streets leading to a one-time **gypsy quarter⁺** around the Iglesia de San Miguel.

The main gypsy quarter, however, is the **Barrio de Santiago⁺⁺**, a hive of narrow streets and lanes uphill north and west of the cathedral en route to the Iglesia de Santiago. Sculptures of some of the *gitano* flamenco artists dot the area, and the **Centro Andaluz de Flamenco⁺** *(Pl. de San Juan 1; tel: (95) 634–9265; Mon–Fri 1000–1400)* occupies the 18th-century Palacio de Pemartín on Pl. San Juan. With a library of books, music and videos, the centre teaches and preserves the tradition of *bulería*, Jerez's version of flamenco. Classes are held in a mirrored dance room and there are occasional performances in the centre.

González Byass €€
c/ Manuel González 12;
tel: (95) 635–7016;
www.gonzalezbyass.es; open
daily; tours on the hour
Mon–Sat 1130–1830, Sun
1130–1330.

Domecq € c/ San
Ildefonso; tel: (95)
615–1500; www.domecq.es;
open Mon–Fri 0930–1330.

Sandeman c/ Pizarro 10;
tel: (95) 630–1100;
www.sandeman.com;
open daily 0900–1400.

La Casa del Jerez
c/ Divina Pastora 1; tel:
(95) 633–5184. Tourist-
oriented shop near Real
Escuela Andaluza del Arte
Ecuestre offers the
opportunity to sample
wines from a variety of
makers and purchase other
souvenirs.

**La Boutique del Caballo
Hipisur** c/ Centro 1; tel:
(95) 632–3055. Everything
but the horse for riders,
from boots and spurs to
saddles and caps.

Check the Oficina de
Turismo or the
Centro Andaluz de
Flamenco for listings of
flamenco performances.

El Laga Tío Parrilla
€€€ Pl. del Mercado (Barrio
Santiago); tel: (95)
633–8334. Flamenco
performances Mon–Sat.
Stop by at midday to
reserve a front table.

Peña Antionio Chacon
€€ c/ Salas 2; tel: (95)
634–7472 has an excellent
show on Saturday nights.

The superb **Museo Arqueológico**✦✦ (€ Pl. Mercado s/n; tel: (95) 634–1350; open summer Tue–Sun 1000–1430; winter Tue–Fri 1000–1400, 1600–1900, Sat–Sun 1000–1430) recapitulates the area's history with such items as a Greek military helmet from the 7th century BC found on the banks of Río Guadelete, Roman amphorae used in trade, Moorish ceramics, Iberian sculpture from the 3rd to 1st centuries BC, a Visigothic sarcophagus and a few models of the city at various periods. Interpretive plaques are entirely in Spanish, but displays are first-rate.

Sherry bodegas riddle the city, although the massive domains of **González Byass**✦✦ and **Domecq**✦✦ are near each other west of the Alcázar. Both offer tours conducted in Spanish and perfunctory English that are opportunities to wander around amid rows of barrels before having a taste and being shuffled off to the company store. Many of the bodegas are closed for tours in late July and August, so call beforehand to reserve space on tours and to confirm hours.

Sherry barons and local gentry have cultivated a love of horses – polo ponies abound – that has given rise to an impenetrable social class. Its finest manifestation is the **Real Escuela Andaluza del Arte Ecuestre**✦✦ (tel: (95) 631–9635; www.realescuela.org) where horses and riders are trained in formal show styles and dressage. Training sessions (€) are open to the public Mon, Wed and Fri 1000–1300. During the summer the Dancing Horses perform an equestrian ballet Tue and Thur at 1200.

The **Feria del Caballo** in early May (tel: (95) 633–1150) is one of the biggest festivals in Andalucía, with music, dance and horse parades. For two weeks before the horse fair the **Festival de Jerez** celebrates with music and dance, especially flamenco (most events at the Teatro Villamarta on c/ Medina). Later in the year, the **Fiestas de Otoño**, a mid-Sept–mid-Oct harvest celebration, bring together everything special about the area: horse races, flamenco and the treading of the first grapes in front of the cathedral.

Accommodation and food in Jerez de la Frontera

El Ancla Hotel € Plaza del Mamelón; tel: (95) 632–1297; www.helancla.com. Classic Jerez décor of yellow and white paintwork, wrought-iron balconies and wooden shutters. The hotel doubles as a popular local bar, which is good for atmosphere, but might mean earplugs on a Saturday night.

Hotel Doña Blanca €–€€€ c/ Bodegas 11; tel: (95) 634–8761; e-mail: info@hoteldonablanca.com; www.hoteldonablanca.com. Quiet hotel off main streets but close to the central city with its own garage for parking. Rates are bargain Sept–Mar, expensive Apr–Aug.

Hotel Jerez €€€ Avda Alcalde Alvaro Domecq 35; tel: (95) 630–0600; fax: (95) 630–5001; e-mail: comercial@jerezhotel.com; www.jerezhotel.com. Gracious hotel in residential area 10 min by taxi from city centre.

San Miguel Hotel € *Pl. León XIII; tel/fax: (95) 634–8562.* The 30 rooms (all shared baths) of this *pension* share the square with the Iglesia de San Miguel.

La Marea € *San Miguel 3; tel: (95) 632–0923.* Don't let the sickly fluorescent glare put you off this excellent fish restaurant specialising in squid and fresh anchovies. The blue-and-white tiles are classic for an urban fish house.

El Mirador de las Almenas € *c/ Pescadería Vieja; no phone.* One of several appealing restaurants on this cobbled side street, with a menu more varied than most, and with filled baked potatoes a welcome change from chips.

Restaurante La Parra Vieja €€ *San Miguel 9; tel: (95) 633–5390; closed Sun.* You can't miss it with the great tile murals outside. The inside has walls covered with *azulejos* and a big wooden bar. Specialises in meats, local fish and shellfish, all grilled on wood fire.

The produce **market** on c/ Doña Blanca, parallel to Coradera and Medina, is surrounded by casual eateries. Pastries and assorted cakes are best bought in the morning from the cloistered nuns at **Madres Dominicas** (*c/ Espíritu Santo 9*) and **Madres Agustinas Ermitañas** (*c/ Santa María de Gracia 2*).

El Puerto de Santa Maria**

Oficina de Turismo
c/ Guadalete 1; tel:
(95) 654–2413; e-mail:
ptoturis@elpuertosm.es;
www.elpuertosm.es

El Vaporcito €
Muelle del Vapor, Pl.
Galeras; tel: (95) 654–2413.
The vapor, an allusion to
steamship days, makes
several runs daily between
El Puerto and Cádiz.

P Free public parking at
Pl. de Toros.

El Convento Avda
Bajamar near the ferry
dock has bars and discos in
the ruins of a monastery.

Semana Santa tel: (95)
654–2413. El Puerto's
Holy Week processions
are very elaborate for a
small town.

The *Santa María*, Columbus's flagship, hailed from El Puerto, and its owner Juan de Cosa served the explorer as pilot. Trade with the Americas made the port wealthy, and many fine 18th-century palaces still stand. Only Casa de la Marquesa de Candia is open to the public, for it houses the **Museo Municipal** (*c/ Pagador 1; open Tue–Fri 1000–1400, Sat–Sun 1045–1400*), with a fair sampling of archaeological finds and modest artwork. The port region along Ribera del Marisco remains the focus of attention for short-term visitors, as it is lined with *marisquerías* (seafood bars) and wine shops selling El Puerto's excellent sherries. A flirtatious social scene goes on at the dockside **Parque Calderón**.

Plaza España, the town centre, is dominated by the **Iglesia Mayor Prioral**, a blend of many styles on a Gothic frame. The Plateresque south entrance and the richly gilded altarpiece in the chapel of the Virgen de los Milagros (El Puerto's patron saint) are extraordinary. The most stirring sight, however, is the **Castillo San Marcos** (*Pl. Alfonso El Sabio; open Tue–Sat 1000–1330*) built by Alfonso X in the 13th century.

Scattered throughout El Puerto are the low concrete blocks of the city's chief **sherry bodegas**. El Puerto sherries are typically light and aromatic, comparable to the manzanillas of Sanlúcar. It is possible to visit the *bodegas* at **Fernando de Terry** (*c/ Santísima Trinidad 2; tel: (95) 648–3000; open Mon–Fri 0900–1300*), which are located in a 17th-century convent with a small museum, and also at **Osborne and Duff Gordon** (€ *c/ Fernán Caballero 3; tel: (95) 685–5211; open Mon–Fri 0930–1300*). Call the day ahead to reserve a place on a tour. Osborne is also Spain's largest brandy producer, and the source of the 50-ton metal bulls found along Andalucían highways.

It takes only minutes to see, but El Puerto's **Plaza de Toros*** (*open Tue–Sun 1100–1330 and 1800–1930*), built in 1880, is one of the most beautiful in Spain as well as the third largest, holding 15,000 spectators. Legendary matador Joselito is quoted in tiles at the entrance: 'He who has not seen bulls in El Puerto does not know what bullfighting is.'

Accommodation and food in El Puerto de Santa María

Hotel Los Cántaros €–€€ *c/ Curva 6; tel: (95) 654–0240; e-mail: reservas@hotelloscantaros.com; www.hotelloscantaros.com*. Exquisite 39-room hotel convenient to, but out of earshot of the lively port.

Opposite
Easter morning at Iglesia
Mayor church, in El Puerto
de Santa María

Las Bóvedas Restaurant €€ *Hotel Monasterio San Miguel, c/ Larga 27; tel: (95) 654–0404*. Superb restaurant as befitting this grand hotel. Chef Joaquín Ramírez has won several awards for his innovative cuisine.

Below
El Puerto de Santa María
Plaza de Toros

Tapas The bustling Ribera del Marisco and adjacent side streets are jammed with tiny bars and *marisquerías* that serve good, mostly fish, *tapas* with the local fino.

Vinoteca Mi Bodega *c/ Micaela Aramburi 20* is a convenient spot a block from the *vapor* to stock up on the sherries of El Puerto.

SANLUCAR DE BARRAMEDA❖❖

ℹ️ **Oficina de Turismo**
Calzada del Ejército s/n; tel: (95) 636–6110; fax: (95) 636–6132; www.aytosanlucar.org; open daily 1000–1400 and 1800–2000 in summer; and 1700–1900 in winter.

🅿️ Parking is tight in Sanlúcar and always 'assisted'. Look for a space around the *alameda* in the centre of town and walk everywhere else.

🚢 **Real Fernando riverboat to Parque Doñana** €€€
Fábrica de Hielo, Bajo de Guía; tel: (95) 636–3813; open daily 0900–2000. Four-hour visits to the park by boat and on foot; departures are every morning at 1000 and in the afternoon at 1600 Mar–May, 1700 Sept, 1600 Oct.

📞 Phone to reserve a spot and confirm tour times at the **Sherry Bodegas: Antonio Barbadillo** € *c/ Sevilla 25; tel: (95) 636–0894; www.barbadillo.com; open Wed & Thur 1230.* **Vinícola Hidalgo** *c/ Banda Playa 24; tel: (95) 636–0516; www.vinicola/hidalgo.es; open Wed, Fri 1145 and 1245, Sat 1230.* **Herederos de Argüeso** *c/ Mar 8; tel: (95) 636–0112; open Tue and Thur 1230.*

Once a world trade port, Sanlúcar is satisfied now to fish and contemplate the marshes of Parque Doñana, just across the Río Guadalquivir estuary. The Mediterranean character of its long beaches contributes to the town's air of aristocratic leisure, an image enhanced by the architecture of the older quarters. While both Columbus and Magellan sailed from Sanlúcar, the city, content with sybaritic pleasures, draws its identity today from sherry and shellfish.

The original city, **Barrio Alto**❖❖, overlooks the Guadalquivir and the Atlantic from a small hill. Segments of its original walls remain, but the highlights are houses and gardens from more recent centuries. The town hall occupies the stunning neo-Mudéjar **Palacio de Orleans y Bourbon**❖❖ (*c/ Cuesta de Belén; tel: 956 38–8000. Open Mon–Fri 1000–1400*), a 19th-century estate with superb gardens to match the inspiring architecture. The neighbourhood at the top of the old city follows suit, although in less ostentatious fashion, with lush patios and

elaborate wrought-iron gates and fences. Nearby is the looming **Nuestra Señora de la O✦✦**, notable for its Mudéjar exterior and ceiling. It is best contemplated over *tapas* and manzanilla from **Plaza de la Paz✦✦**.

By contrast, the **Barrio Bajo✦✦**, or lower city, is a bustling business district built on the silted-in shores of the harbour. **Plaza del Cabildo✦✦**, by the former town hall, is the liveliest square, ringed with bars serving *tapas* and manzanilla. Some **manzanilla bodegas✦✦** are located nearby. The central *alameda* leads down to the sea and the concrete walkway between Paseo Marítimo and the beaches.

Sanlúcar's beaches are small and interrupted by mudflats except at the **Bajo Guía✦✦✦**, the fishing port – or fish-eating port. Excellent restaurants and bars line the port, offering some of the finest seafood in all of Andalucía. The classic meal is a plate of *langostinos* complemented perfectly by the local manzanilla sherry. Sanlúcar is unusual in combining good *tapas* and restaurant dining, and regulars of its establishments routinely mix orders from both menus as they stretch their hours of dining in the afternoon sun.

Below
Enjoying *langostinos*

For those who want more than a good meal and sunbathing, the **Centro de Visitantes de Doñana** (*Fábrica de Hielo, Bajo de Guía s/n; tel: (95) 638–1635. Open daily 0900–2030*) offers static and audiovisual exhibits of Doñana flora and fauna, and recounts the history of the lower reaches of the Río Guadalquivir. Guided visits to Parque Doñana can be arranged here.

Accommodation and food in Sanlúcar de Barrameda

Hostal Blanca Paloma € *Pl. San Roque 15; tel: (95) 636–3644.* Very friendly and spotlessly clean *pensión* with five rooms on each of two floors, one shared bath per floor. Centrally located in the old city on fairly quiet square. No air conditioning.

Hotel Los Helechos €€ *Pl. Madres de Dios 9; tel: (95) 636–1349; fax: (95) 636–9650; e-mail: info@hotelloshelechos. com; www.hotelloshelechos.com.* A veritable fantasy in tiles, with a gorgeous central courtyard in the old city. Located on square of convent where nuns sell their own pastries.

Above
The Alcázar in Jerez

Posada del Palacio € *c/ Caballeros 11; tel: (95) 636–4840; fax: (95) 636–5060.* Adjacent to the grand palace that serves as the town hall, this modest 18th-century noble house has a sunny central courtyard and large rooms lined with tiles and filled with hefty pine furniture.

Tartaneros Hotel € *c/ Tartaneros 8; tel: (95) 638–5378; fax: (95) 638–5394.* A Mudéjar revival exterior encloses elegant neo-Victorian common areas and 22 fairly spare but serviceable rooms close to the action of the lower town. The décor includes many statues of Negro servants.

Casa Bigote €€ *Bajo de Guía; tel: (95) 636–2696; closed Sun.* Brilliantly prepared and served *langostinos* at tables so close to the sea wall that you can feel sand between your toes. The restaurant also has a salty *taberna* attached.

Manzanilla La Gitana € *Pl. Cabildo 15; no tel.* Order inside at the bar and bring your own food to the café tables in the busy plaza. Large menu includes fish (including shrimp and prawns) priced daily by the kilo. Exquisite quick food.

Mirador de Doñana € *Bajo de Guía; tel: (95) 636–3502.* Wonderful *tapas* bar and restaurant overlooking the river, specialising in seafood dishes, including an unbeatable *sopa de marisco* (fish soup).

Restaurante Mirador de Doñana €€ *Bajo de Guía; tel: (95) 636–4205.* Possibly some of the finest fish anywhere in Spain. Great views of the harbour and the edge of Parque Doñana from the air-conditioned dining room.

Feria de la Manzanilla *tel: (95) 636–6110.* Sherry festival in late May to early June.

Carreras de Caballos *tel: (95) 636–6110.* August horse races on beach (except third week) have been a tradition since 1845.

Manzanilla, the other 'Sherry'

Sanlúcar alone produces manzanilla, a delicate variety of *fino* with a nutty, salty tang that connoisseurs hold in high regard. It is the driest of sherry varieties and acquires a straw colour on ageing. Only in Sanlúcar does sherry take on these distinctive qualities; attempts to replicate it using Sanlúcar grapes elsewhere fail miserably. Fittingly, it is the perfect match for seafood. In Sanlúcar it is always served ice-cold. The largest producer is Bodegas Barbadillo, which also makes a slow-ageing sherry that is left 15 years in the *solera* – rather than the usual 4. The best-selling brand of manzanilla is La Gitana, bottled by Vinícola Hidalgo. Many *tapas* bars in Sanlúcar are distinguished less by their names or menus than by which particular brand of manzanilla they serve.

Right
Manuel González, founder of the González Byass sherry company

Suggested tour

Total distance: 90km, 100km with detour.

Time: 4 hours.

Links: Connects to Cádiz (*see pages 98–107*) by ferry at El Puerto de Santa María.

Above
Easter in Jerez

Route: From **SANLUCAR DE BARRAMEDA ❶**, tour the beaches by driving west 9km on the A480 to **Chipiona**, a quintessential modern beach community, then south along the beaches on the CA604 to **Rota**, doubling back from the cape on the CA603 to head 21km to **EL PUERTO DE SANTA MARIA ❷**. From El Puerto, follow the N443 north toward Jerez, turning off to **Ermita de San Cristóbal** in 14km, on the CA201. This scenic drive passes through vineyards before reaching a Y-junction.

Take the right-hand fork, where the paved road gives way to dirt, for a 3km journey to the **Monasterio de la Cartuja**. Visit the **Yeguada de la Cartuja**, an estate where the Spanish Carthusian thoroughbred line was developed five centuries ago (*open Sat only*).

Back on the CA201, continue into **JEREZ DE LA FRONTERA ❸**. Return 22km to Sanlúcar on the C440.

Also worth exploring

Located 34km northeast of Sanlúcar on the A471, **Lebrija** is a striking little wine-making centre founded by the Romans. Around the Plaza de España, lined with palm trees, ruins of a Moorish fortress stand next to the Mudéjar-style Iglesia de Santa María del Castillo. More interesting is the Iglesia de Santa María de la Oliva, which was adapted from an Almohad mosque in the 13th century, and enlarged in the 15th and 17th centuries. Between Lebrija and Sanlúcar the countryside of sandy hills terraced with vineyards offers long, picturesque vistas.

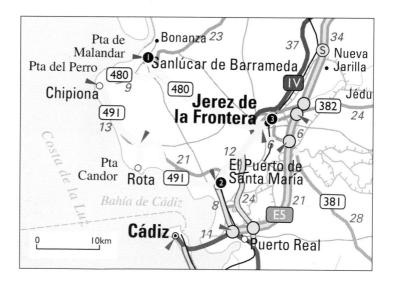

The White Villages

Ratings

Architecture	●●●○
Nature and wildlife	●●●●
Outdoor activities	●●●○
Scenery	●●●●
Gastronomy	●●●○○
History	●●●○
Shopping and crafts	●●●○○
Museums	●○○○○

Many years ago the villages of the Sierra Grazalema were dubbed *Los Pueblos Blancos*, or 'the White Villages'. They are no whiter than most Andalucían mountain villages, but the name stuck for this sequence of towns that seem crowned with snow from a distance. Their fortifications marked the border between Muslim and Christian holdings for many centuries, but their character has always been formed more by the mountains than by the ruling cultures. While Arcos de la Frontera on the west is a ducal town of many churches and monuments, most of the White Villages are simple agricultural villages surrounded by extraordinary landscapes. This is a region for leisurely exploration through scenic drives or by hiking mountain trails. The area around the White Villages holds some of Spain's best trout fishing, and the villages produce some surprisingly good table wines, cured meats and cheeses.

ARCOS DE LA FRONTERA✦✦✦

ⓘ Oficina de Turismo
Pl. Cabildo; tel: (95) 670–2264; fax: (95) 670–2226; e-mail: turismo@ ayuntamientoarcos.org; www.ayuntamientoarcos.org; open Mon–Fri 1000–1300 and 1530–1830, Sat 1000–1400.

ⓟ Parking inside the old city is confined primarily to Pl. Cabildo. Use the ticket machines for short-term parking or get a parking pass from your hotel.

Declared a national artistic monument in 1961, Arcos rises high on a limestone ridge above the Río Guadalete and an artificial lake that irrigates the valley's orange groves. Above all, it is a city of contemplation and reflection, full of former convents and 18th-century palaces built on old Arabic streets after the 1755 earthquake. In 1255, King Alfonso X knighted all the residents, and most palacios bear a coat of arms carved in limestone above the entry lintel. A large part of the Arcos experience is staying in one of these historic buildings until the frenzy of touring has dissipated and an appetite for exploration is restored. Many travellers find Arcos a convenient base for visiting the Parque Sierra de Grazalema, Jerez and even the Costa de la Luz.

The old city is crowned with a **Moorish fortress✦** built when Arcos was an independent *taifa* (kingdom) in the 11th century. Now the castle is the country getaway home of a ducal family based in Madrid

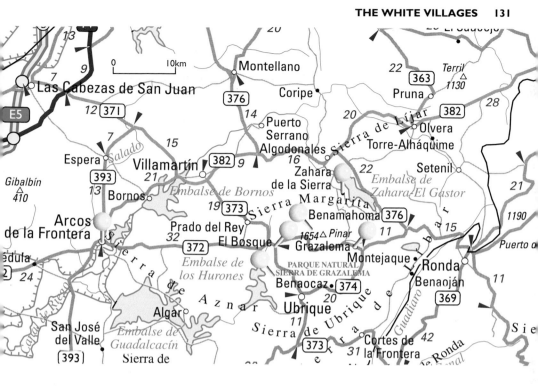

Galería de Arte San Pedro c/ San Pedro 7. Displays local ceramics, wood carvings and paintings in galleries surrounding a patio and fountain.

Semana Santa tel: (95) 670–2264. Features processions through the narrow streets of the old town.

Fiestas de San Miguel tel: (95) 670–2264. These celebrate the patron saint in late Sept with typical dances and traditional running of the bulls.

and can only be viewed from the outside. Below it spreads the city's main square, the Pl. Cabildo, flanked by the *parador* and an old ducal residence now containing the tourist office and the *ayuntamiento* (town hall); a splendid statue of the town's patron saint, San Miguel, crowns the doorway. Also on the plaza is the **Balcón de Arcos✦✦** and the **Iglesia Santa María✦✦** (€ *open daily 1000–1300 and 1600–1900*). The 7th-century Latin-Byzantine church foundation sits beneath a Moorish mosque on which the later Roman Catholic church was built. It is said that the *mihrab* still exists behind the main altar. The side facing Pl. Cabildo, where tourists enter, ranges from Renaissance on the right to baroque in the middle and Gothic on the left – a timeline of the centuries it took to build and rebuild the church.

The best circuit of Arcos is to walk from Pl. Cabildo down c/ Escribanos past the **Convento de las Mercederías Descalzas✦**, the only active cloister in Arcos, to Pl. Boticas. A right turn down c/ Oliveras Veras passes the active theatre by the same name and leads to the head of **c/ Maldonado✦**, a street celebrated by poets for its beautiful courtyards, sometimes visible from the street. Continuing downhill leads to the **Mirador de Abades✦**, which overlooks the lake and river. Otherwise, a left turn at the end of Maldonado comes out in the plaza of the **Iglesia San Pedro✦**, a Gothic church with excellent Renaissance statues of the four evangelists and a rather heroic San Pedro. Across the square is the **Palacio del Mayorazgo✦**, a 17th-century nobleman's palace with two

travellers passing through are found on the east side. Hikers often prefer to start the 5km Benamahoma–El Bosque trail from Benamahoma so that the walk is downhill most of the way.

EL BOSQUE*

ⓘ Centro Recepción del Parque de Grazalema *Avda Diputación s/n; tel: (95) 672–7029. Open Mon–Thur 0900–1400, Fri–Sun 0900–1400 and 1600–1800. Sells hiking maps, guides to flora and fauna, and provides information about excursion operators.*

This minuscule village is the western gate to the Parque Natural Sierra de Grazalema. The town sits at the base of the Sierra Albarracín along the **Río Majaceite***, a shallow but icy-cold trickle that is Europe's southernmost trout stream. Banks are marked for fishing access. One of several excellent hiking trails follows the river upstream to the village of Benamahoma.

Accommodation and food in El Bosque

Albergue Molino de En Medio € *Av de la Diputacion; tel: (95) 671–6212.* Riverside youth hostel geared towards family camping with shared rooms of 2–3 beds.

Camping La Torrecilla € *Carretera El Bosque–Ubrique km1; tel: (95) 671–6095; www.campinglatorrecilla.com; closed in winter.* Tranquil camping in the heart of the Parque Natural Sierra de Grazalema; also offers air-conditioned *cabañas*.

Las Truchas € *Avda Diputación s/n; tel: (95) 671–6061.* Situated at the entrance to the natural park along the Río Majaceite, Las Truchas is an upmarket country hunting lodge with downmarket prices. Restaurant with large fireplace serves trout from the river.

Mesón Majaceite € *next to Albergue Juvenil; no tel.* Extremely casual dining less than 10m from trout farm; features several local trout preparations.

GRAZALEMA**

ⓘ Oficina de Turismo *Pl. España 11; tel: (95) 613–2225; open summer 1000–1400 and 1700–2000, winter 1000–1400 and 1600–1900, closed Mon.* Upper level sells excellent selection of local crafts and food products.

☾ Market day is Tuesday in the car park behind *c/ Los Asomaderos.*

The Berbers from Saddina who founded Grazalema on this rocky ledge in the late 8th century must have been in ecstasy, for even today water bubbles in 13 public fountains within the town. Never fortified, Grazalema was never levelled either. The fertile Río Guadalete valley makes the town an agricultural centre in the Sierra de Grazalema. The range's soaring peaks rise all around the town, trapping so much moisture that the western limits of Grazalema are soggy, with more than 1100mm of rainfall per year. Yet the rest of the town lies within the rain shadow of those peaks, sprawling in the sun on its ledge above a green valley. This location is ideal for hiking expeditions into the park.

Accommodation and food in Grazalema

Artesanía en Lana Anexo *Pl. España 18.* Displays beautiful locally woven blankets, shawls and ponchos.

Fiestas Mayor de Nuestra Señora de Los Angeles *tel: (95) 613–2225* take place last weekend in Aug.

Camping Tajo Rodillo € *Periferia Villa; tel: (95) 613–2063.*

Hostal-Restaurante La Casa de las Piedrasa € *c/ Las Piedras 32; tel: (95) 613–2014.* Traditional rooms over restaurant make budget base. Restaurant features local cuisine, with casserole of suckling goat a house speciality.

Villa Turística de Grazalema € *El Olivar s/n, 500m north of village centre; tel: (95) 613–2136; www.tugasa.com.* Operated by a branch of provincial tourism, the 'village' includes both hotel rooms and small self-catering flats.

Restaurante Cádiz el Chico €–€€ *Pl. España 8; tel: (95) 613–2027.* Serious country gourmets should inquire here for local specialities: roast lamb and venison, *tagarnina* (thistle stew), wild mushrooms, wild asparagus soup, rabbit, partridge with mushrooms, and wild trout cooked with a slice of mountain ham inside.

Below
Grazalema

Parque Natural Sierra de Grazalema❖❖

Pinzapo €€–€€€
c/ Las Piedras 11,
Grazalema; tel: (95)
613–2225, open Tue–Sun
1000–1400 and winter
1600–1900, summer
1800–2000, to book guided
tours and also arrange horse
riding tours. The office also
issues permits for
restricted areas of the
park.

Horizon €€–€€€
c/ Corrales, Tercero, 25;
tel: (95) 613–2363;
www.horizonaventura.com to
arrange hikes and canoe
trips in the reserve area as
well as canoe trips, rock-
climbing, cycling and caving
in other parts of the park.

The Grazalema massif is the most westerly sector of Cordillera Bética, the ranges that divide Andalucía's uplands from the coastal zone. The bald-top limestone cliffs of the Sierra del Pinar make up the heart of the park, where the top of the treeline is populated with the rare Spanish fir or *pinsapo*, a relic of the last ice age. Declared a biosphere reserve by UNESCO in 1977, this block of the park forms a triangle with points at El Bosque, Grazalema and Zahara de la Sierra. Access is controlled and hikers must obtain permits from the park authorities in Zahara. In practice, permits are only granted to guided groups, as authorities fear a forest fire that would render the *pinsapo* extinct. Guided walks along the main trails of this region – taking about six hours – can be arranged in Grazalema and Zahara.

The key to hiking in the park is the well-marked 1:50,000 scale topographic map, which can be purchased at park information centres. Outside the reserve area, some of the best half-day self-guided hikes lie southwest of Grazalema. A superb 20-min hike (each way) begins behind Camping Tajo Rodillo outside Grazalema to the 1100m peak of Llano del Endrinal with outstanding views. Three km west, towards El Bosque, is the Puerto del Boyar trailhead, 5km along a green river valley to the rock-climbing area called Salto del Cabrero ('Goatherd's Leap'). Another trail continues a further 5km south to the village of Benaocaz on the CA3331.

Right
Parque Natural
Sierra de Grazalema

ZAHARA DE LA SIERRA**

ⓘ **Oficina de Información del Parque de Grazalema**
c/ San Juan s/n; tel: (95) 612–3114; open Mon–Sat 0900–1400 and afternoons 1700–2000 in summer. Information and reservations for guided tours in the *pinsapo* reserve sector of the park. Office also assists with reservations for horse and canoe rentals.

🫒 **El Vínculo** *CA531*, 1km south of town; tel: (95) 612–3002. This mill has pressed local olive oil since 1640 and has the usual show-and-tell demonstration. The richly flavoured oil from two strains of olives is, of course, for sale.

🎈 **Lijarsur** *c/ Ronda 7, Algodonales; tel: (95) 622–1351;* www.lijarsur.com; open Fri–Sun. Offers hot-air balloon rides and paragliding, weather permitting.

From the Algodonales road north of town, Zahara appears like a mirage on a bluff above the reservoir with high mountains behind it. This quintessential white town is capped by a 12th-century **Nazari castle**** built over a Roman fort. The castle is reached by a marble cobble path from the Arco de la Villa hotel behind the 18th-century Baroque **Iglesia Santa María de Mesa***, one of the bookend churches at opposite ends of the main street, c/ San Juan. Halfway up the hill are the ruins of a 15th-century church, now being restored. From the castle, a vast bowl of a valley unfolds below. Because Zahara stands at the northern gateway to the most protected area of the Parque Natural Sierra de Grazalema, it serves as the principal base for guided hiking excursions.

Accommodation and food in Zahara de la Sierra

Arco de la Villa € *Pas. Nazari s/n; tel: (95) 612–3230.* All 17 rooms in this hotel built into the side of the cliff below the old castle have spectacular views at bargain prices. The bar-restaurant, open to all, features mountain cuisine with an emphasis on fresh pork.

Hostal-Restaurante Marqués de Zahara € *c/ San Juan 3; tel: (95) 612–3061; www.Marquesdczahara.com.* The ten rooms of this former mansion circle the courtyard that serves as the reception area and bar. The small restaurant offers typical mountain cuisine.

Los Tadeos € *Paseo La Fuente; tel: (95) 612–3086.* Small, friendly hostel with a bar/restaurant.

Suggested tour

Total distance: 83km, 93km with detour.

Time: 6–8 hours.

Links: The easternmost part of this tour connects to heart of the Frontera (*see pages 108–17*) at Ronda, while on the west it links to Sherry country (*see pages 118–29*) through Jerez de la Frontera.

Route: Leave **ARCOS DE LA FRONTERA** ❶ heading east on the A372 towards **EL BOSQUE** ❷. The route traverses rolling green hills emblazoned with patchwork plantings of grain and vegetable crops and lush wildflowers along the roadside as evidence of the moisture trapped on the west side of the sierra. It is a 32km drive to El Bosque, unmistakable against the backdrop of the Sierra Albarracín.

Detour: Just before entering the village, turn sharp left at Hotel Las Truchas and drive 300m to the trailhead for the El Bosque–

Benamahoma trail along the Río Majaceite. This 5km trek is officially rated as 'medium-difficult' in this direction, but should take no more than two hours for walkers in moderate cardiovascular condition. Bring insect repellent and binoculars; many bird species live near the trail, and otters sometimes appear in the river. Check the bus schedule at the park information centre to return.

The A372 continues east for 4km past **BENAMAHOMA ❸**, which lies 2km off the main road. Over the next 14km the road rises through increasingly steep switchbacks along sharp mountain ridges with stunning views if the region is not swaddled in cloud. The descent begins abruptly, often announced by a burst of blue sky and sunshine, down the eastern face of the Sierra Albarracín into the Río Guadalete valley and **GRAZALEMA ❹**. From the west side of town, the CA531 heads north over the highest pass in southern Andalucía, **Punto de las Palomas**✢✢, at 1157m. A mirador with splendid views stands above the road. This spot is also a bus stop and the crossroads of hiking paths to some of the highest summits in the **PARQUE NATURAL SIERRA DE GRAZALEMA ❺**. The CA531 swishes through the hills over a deep valley as it continues a further 12km to the steep turn-off for **ZAHARA DE LA SIERRA ❻**, just past an ancient olive oil mill. Trapped in the rain shadow of the Sierra Pinar, this dry country is irrigated from the turquoise-coloured reservoir that fills the floor of the valley. Follow the CA531 out of town, taking the Algodonales turn-off that passes over the reservoir dam. Pull into the turn-off on the far side of the dam for a spectacular view of Zahara. **Algodonales**✢ lies just 10km north, remarkable mostly for its handsome neo-classical church. Just north of town is the junction with the A382 and A376 highways, offering a speedy return to Arcos (A382 west) or a quick connection to Ronda (A376 east).

Also worth exploring

Ubrique✢✢ is the least rural and least white of the White Villages. Its artisans are famed for their saddlery and other leather work, and the town is a prosperous community of glass-fronted shops selling chic goods that include cigar cases, wallets, handbags, jackets and luggage. It is easily reached from El Bosque 13km southeast on the A373, or from Grazalema it is a 21km journey southwest on the A374.

Parque Doñana and environs

Doñana consists of a vast nature reserve and surrounding buffer zones that occupy the Andalucían coast from Huelva south to the Río Guadalquivir. Doñana's inland wetlands, a critical habitat for Europe's waterfowl population, stretch from the coast more than halfway to Sevilla. The park functions as a roadblock to traffic, often forcing long detours, but preservation of this natural treasure far outshadows any inconvenience. Public access to the national park at the core of Doñana is limited to protect its delicate environment, but the wildlife spill over into the less restricted buffer zones. Moreover, certain enclaves within Doñana are exempt from the strictest controls, resulting in access to bathing beaches at Playa Mazagón and Playa Matalascañas. The village of El Rocío, home to one of Spain's holiest pilgrimage sites, sits in the middle of the park as a gateway to guided tours to the interior.

ALMONTE❖

The A483, the only north–south road through Doñana, bypasses the handsome municipal centre of Almonte, and so do most visitors to the park. Two good reasons to follow the road into town are the delightful churches and the excellent local cuisine. Spotless white streets converge on **Plaza Virgen de los Reyes❖** between the 16th-century *ayuntamiento* and the 18th-century **Iglesia de la Asunción❖** (*open daily 1000–1400 and early mornings for Mass*). The latter is an architectural curiosity, as its design was influenced by Mexican colonial churches. Two tiny hermitages (with haphazard opening hours) are the 17th-century temple of **Ermita del Cristo❖** (*c/ del Cerro s/n*), wedged into the corner of a small plaza, and the **Ermita de San Bartolomé❖** (*c/ de Santiago s/n*).

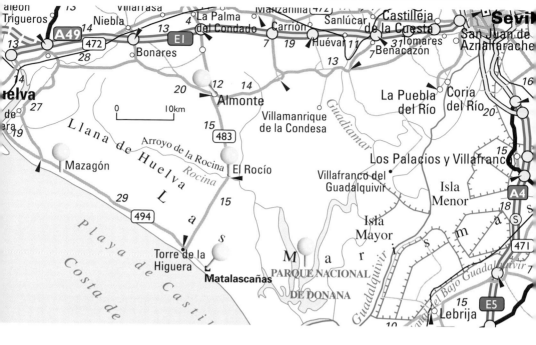

On Pl. Virgen de los Reyes, several small bar-restaurants offer dining-room and outdoor service. Good midday fare consists of local bread, a Condado wine made on the outskirts of town and a bowl of either *sopa marismeña* (chicken and rabbit soup) or *sopeao* (a variety of *gazpacho* with onion).

MAZAGON*

Most of the beaches of the Coto Doñana lie within the protection of the buffer zone of the park's reserve, but restrictions are eased for beaches around the fishing village of Mazagón and the purpose-built leisure community of Matalascañas. With a good variety of lodging, Mazagón makes a superb base for touring both the Columbus Trail (*see Huelva and environs, pages 148–55*) and for making forays into the park. The town sits on the mainland across a narrow channel from the southern tip of the barrier island Isla de Saltes, which stretches 15km southeast from Huelva harbour. Small fishing boats fill the marina nestling beneath El Picacho lighthouse, and the occasional pleasure craft anchors here overnight. The virtually deserted brown-sand **Playa Mazagón*** stretches 7km back toward Huelva, while the Playa de Castilla begins southeast of town. Most of the latter is off-limits as either protected land within Parque Doñana or as a military preserve surrounded by barbed wire. A low-tech amusement park supplies much of the evening entertainment.

Accommodation and food in Mazagón

Camping Playa Mazagón € *Cuesta Barca s/n; tel: (95) 937–6208; fax: (95) 953–6256; www.campingplayademazagon.com.* A few minutes' walk from the beach at the southeast end of town near the lighthouse.

Hotel Carabela Santa María €–€€ *Avda los Conquistadores s/n; tel: (95) 953–6018; fax: (95) 937–7258; www.hotelcarabelasantamaria.com.* This 80-room modern hotel opened in July 1998 as a rather elegant in-town option within walking distance of the beach.

Parador de Mazagón €€€ *Playa Mazagón; tel: (95) 953–6300; www.parador.es.* Modern *parador* 2km south of town with motel-style rooms open to the interior pool, which looks west to the ocean. Spectacular views from high bluffs over the beach. Also known as Parador Cristóbal Colón. Excellent dining rooms specialise in local shellfish and crustaceans as well as Jabugo hams, ribs and pâtés.

Cafetería Europa €–€€ *Avda Conquistadores 18; tel: (95) 937–6107.* The harbour end of Mazagón's main thoroughfare is lined with small restaurants and cafés, all of them virtually ignoring their printed menus in favour of serving the catch of the day. The chef at Europa is as particular and proud as his kitchen is small, refusing to send out condiments because he seasons each dish 'perfectly'.

PARQUE DOÑANA✦✦✦

❶ **Centro de Visitantes El Acebuche** *A483 km26; tel: (95) 944–8711; fax: (95) 944–8576; www.mma.es; open daily 0800–2000.* Displays on Doñana ecosystems, audiovisual presentation, souvenir shop, information and reservations for guided tours.

Centro de Informacíon La Rocina *A483 km16; tel: (95) 944–2340; open daily 0900–2100.* Park information and access to creekside path.

Once a hunting preserve of dukes, kings and sherry barons, the Coto de Doñana was recognised as a critical waterfowl habitat in the 1960s, and portions of what became the Parque Doñana were set aside in 1964. The central core of the Parque Nacional (the most protected zone) was established in 1969. The buffer zones, known as the Parque Natural, are administered by the regional government of Andalucía, and are open to limited agricultural and tourism uses.

The park consists of three distinct ecological zones. The dunes and wet interdune valleys (*corrales*) represent waves of shifting sand steadily blown and washed inland from the Atlantic. The wild camels that once wandered these dunes recently died out. A narrow strip of evergreen woodland with a substantial deer population separates the dunes from the wetlands. Most of the park consists of *marismas*, seasonal marshes that flood each spring and turn to salty dry plains in the summer. Hundreds of thousands of waterfowl, from ducks to flamingos, take refuge in the shallow *marismas* in the winter and late spring. Due to its critical location on the Europe–North Africa flyway, more than half of Europe's migratory birds depend on Doñana.

There are two easy options for casual visitors to sample Doñana. Storks nest atop the visitor centre at **El Acebuche**✦✦, where a boardwalk trail leads to blinds where waterfowl can be observed. The

**ℹ Cooperativo
Marismas del Rocío**
€€€ *Pl. Acebuchal 16, El
Rocío; tel: (95) 843–0432.*
Reservations for Land
Rover tours inside the
reserve. Trips daily at 0830
and 1700.

Ⓠ Doñana Ecuestre
€€ *Avda La Canaleja
s/n, El Rocio; tel: (95)
944–2474.* You can hire
horses here for a couple of
hours or a full day. The
company also organise
4-wheel drive tours of the
park.

Arroyo de la Rocina✶✶ protected area is traversed by a 3.5km path along reedy marshes and then a 7km path through pine forest and heather to **Palacio El Acebrón**✶, which has audiovisual displays on the relationship that local people have always had with the marsh.

El Acebuche is the departure point for guided Land Rover tours to the interior reserves. Other trips on horse, bicycle or by barge can be arranged at the centre or else in El Rocío or Sanlúcar de Barrameda (*see Sherry country, pages 118–29*).

Right
A boardwalk in the Parque
Doñana

PLAYA MATALASCANAS❖❖

Oficina de Turismo
Avda de las Adelfas; tel: (95) 943–0086; fax: (95) 944–3808; open Mon–Fri 0930–1400, Sat 1000–1400; closed Sunday.

Built as a coastal resort despite complaints about the threat to Coto de Doñana as a natural preserve, the clumps of small stucco villas and expansive beachside hotels stand in strong contrast to the nearby swamps. Yet park boundaries keep the resort in check, and the paved seaside promenade is a lively scene on a stunningly beautiful beach, part of Playa Castilla. The cleanliness of the beach is underscored by the dozens of shellfishermen plying its sands. With thousands of rooms only 4km from Parque Doñana's main visitor centre, Matalascañas is a popular base for exploring the park.

Accommodation and food in Playa Matalascañas

Camping Rocío Playa € *A494, Playa Matalascañas; tel: (95) 943–0238.* Unusually good camping community with mobile homes and cabins as well as pitches. Superb beach stretching to the horizon.

Hotel Tierra Mar €–€€ *Playa Matalascañas; tel: (95) 944–0300; fax: (95) 944–0720; www.atlanticclub-hotels.com.* Rather elegant and extremely well-maintained concrete tower hotel on the beach, complete with large pool and nightly entertainment. Essentially a resort destination.

Below
The Parque Doñana viewed through one of the hides on the reserve.

Restaurante Bajo Guía €€ *Paseo Marítimo; tel: (95) 944–0037.* Barbecue and rotisserie chicken in addition to the fish specialities of the coast. One of the nicest restaurants along the decidedly casual beachfront walkway.

EL ROCIO❖❖

ⓘ Oficina de Turismo *Avda Canaliega s/n; tel: (95) 944–3008; www.donana.es.* Provides information on El Rocío.

◖ Hotel Puente del Rey €–€€ *Avda Canaliega s/n; tel: (95) 944–2575; fax: (95) 944–2070.* Large and attractive hotel along the A483; makes a good stopover for visiting Parque Doñana. Just don't expect much evening hoopla beyond nocturnal wildlife.

The village of El Rocío is home to the image of the Virgen del Rocío (Virgin of the Dew), affectionately known as the 'white dove'. According to legend, a 13th-century Almonte shepherd discovered the carving inside a hollow tree and the image miraculously returned to that spot whenever it was removed. The villagers built a shrine at El Rocío, where many miracles have been reported over the centuries. The current shrine, built in 1964, is the **Basílica Paloma Blanca❖❖** *(Pl. Ermita; open daily 0830–1930).* A steady stream of the faithful files through daily.

On the Saturday, Sunday and Monday of Pentecost, or Whit Sunday – the seventh Sunday after Easter – up to a million pilgrims descend on the village for the Romería del Rocío. More than 70 brotherhoods make pilgrimages by horse and ox-cart over several days while dressed in flamenco garb and drinking heavily. The culminating moments, when the brotherhoods surge at the image, are televised throughout

Spain. A more sedate version is enacted every seven years (next in 2005) on the third weekend of Aug. Called El Rocío Chico, it features only the brotherhoods of Almonte.

This phenomenon has a curious effect on El Rocío. Most buildings belong to the brotherhoods, and stand empty except during the pilgrimage and a few other days of obligation. The village streets are sanded, and area residents often resort to horseback for transportation. Hitching posts stand outside most buildings. As a result, the village has a surreal, TV-western feel.

Yet because El Rocío is surrounded by the marshlands of Doñana and lies on the A483, it serves as a base for serious birdwatchers and other naturalists. The Río Madre de las Marismas ('Mother River of the Marshes') begins at the edge of the village, and the Spanish Ornithological Society has set up excellent blinds for observing waterfowl, the **Observatorio Madre del Rocío*** (*by river, 150m east of Hotel Toruño; open Mon–Thur 0900–1500 and Fri–Sun 1030–1330 and 1430–1730*).

Suggested tour

 Club Hípico El Pasodoble €€€
A494; tel: (95) 944–8241 operate two- and four-hour guided horse rides on trails in the dunes and beaches of Parque Doñana near Playa Matalascañas. Call for timetable.

Total distance: 102km.

Time: 5 hours.

Links: Connects to Huelva and environs (*see pages 148–55*) through Moguer.

Route: Following the A494 south from **MAZAGON** ❶ the road rarely passes in sight of the beach, although for the first few kilometres houses of the well-to-do on the beach side are evident behind screens of trees and other landscaping. Soon the strip between the highway and the beaches becomes a military reservation and then a section of **PARQUE DONANA** ❷. There are several turn-offs to campsites, each of which is a self-contained community.

Detour: Just before reaching Playa Matalascañas a turning on the right leads to the riding stable, **Club Hípico El Pasodoble**, which offers a chance to see the dunes and ride along the long beaches.

PLAYA MATALASCANAS ❸ is worth the visit for the sheer immensity of the EU blue-flag beach, where shellfishermen and surf swimmers share the strand. From the roundabout west of the beach town, the A483 heads northeast towards El Rocío, with the major access points to **PARQUE DONANA** at El Acebuche in 4km and La Rocina in another 11km. The drive through this territory captures the geographic ironies of Doñana – a desert that meets the ocean and is cross-hatched by *arroyos* (streams) and marshes. The landscape has a surreal quality, sometimes resembling barren desert where only low scrub can survive in the drifting sands, and at others appearing like an African savannah of low grasses with flattened lollipop trees. The dominant vegetation is broom, which blooms bright yellow in the spring, and umbrella pine; but in the uplands (never very far 'up') the pines stretch 10m tall or more in the dry *bosque* (woodland).

The drive from Acebuche to Las Rocinas passes through agricultural land heavily planted with strawberries, oranges, and, to a lesser extent, olives. The tiny community of **Los Mimbrales** appears to exist almost solely for the benefit of low-income farm workers. **EL ROCIO** ❹ can seem deserted, but is worth a visit to see the shrine; adjacent casual bars offer pilgrims bargain fare.

The 15km drive on the A483 from El Rocío to **ALMONTE** ❺ crosses rolling landscape planted extensively with grapes for the vermouth of Almonte and the light Huelvan white wines produced at **Rociana del Condado**, 10km northwest of Almonte on the A484. The 15km drive west from Rociana to **Lucerna del Puerto** is a sampler of both the upland *bosque*, where deer and wild boar roam, as well as hillside vineyards. In another 13km, turn left on to the A494 past Moguer (*see page 150*) and in 4km turn left again on to the HV6231. This narrow country road is one of the few paved rights of way through the edges of the park, passing 25km over *arroyos* and through wild country before returning to Mazagón at the lighthouse east of town.

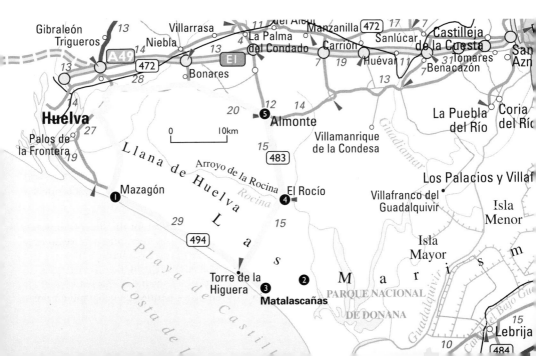

Huelva and environs

Ratings

Beaches	●●●●
Architecture	●●●○○
Gastronomy	●●●○○
History	●●●○○
Entertainment	●●○○○
Nature and wildlife	●●○○○
Museums	●○○○○
Shopping and crafts	●○○○○

The high mountains of the Sierra de Aracena drain in dozens of rivers and streams that empty into the Atlantic near Huelva, creating an intricate coastline of lagoons, marshes and estuaries. Phoenicia established the city as a shipping centre for inland ore deposits, and Huelva is still an industrial port. Yet the old city within the industrial ring has a gentle charm and makes a good base for historic and natural exploration. Even today, the region draws much of its identity from associations with Christopher Columbus, and the principal attractions lie in the villages that provided the political persuasion, navigational skill and manpower for his voyages. The coast west of Huelva is treasured by Spaniards for the pine-topped dunes of some of Europe's cleanest white-sand beaches. Despite pockets of overdevelopment, much of its wild beauty is preserved as parkland free from resorts.

COLUMBUS TRAIL❖❖

ℹ Oficina de Turismo *Paraje de la Rabida s/n; tel: (95) 953–0535; open Tue–Fri 1000–1400 and 1700–2100, Sat–Sun 1000–2000.*

ℹ Monasterio de la Rábida € *tel: (95) 935–0411; open Tue–Sun 1000–1300 and 1600–1900. Guided tours are every 45 mins. Tours in English are also available for a small fee.*

Just south of Huelva along the silted-in Río Tinto are several sites associated with Christopher Columbus, known in Spain as Cristóbal Colón. The towns give Columbus his due, but remind visitors that the explorer hardly sailed alone. When Columbus embarked on his historic voyage on 3 August 1492, two of his three vessels were commanded by the Pinzón brothers of Palos, who also recruited a crew of 120 men from Palos and nearby Moguer.

Convinced that he could reach the East Indies by sailing west, Columbus spent several frustrating years trying to persuade the Portuguese, French, English and Spanish courts to fund a voyage. The **Monasterio de la Rábida**❖❖, about 9km from Huelva, is the modest 14th-century Franciscan monastery where Columbus's luck changed. Abbot Juan Pérez, former confessor of Queen Isabela, interceded on Columbus's behalf and won the queen's backing.

The guided tour, conducted in Spanish by a monk in robe and sandals, begins with 1930s murals depicting the explorer's life and exploits. Other portions of the monastery are little changed since 1492, and the tour passes through the austere refectory where Columbus dined, the cell where he discussed his plans, and the chapel where he and his men prayed prior to departure. The monastery notes its historic role with models of the caravels, navigation charts, a room full of flags and a box of earth from each nation of the Americas.

The harbour where the expedition departed silted up long ago, but a lagoon below the monastery, **Muelle de las Carabelas**✶ (tel: (95) 953–0597; open in winter Tue–Sat 1000–1700 and in summer Mon–Sat 1000–1400 and 1700–2100; Sun 1100–2000), displays full-size replicas of the Niña, the Pinta and the Santa María. The ships are meagrely interpreted, but walking their confined spaces hints at the adventure and hardship of an extended voyage into the unknown. The largest, the Santa María, stretched only 29m. They landed in the Bahamas on 12 October 1492, and returned to Palos de la Frontera on 15 March 1493.

Tidy little **Palos de la Frontera**✶✶, 4km northeast of La Rábida, does not look like a one-time major port, but the ayuntamiento on c/ Colón hands out a sketchy map identifying the main Columbus sites. The explorer and his crew attended Mass at **Iglesia de San Jorge**✶ (open only during service hours), and plaques on the plaza honour all of Palos's seamen and, in a recent gesture of political correctness, the women who waited at home. **La Fontanilla**✶, a medieval brick well where the crew drew water for the voyage, now anchors a new park. Palos reveres Columbus's captains, Martín and Vicente Alonso Pinzón; **Casa Martín Alonso Pinzón**✶✶ (c/ Colón 24; open Mon–Sat 1030–1330, 1730–1930; Sun 1030–1330) is now a town museum with displays related to the brothers and other town history, including a scale

Convento de Santa Clara € *Pl. Monjas, Moguer; open Tue–Sat for tours at 1100, 1200, 1300, 1630 and 1930.*

Casa Museo Juan Ramón Jiménez € *c/ Juan Ramón Jiménez, Moguer; open daily for tours at 1015–1315 and 1715–1915.*

Below
Model of Columbus' ship, the *Santa María*, in Huelva's Muelle de las Carabelas museum

model of *Plus Ultra,* a seaplane that mirrored the Columbus voyage by crossing the Atlantic from Palos to Buenos Aires in 1926.

Nearly half the crew for Columbus's first expedition and succeeding voyages were recruited from **Moguer✦✦**, the most charming town on the Columbus Trail. After his first voyage, the explorer spent a night in prayer here at the Mudéjar-style **Convento de Santa Clara✦**, fulfilling a pledge of thanksgiving for weathering a storm off the Azores. Today the nuns have made way for a religious art museum.

Moguer's other claim to fame is as the birthplace and home – until he fled to Argentina to escape persecution by Franco – of Nobel laureate author Juan Ramón Jiménez. Every student of Spanish knows his classic *Platero y yo* about his donkey, and the town is dotted with tiled plaques quoting from the story. A walking tour from the tourist office is exasperatingly vague and Moguer, like much of Huelva, does not seem to believe in signage. But perseverance pays off with a tour of sites a casual visitor might otherwise miss, including a shop selling the local convent pastries, *quesadillas de Santa Clara,* at c/ Vendederas 26. Serious fans of Jiménez might wish to peruse his manuscripts and memorabilia at **Casa Museo Juan Ramón Jiménez✦**.

Accommodation and food on the Columbus Trail

La Hostería de la Rábida € *in grounds of Monasterio; tel: (95) 935–0312.* Five rooms with austere grace sit over the conference rooms, bar and large dining rooms. Great view to the caravels and the huge Columbus statue in Huelva harbour.

Hotel-Restaurante La Pinta € *c/ Rábida 79, Palos de la Frontera; tel: (95) 935–0511; fax: (95) 953–0164.* Close to the main square of Palos but sufficiently removed to be quiet. Simple, somewhat old-fashioned rooms. The restaurant serves local fish and – something of a relief – regional beef and veal.

Maison Restaurante La Parrala €€ *Pl. Las Monjas 22, Moguer; tel: (95) 937–0452; closed Mon.* On the pedestrian street leading to the Convento, with broad menu emphasising regional seafood and pork dishes. Décor on the elegant side for Moguer, but menu prices are quite a bargain.

HUELVA✢

ⓘ **Patronato Provincial de Turismo** *Avda de Alemania 14; tel: (95) 925–7403 or (95) 925–7403; fax: (95) 921–0548; www.ayuntamientodehuelva.es.* Provides information for the entire province.

Oficina de Turismo *Pl. de las Monjas; tel: (95) 928–3931; www.andalucia.org; open Mon–Fri 0900–1900, Sat–Sun 1000–1400.*

The petrochemical plants on Huelva's periphery spew ominous smoke and grimy ketones, but this small city on the peninsula between the confluence of the Odiel and Tinto rivers makes a good base for exploring the Columbus Trail.

Hit hard in the 1755 earthquake, Huelva now consists of a pleasant blend of 18th- and 19th-century *palacios* with handsome small-scale modern buildings. The main square is **Plaza Monjas✢**, the hub for pedestrian streets lined with shops, bars and restaurants and dotted with contemporary sculpture. Near the plaza on the corner of M. Nuñez and Concepción stands **Iglesia de la Concepción✢**, a postquake reconstruction of a 14th-century church with excellent paintings by Zurbarán.

The **Museo de Huelva✢** *(tel: (95) 925–9300; open Tue–Sat 0900–2000; Sun 0900–1500),* in an attractive modern building at Avda Sundheim 13, mixes art and history. The archaeological collections deal with ancient Tartessos and subsequent Phoenician, Greek and Roman occupations. The fine arts collection is drably academic, but temporary exhibitions are often ambitious.

At the eastern end of Avda Sundheim on Pl. de España, a steep set of stairs leads to **Barrio Obrero Reina Victoria✢✢**, a residential district built in 1917 by the Río Tinto mining company to house its workers. The stairs emphasise the separation from the rest of the city, as does the English bungalow style of the lovingly maintained – and muchmodified – houses with colourful gardens. Many elderly residents claim to have spent their lives in this enclave, and gladly regale Spanishspeaking visitors with *barrio* history, sometimes inviting them in for tea.

The **Sanctuario de Nuestra Señora de la Cinta✢✢** *(off Avda Manuel Siurot; tel: (95) 915–5122; open Mon–Sat 0900–1330 and 1700–1930)* stands 2km north of the city centre on high cliffs over the Río Odiel. Mustering all the divine intervention he could manage, Columbus also visited this peaceful chapel before his first voyage. The attached convent draped in bougainvillaea and surrounded by gorgeous gardens epitomises the grace of monastic life.

Fiestas Colombinas
tel: (95) 925–7403.
Week-long fiesta
commemorating the
navigator begins 3 Aug.
Best corridas take place
during the fiesta in the
Plaza de Toros *Pas.*
Independencia; tel: (95)
925–1500.

Huelva may be an industrial city, but just across the unpolluted Odiel estuary from the city is the **Paraje Natural Marisma del Odiel**, a 72-sq-km region of marshes frequented by a large variety of birds, including osprey and both the grey heron and the purple heron. Many greater flamingos and up to a third of Europe's spoonbills winter here. The **Centro de Visitantes Calatilla** *(tel: (95) 950–9011; mobile: 660 414–920; open Fri, Sat and Sun 0900–1400 and 1700–2000)*, at the southern end of the first island of the reserve, can arrange guided visits by horse, boat and 4-wheel drive (€€).

Accommodation and food in Huelva

Hotel Los Condes € *Alameda Sundheim 14; tel: (95) 928–2400; fax: (95) 928–5041; e-mail: info@hotelloscondes.com; www.hotelloscondes.com.* More modest digs opposite the museum.

Hotel Luz Huelva €€ *Alameda Sundheim 26; tel: (95) 925–0011; fax: (95) 925–8110; www.nh-hotels.com.* Modern, 115-room hotel geared to business people offers terraces and access to swimming pool, tennis and golf.

Mercado del Carmen *c/ Carmen* is the city's main meat, fish and produce market and is surrounded by stalls and shops selling bread, sausages, cheese, olive oil and local hams.

Restaurante Doñana €€ *c/ Gran Vía 13; tel: (95) 924–2773.* Emphasises local fish; the sardines with red peppers are especially good.

WEST TO PORTUGAL**

Oficina de Turismo
Avda de Madrid s/n, Isla
Cristina. s/n; tel: (95)
933–2694; fax: (95)
933–2806; open Mon–Fri
1000–1400 and 1730–
2000, Sat–Sun 1000–1400.

The Atlantic beaches west of Huelva to the Portuguese border fall under the rubric of the Costa de la Luz *(see pages 90–7)*, and their pristine sandy strands rank among some of Europe's finest. Resort development lags behind other beach districts in Spain, and the principal clientele is domestic. The region has superb camping, however, and many of the most beautiful beaches with best surf are located not near the resorts, but near the campsites. The N431 offers a direct route between Huelva and the border with Portugal, but the resorts and fishing villages invariably lie a few km south of the highway on lagoons and peninsulas that dangle from the mainland.

The oldest beach community of this coast is **Punta Umbría**, just a few km from Huelva as the gull flies, but about 21km by road. On the western banks of the Río Odiel, Punta Umbría is sandwiched between the river and a striking west-facing beach of coarse brown sand. The town has flourished as a getaway for Huelvans, who hop over on the ferry in July and Aug. A bustling summer venue, Punta Umbría has an old-fashioned charm compared to more built-up sections of the Huelvan coast.

El Rompido, with its combined church and town hall, is a gritty fishing village which at the same time has striking beaches and many good bars and restaurants. A long sandbar shelters sandy beaches on both sides of an estuary from the brunt of the Atlantic Ocean. High dunes covered with umbrella pines and junipers stand behind the beaches.

The most overdeveloped resort areas lie west of the Río Piedras. While **El Terrón** is just a small fishing port on the marshes of the Río Piedras, the neighbouring village of **La Anchilla** has mushroomed beyond recognition. The west end of town has spread around the pioneer Confortel resort with a riot of high-density construction that now identifies itself as 'Islantilla', a blending of the names of La Anchilla with that of the well-established beach community, **Isla Cristina**. Ironically, while La Anchilla and Isla Cristina embody the worst excesses of beach resort development, between them lies a pretty provincial park with the finest beaches of the area, complete with majestic surf. They are best enjoyed by settling at a campsite across the highway and walking through the park to the beach.

On the Río Guadiana border with Portugal, half of **Ayamonte*** perches on a high bluff above the estuary while the other half puddles around the fishing port. Much of the town's pre-development character remains because its best beaches are 7km south of centre on the Isla Canela peninsula. Most of Isla Canela's resorts stand across the main road from the beach, and few rise more than six storeys.

Below
Ayamonte

🍴 Bar-Restaurante La Patera € c/ Nao 1, El Rompido; tel: (95) 939–9320; closed Mon. Bustling semi-formal fish restaurant with striking tiled bar and delightfully funky café opening on to beach.

Espuma del Mar € Paseo de los Gavilanes s/n; tel: (95) 947–7295. Catch-of-the-day seafood with an inexpensive daily menu and outside tables for dining alfresco.

Bar-Restaurante El Velero € Pas. Ría, Punta Umbría; tel: (95) 931–5315. Family-run fish restaurant across the street from the docks and fish market. Great seafood gazpacho.

Accommodation and food in the Huelva area

Camping Catapum € HV4111 just east of El Rompido; tel: (95) 939–0165. Just across the road from stunning white-sand beach where many sailing boats anchor.

Camping Giralda € Carretera Isla Cristina–La Antilla km1.5; tel: (95) 934–3318; e-mail: campinggiralda@infonegocio.com; www.campinggiralda.com. Superb campsite across the road from pine-filled littoral park, with beach 90m away.

Confortel Islantilla €€€ Carretera Isla Cristina–La Antilla km5; tel: (95) 948–6017; fax: (95) 948–6211; e-mail: islantilla.confortel@once.es; www.confortelhoteles.com. This giant resort with 27-hole golf course pioneered large-scale development on the Costa de la Luz.

Hotel Ayamontino Ría €€ Avda Ría 1, Punta Umbría; tel: (95) 931–1458; fax: (95) 931–1462. Riverside hotel near the bustling summer café scene.

Hotel Emilio € c/ Ancha 21, Punta Umbría; tel: (95) 931–1800; fax: (95) 965–9051; www.guiadehuelva.com/hotelemilio. Old-fashioned beach hotel on the river side of town.

Hotel Los Geranios € Avda Playa s/n, Isla Cristina; tel: (95) 933–1800; fax: (95) 933–1950. Delightful 30-room hotel near best Isla Cristina beach, Playa Central.

Hotel Riu Canela €€€ (half board) Pas. Gavilanes s/n, Ayamonte; tel: (95) 962–1006; fax: (95) 947–7170; www.riv.com. Self-contained resort with 347 rooms, facing onto Playa Isla Canela.

Mesones Juan Macías €–€€ Paseo de la Ribera 2; tel: (95) 947–1695. Famous local charcuterie with plenty of meaty choice and inexpensive raciones.

Parador de Ayamonte €€ El Castillito s/n, Ayamonte; tel: (95) 932–0700; fax: (95) 902–2019; www.parador.es. Elegant traditional Spanish décor is upstaged by the surrounding views. Restaurant specialises in coastal clams, and the mountain hams of Jabugo (see pages 160–1).

Restaurante La Esperanza € Pl. Pérez Pastor 7, Punta Umbría; tel: (95) 931–1045; open Jul–Sept only. Good range of daily specials, most of local fish.

Suggested tour

Total distance: 170km, 210km with detour.

Time: 8 hours.

Links: This tour connects to Parque Doñana and environs (see pages 140–47) through Moguer.

Route: Drive south out of **HUELVA** ❶ on the N442 through the petrochemical complexes that line the harbour where the Odiel and Tinto rivers converge. A vast statue of Columbus looms over the estuary, looking more like Godzilla than a visionary explorer. After 2km the landscape suddenly changes with a left turn at a small roundabout on to the H640; a huge sign announces the **COLUMBUS TRAIL** ❷. The turn-off on Avda de América to **La Rábida** steps back 500 years into a park-like landscape. Follow Avda de América, marked with seals of the American republics rendered in tiles, to **Palos de la Frontera**. Continue 8km along the A494 through strawberry fields (watching for roadside stands) to **Moguer**. After another 4km take the A472 southwest for 8km to return to Huelva.

Detour: From Huelva, cross the Río Odiel bridge and immediately turn left, then right on to Carretera Islas. This road runs 20km down the centre of the **Paraje Natural Marisma del Odiel**. Most of the birds are found in the salt lagoons at the southern end of the park.

From the Río Odiel bridge, the A497 leads 8km west to Punta de Sebo and another 14km southeast to the beach at **Punta Umbría**. Head west on the beach road 16km toward **El Rompido**, then north 8.5km on the N411 to **Cartaya**, following signs for 12.5km through **Lepe** to **La Antilla**. The beach road resumes, going west 10km to the chic **Isla Cristina** resort, then north 5km on the H412 to connect to the E31/N431, which reaches **Ayamonte** in 10.5km.

Return 53km to Huelva on the N431 through rolling landscape, planted in oranges and peaches on the western end, and in strawberries on the east. Driving through Lepe in early April with the windows down, the delicious perfume of orange blossoms makes for a heady experience.

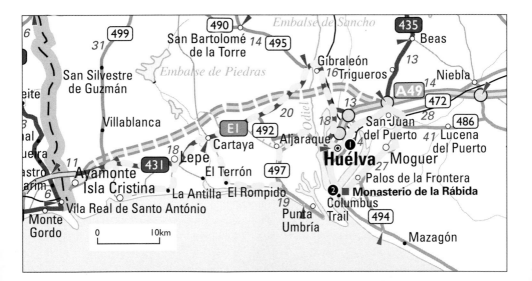

Huelva's high country

Ratings

Gastronomy ●●●●●

Outdoor
activities ●●●●●

Nature
and wildlife ●●●●○

Architecture ●●●○○

Shopping
and crafts ●●●○○

History ●●○○○

Entertainment
●○○○○

Museums ●○○○○

Compared to the big cities of Huelva in the south and Sevilla to the southeast, the rolling hills of the Sierra Aracena seem to belong to another country. In fact, the residents even *sound* foreign, as the local Spanish carries an accent closer to Portuguese than Castilian. The moist uplands are verdant and lush, supporting vast stands of cork oaks and chestnuts amid olives and oranges. Few other parts of Andalucía are so conscious of high-quality foods, perhaps because the best dry-cured hams in the world come from these hills, along with an astonishing variety of honeys and extraordinary sheep and goat cheeses that are rarely exported. Most of the region lies within the Parque Natural Sierra de Aracena y Picos de Aroche, and well-marked hiking trails link many of the villages. The easy terrain makes Sierra Aracena the most welcoming hiking region in Andalucía.

ALAJAR❖

La Posada € c/ Médico Emilio González 2; tel: (95) 912–5712; e-mail: laposadaalajar@ telefonica.net has eight rooms with bath and a modestly priced (€) restaurant.

This typical mountain town of whitewashed buildings spreads out from a centre defined by the *ayuntamiento* (town hall) and a crumbling 18th-century church. Alájar is the area's market centre (Thursday is market day), but most visitors skip the valley town for the **Peña de Arias Montano❖❖** perched high above on a limestone bluff. Named after the 16th-century humanist cleric who was Felipe II's confessor and who retreated to this overlook to meditate, the site is one of the few commanding seats of power in Andalucía without the ruins of a fortress. Stories are told of pre-Christian mystics using the *peña* for vision quests and other shamanistic activities, and a certain counter-cultural contingent still comes in search of the hallucinogenic *amanita muscaria* mushroom. The 16th-century hermitage of the **Virgen de los Angeles❖** has some striking tiles and *trompe l'oeils* of saints. The more

secular side of the *peña* includes a lively group of vendors selling local ceramics, honey, cheeses and bee pollen.

Every year on 6–7 September at the **Romería de Nuestra Señora de los Angeles** the young men of the village race horses around the cobblestone streets and up the precipitous hill to the shrine while other pilgrims make the *romería* on foot.

ALMONASTER LA REAL✦✦✦

ℹ Oficina de Turismo
Ayuntamiento, Pl.
Constitución 1; tel: (95)
914–3003; open Mon–Fri
1000–1400.

🍴 Restaurante Las
Palmeras €–€€
Carretera s/n; tel: (95)
914–3105. Big, sunny patio
fronts a casual dining room.

▲ Fiesta de la Santa
Cruz and **Romería**
Santa Eulalia *tel: (95)*
914–3003. Both held in
May, featuring flamenco and
processions, respectively.

Two fine churches define the hills of this pleasant agricultural town. The northern hill is crowned with a 14th-century Mudéjar church. On top of the southern hill is a stunning **rural mezquita**✦✦✦ left virtually intact when it was Christianised in the 13th century. The mosque embodies the history of the region. The granite and marble columns that support horseshoe brick arches were salvaged from Roman and Visigothic buildings. Roman, Visigothic and Arabic marble capitals top the columns. Although a Gothic altar was added, the mosque's keyhole-shaped *mihrab* and square minaret were left intact. Variously attributed to the 8th or 10th centuries, it is the oldest relatively intact mosque in Iberia and an uplifting venue for occasional chamber music recitals. If the door is locked ask for a key in the *ayuntamiento*, or ask a local policeman. Curiously, Almonaster's bullring has been grafted onto the side of the mosque, and *corridas* are staged during the first week of May and in August. The children of the town often watch from the top of the minaret.

Accommodation and food in Almonaster la Real

Hostal Restaurante Casa García € *Avda San Martín 2; tel: (95) 914–3109; fax: (95) 914–3143.* Charming small complex has 22 rooms with private bath, a restaurant serving country cuisine and grilled meats (€–€€) and a lively bar and patio, plus pool.

ARACENA✦✦✦

ℹ Centro de
Visitantes Cabildo
Viejo *Pl. Alta; tel: (95)*
912–8825; open daily,
1000–1400 and 1600–1800
in the former town hall
provides information on
the Parque Natural Sierra
de Aracena and Picos de
Aroche.

Centro de Turismo
Rural *at the Gruta de las*
Maravillas; tel: (95)
912–8206 provides
information and helps with
lodging reservations in the
surrounding area.

The natural choice as a base for exploring the Sierra Aracena, this handsome town claims two major 'attractions' in its hilltop castle and its network of underground grottoes. The **Gruta de las Maravillas**✦✦ (*€ entrance at Pozo de la Nieve; tel: (95) 912–8355; open daily 1000–1300 and 1430–1800*) ranks among Spain's largest and most impressive caves. Parts of the film *Journey to the Centre of the Earth* were shot here, though not in the final cavern, the Room of the Buttocks, whose rounded formations are enhanced by strategic lighting. It's best not to arrive too late in the day since tours (lasting 45min–1hr) will not depart unless there are at least 25 people. The Gruta's popularity has spawned a cluster of shops, restaurants and bars around the entrance.

No such commercialisation attends the **Iglesia Nuestra Señora de los Dolores**✦✦. The complex includes a castle where Moorish, Portuguese and Castilian fortifications have been reduced to generic ruins by time. The Gothic-Mudéjar church, on the other hand, remains in fine condition seven centuries after its construction by the Knights Templar, the independent army that waged a permanent holy war against the Muslim 'infidels' in western Europe and the

Tren Turístico Parque Natural Sierra de Aracena y Picos de Aroche € *Tel: (95) 912–8825.* Departs from Pl. San Pedro for one-hour tours of monuments and natural areas, daily 1030–1830.

Complejo Finca Valbona €€€ *Carretera de Carbonera km 1; tel: (95) 912–7711* offers horse riding and bicycle touring. Ask for information at Hotel Sierra de Aracena.

Fernández Jamón de Jabugo *c/ San Pedro s/n* sells local ham (some vacuum-packed for travel) as well as local cheeses and baked goods.

Holy Land. Committed to exploring multiple mystic paths to enlightenment (read: heresies) and possessed of sufficient clout to unnerve Europe's monarchs, the Knights fell foul of both religious and civil authorities and were abolished in 1312 by papal bull. The main altar is an impressive agglomeration of liturgical imagery. The wrought-iron screens on the side chapels are some of the finest in Andalucía.

Aracena's **Feria de Agosto** (*tel: (95) 911–0355*), held the third week of Aug, features music, dancing and bullfights.

Accommodation and food in Aracena

Camping Aracena € *Carretera Sevilla–Rosal de la Frontera; tel: (95) 950–1004; www.vayacamping.com.* The campsite is about 5km out of town.

Hotel Los Castaños € *Avda Huelva 5; tel: (95) 912–6300; fax: (95) 912–6287.* The town's business hotel also has a modest restaurant.

Hotel Sierra de Aracena € *c/ Gran Vía 21; tel: (95) 912–6175; fax: (95) 912–6218.* Popular with hikers, this 43-room hotel has a fireplace in the lobby to ward off the evening chill.

Mesón de Pedro Restaurante € *c/ Gran Vía s/n; tel: (95) 912–6298; closed Mon.* Low-key spot to sample local ham served country-style.

Montecruz €€ *Plaza de San Pedro; tel: (95) 912–6013.* Stunning view of the castle, and you can eat on an outdoor terrace in summer. Starters include such local specialities as *migas* (fried breadcrumbs).

Right
Aracena

JABUGO*

Fernández *Carretera San Juan del Puerto s/n* is one of many shops in town selling local ham, including small vacuum-packed portions.

There is really only one reason to visit Jabugo: its legendary *jamón ibérico* produced in prodigious quantities from the local *patas negras,* or black-footed pigs. Actually, the pigs are entirely black, or at least a smudgy grey or deep brown, and can be seen all around Jabugo, grazing in pastures and particularly in orchards of oak trees, where they are fattened on acorns in the autumn. The hams are packed in salt and matured in cool cellars for up to two years. Identified as *jamón ibérico* to differentiate the product from mere *jamón serrano* (mountain ham from white pigs aged as little as two weeks), the Jabugo hams are graded from one to five 'j's (or *jotas*). Even Italian gourmets concede that Jabugo *cinco jotas* (top-grade) hams are superior to the best *prosciuttos.* As expected, ham pervades

Above
Jamón serrano (mountain ham)

Right
Jabugo's legendary pigs

the local cuisine as a flavouring and as a garnish, and can be tasted at every restaurant and bar.

Accommodation and food in Jabugo

Finca La Silladilla €€€ *N433 in El Repilado, direction Los Romeros; tel: (95) 950–1350; www.visionrent.com.* Four farm buildings have been tastefully converted to luxurious cottages with handcrafted furniture, Portuguese tiles and all mod cons, including jacuzzis. Swimming pool and wheelchair access.

Mesón Cinco Jotas €–€€ *Carretera San Juan del Puerto s/n; tel: (95) 912–1071; closed Mon pm.* Fancy dining room run by one of the area's major ham producers serving the local delicacy as *tapas* and in a variety of dishes.

PARQUE NATURAL SIERRA DE ARACENA Y PICOS DE AROCHE*

The mix of granite bedrock with limestone intrusions gives these low mountains a more varied landscape than any other hills in Andalucía. The Atlantic moisture and altitude create a primarily temperate climate with some subtropical species intruding at the lower altitudes. The forests, chiefly of nut trees, are home to wild boars, martens, badgers and otters as well as many vultures, eagles and hawks. Like most nature parks in Andalucía, the Sierra de Aracena has murky boundaries and distinctions between public and private property, though fences and signs announcing 'coto privado' should be respected. Proper respect could be lifesaving, as *toros bravos*, or fighting bulls, are often grazed behind some of these fences.

This park is hiker-friendly, with many km of marked trails that cross highly varied landscape between villages. These include such straightforward routes as the PRA-5-2 path northeast of Almonaster, marked 4km to the **mirador Cerro San Cristóbal***. This former Roman quarry track leads to the highest point in these mountains, taking a few hours each way. Vehicles with high undercarriage and all-wheel drive can also tackle this route.

A somewhat longer circuit leaves Aracena on the west end of town next to the A470 road and passes through a broad valley 6km to the village of **Linares de la Sierra***. At Linares, the PRA-3-8 path continues 4km across hillsides through Los Madreños to Alájar. After doubling back to Linares, the PRA-3-9 path, which begins at the stone bridge over the river, climbs across rocky hillsides for 6km back to Aracena.

Veteran hikers claim that the Sierra de Aracena offers Spain's best hiking, and it is easy to string together other similar day hikes between the villages with the maps and brochures available from the park centre and local tourist offices.

Suggested tour

Total distance: 76km, 85km with detours.

Time: 5 hours.

Links: This route connects to Huelva and environs (*see pages 148–55*) via the N435, and to Sevilla (*see pages 164–79*) via the N433 and N630.

Route: Begin at **ARACENA** ❶ (109km north of Huelva or 90km northwest of Sevilla) with tours of the castle and caves. Midway between the two, join the N433 west, signposted for Portugal, for the beginning of a drive through intensely green countryside with red limestone soil, hills covered with terraced olive groves and occasional fenced compounds where black pigs snuffle along rooting for food. Unlike most of Andalucía, the Aracena hills are a patchwork of small farms where stone walls and hedgerows mark the careful division of property.

Detour: After 10km the road passes a turn-off for **Fuenteheridos**✦. There is little of note in the village, but the road due south quickly becomes an extremely scenic, twisting drive through high hills covered with chestnut trees and deep valleys lined with farms. Several dirt roads diverge from the main paved path for bucolic exploration.

Back on the N433 and 5km further west, **Galaroza**✦ is another village favoured as a base by hikers. On the west side of town, turn right on to the N435 and follow signs 8km to **JABUGO**. Leave Jabugo on the N435 and in 11km make the sharp right turn on to the A470 to travel 7km west to **ALMONASTER LA REAL** ❷.

Detour: Just before entering town, detour 4km by vehicle or on foot to the **Mirador Cerro San Cristóbal**✦, the highest point in the area.

Return eastward on the A470 from Almonaster for 16km through a cork oak forest, passing the spire of the church at **Santa Ana La Real**✦ along the way. Typical of churches in this area, its belltower contains a fine 19th-century clock and the conical steeple is covered with black, blue and white tiles. The old cork oaks that overhang the road are as gnarled as ancient olive trees, most of them old enough to have been harvested many times. After driving through the village of **ALAJAR** ❸, make a double-back left turn to the hermitage at Peña Arias, driving 1km to the summit. From here the A470 continues 11.5km east through more cork forest to return to Aracena.

Also worth exploring

Las Minas Río Tinto, 34km south of Aracena on the A479, is a community where open-pit mines (copper, silver and iron ore) have been operated by various overseas empires – the Phoenicians, the

Romans, and from the 1870s to the 1950s, an Anglo-German consortium. The scale is mind-boggling, and one of the pits can be toured. An excellent mining museum (€ *Pl. Museo s/n; open daily 1030–1500 and 1600–1900*) deals with the geology and impressive mechanics of the mines. There are also train rides available on the 30km Ferrocarril Turístico-Minero (€€ *tel: (95) 959–0025; runs daily Jul–Sept at 1300; call for weekend hours the rest of the year*).

Ratings

Architecture ●●●●●

History ●●●●●

Museums ●●●●●

Gastronomy ●●●●○

Parks
and castles ●●●●○

Shopping
and crafts ●●●●○

Entertainment
●●●○○

Nature
and wildlife ●○○○○

Sevilla

Not just the capital, Sevilla is the regent queen of Andalucía: imperial, majestic, encrusted with monuments and teeming with life. Many visitors barely venture beyond the Alcázar and the Cathedral, centres of secular and religious power. Yet Andalucía matches its myths in Sevilla, where women model themselves on Bizet's sultry Carmen and men aspire to the grace of matadors. Power and glory are manifest in the Alcázar and the Plaza de España, implicit in the quiet halls of a Carthusian monastery and elegant gardens of Parque de María Luisa. Sevilla grew fat on the gold of the New World and stylish from the attentions of the Bourbon nobility. Yet some of its finest surprises – a beautiful church, a hidden garden or the golden notes of a *sevillana* tune – lurk in the old port district of Triana, the medieval maze of Santa Cruz and the working-class streets of Macarena.

Sights

 **Oficina de Turismo de la Junta de Andalucía** *Avda Constitución 21; tel: (95) 422–1404; www.turismosevilla.org; open Mon–Fri 0900–1900; Sat 1000–1400, 1500–1900; Sun 1000–1400.* Provides information for all of Andalucía.

Barrio de Macarena✲

Ironically, c/ San Luis, the main thoroughfare through this working-class neighbourhood, is also known as Camino Real, for it is the traditional route by which monarchs enter Sevilla. They pass through the remains of the 12th-century defensive walls at **Puerta Macarena✲**, which dates from the 16th century when defence was less a consideration than the accommodation of royal coaches. Walking down c/ San Luis gives a good sense of the private side of the city. By the old walls, the street begins at the **Basílica de la Macarena✲**, built in the 1940s to contain the elaborately carved 17th-century image of the city's best-loved Virgin: the Esperanza Macarena. The image, mounted in a silver alcove, inspires ferocious devotion and is the

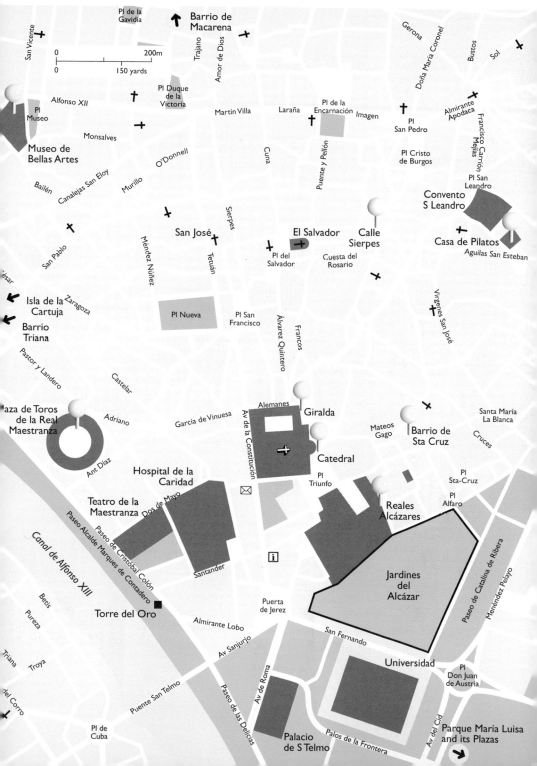

Oficino de Turismo
*Pas. de las Delicias 9;
tel: (95) 423–4465; open
Mon–Fri 0830–1830 and Pl.
Concordia s/n; tel: (95)
490–5267.*

**Basílica de la
Macarena** € *c/
Bécquer 1; open daily
0930–1300 and 1700–2000.*

Iglesia de San Luis *c/ San
Luis; open Wed–Thur
0900–1400, Fri–Sat
0900–1400 and
1700–2000.*

centrepiece of Holy Week activities in Sevilla. Several delightful Mudéjar Gothic churches line c/ San Luis east of the basilica, each sparingly cut from salmon-coloured limestone. **Iglesia de San Luis** is a radical departure, as its exterior represents the extremities of Baroque ornamentation. Although the façade is in very poor condition, the interior of the church has been restored, and a crystal mirror in the centre aisle reflects the striking frescoes of the ceiling. C/ San Luis concludes in **Plaza San Marcos**, the traditional gathering place for Sevilla's religious brotherhoods.

Museo de Murillo
c/ Santa Teresa 8; tel:
(95) 421–7535; open
Mon–Fri 1000–1300 and
1600–1900, Sat–Sun
1100–1400.

**Hospicio de los
Venerables Sacerdotes**
€ Pl. Venerables Sacerdotes;
tel: (95) 456–2696;
www.focus.abengoa.es; open
daily 1000–1400 and
1600–2000.

Barrio de Santa Cruz***

After the reconquest of Sevilla, Fernando III brought Jews to help administer the royal palace. They settled in the maze of streets that spread out from the Cathedral and Alcázar. Although the streets nearest the Cathedral are lined with restaurants and shops, the old quarter still retains the charm of its whitewashed houses with potted geraniums hanging in windows and from roof ledges along the narrow, twisting streets. Specific sites within the *barrio* include the **Museo de Murillo***, the house where the painter lived at the end of his life, and the **Hospicio de los Venerables Sacerdotes***, a rest home for aged and infirm priests that was transformed in 1991 into a cultural centre. The admission price to art exhibitions also gains limited access to the rooms of this in-city *palacio,* organised around an exceptionally fine courtyard with fountain.

Barrio Triana***

Southwest of the city centre across the Río Guadalquivir, Triana is the traditional *gitano*, or gypsy, quarter and one of the birthplaces of flamenco. As commemorative plaques throughout the neighbourhood note, Triana was also the cradle of many great bullfighters. Today Triana is principally a working-class district distinguished for its *alfareros*, makers of decorative tiles. These *alfarerías* are concentrated along c/ San Jorge and surrounding streets, where tailors producing flamenco garb are also found. The ceramics industry is more than 2000 years old, originally producing *amphorae* to transport oil and wine in Roman times. Legend holds that Christian martyrs Santa Justa and Santa Rufina were potters from Triana, and they have been adopted as patron saints of the *barrio* in general and of potters in particular. The ceramic tradition continued to flourish during the Moorish centuries, when the decorative tiles in blue, white, green and black came to be known as *azulejos*. The interiors of most buildings in Triana (indeed, many throughout Sevilla) are lined with these tiles in profusion. The painted tiles depicting scenes and religious images are an 18th-century development, and in the 20th century Triana tilemakers began producing large mosaic scenes.

Triana is a neighbourhood of great intrinsic charm, where what appears to be a fisherman's bar may also advertise that it has a private salon to celebrate baptisms, communions and reunions. The riverfront at the foot of Puente Isabel II, the so-called Puerto de Triana, has a concentration of *cervecerías* and *marisquerías* that set up tables all along the river wall during warm weather. Further east along the river, approaching Puente San Telma, the banks are covered with restaurants whose terraced gardens offer great views back across the river. Halfway between the two bridges, the small **Capilla de los Marineros*** houses the image of the Virgin known popularly as the Esperanza de Triana, a rival to the Macarena during Semana Santa festivities.

Left
The elegant Plaza de Cabildo

Casa de Pilatos
€–€€ Pl. Pilatos; tel:
(95) 422–5298; open daily
0900–1900. Free on Tue
1300–1700 with EU
passport. Admission price
doubles to add guided tour
of upper floor.

Calle Sierpes*

The pedestrianised street of Sierpes, so-named for its supposedly serpentine course, is the commercial heart of Sevilla. Many of its shops sell the more expensive souvenir items, such as the traditional *mantillas* (lace headdresses), flamenco costumes, painted fans and castanets, and it is dotted with small booths authorised to sell bullfight tickets. Somewhat marred by the presence of many beggars, Sierpes, its parallel street of Tetuán and some of the small side streets nonetheless lure many visitors.

Commercialism has triumphed over history along the route: now only plaques mark the former site of the jail where Cervantes conceived the story of Don Quixote while imprisoned for embezzling tax revenues and the former gardens of Nicolás Monardes, where the first tomatoes, potatoes, tobacco and castor bean plants from the New World were grown. But the district is not without interest, even for the souvenir-shy, as one end contains the wonderful baroque **Ayuntamiento*** on Pl. San Francisco, and the other the comprehensive department store, El Corte Inglés, on Pl. Duque de la Victoria.

Casa de Pilatos**

One of the city's finest mansions, on the edge of Barrio Santa Cruz, was commissioned by the governor of Andalucía, Don Pedro Enríquez, after his son, the Marqués de Tarifa, made a pilgrimage to Jerusalem in 1519. The Marqués recorded the route that Jesus took from Pilate's house to Golgotha, and then created a similar set of landmarks in Sevilla. These still form the main staging posts along the Way of the Cross followed by the religious brotherhoods on their penitential processions during Semana Santa (Holy Week). The family palace, naturally, takes the place of Pilate's residence.

There is nothing terribly penitential about this palace, which is a fabulous hybrid of Gothic, Renaissance and Mudéjar styles. After the Civil War the Medinaceli ducal family reclaimed this ancestral home and restored it to its original splendour. Family members still occupy some chambers of the upper level, so tours of that section are strictly guided. Visitors may wander freely on the lower level, which includes extraordinary gardens and the main patio. The archway into the patio is covered with a magenta blaze of ancient bougainvillaea for much of the year, and the patio itself contains four striking statues that are true antiquities, including a 5th-century BC Greek Athena and three Roman pieces. In their own way, the beautiful Renaissance gardens are more enjoyable than the grander plantings at the Reales Alcázares, not least because the palace's location off tiny streets keeps the bus tours away.

These narrow surrounding streets are worth a stroll as well, if only to browse around some of the city's better antique shops or stop off at the **Convento de San Leandro*** to purchase sweets from the nuns' *retorno*.

Cathedral and La Giralda ✦✦✦

Sevilla's cathedral leaves no doubt as to who triumphed in the struggle between Moors and Christians. Completed in 1507 on the site of the great Almohad mosque, the cathedral is 160m long and 140m wide; only St Peter's in Rome and St Paul's in London have more floor space.

But the builders did not quite obliterate the mosque. Visitors enter through the Patio de los Naranjos where more than 60 orange trees and an ablutions fountain remain. The 90m brick tower on the east side of the cathedral, La Giralda, was originally the minaret of the mosque. Its elegant proportions and fine detailing – including a 16th-century addition from the belltower up – stand out from the rather unwieldy bulk of the cathedral. The recently restored Giralda is one of Sevilla's most prized monuments, and the bronze weathervane representing faith, *El Giraldillo*, has become the *de facto* civic symbol. Ramps permit an easy climb to the belltower for views of the city and a bird's-eye perspective of the cathedral itself.

🛈 **Catedral and La Giralda** € *Open Mon–Sat 1100–1700, Sun 1000–1330 (Giralda) and 1430–1800 (Cathedral).*

The cathedral's five naves and innumerable chapels are a treasure trove of art and history. Sevillana girls often pray for a boyfriend before the Murillo painting of St Anthony, patron of the lovelorn, in the Capilla de San Antonio, on the north side. On the south side, Columbus and other explorers used to pray in the Capilla de la Virgen de la Antigua before embarking on their voyages. The explorer's tomb stands nearby, his supposed remains having been returned from Cuba in 1899. Carved pallbearers proclaim the importance of the year 1492: one pierces a pomegranate – the symbol of Granada, the last Moorish city to fall to the Christians – with his sword; another holds an oar to row to the New World. In fact, the gold that gleams within the cathedral came from America, and reflects Sevilla's 16th-century 'golden age' as a leading port.

The Gothic *retablo mayor* on the main altar is believed to be the largest altarpiece in the world, with more than 1000 biblical figures in carved, gilded and polychromed wood. Art lovers can spend a day wandering from chapel to chapel. The Capilla de San Pedro has nine paintings of the saint's life by Zurbarán. The Sacristía de los Cálices

Above
The cathedral

Isla Mágica €€€
*Isla de la Cartuja; tel:
(95) 446–1493; open
Apr–Sept daily 1100–2400.*

**Centro Andaluz de
Arte Contemporáneo**
*€ Isla de la Cartuja; tel: (95)
448–0611; open Tue–Sat
1000–2300, Sun
1000–1500.*

has a Goya painting of the 3rd-century *sevillana* martyrs, Santa Justa
and Santa Rufina, and a Zurbarán painting of San Juan Bautista.
Artwork in the Sacristía Mayor includes more works by Murillo and
Zurbarán, and two huge monstrances carried in the Corpus Christi
processions – a true sign of religious devotion, not to mention
strength.

Isla de la Cartuja*

The island of Cartuja, between two branches of the Río Guadalquivir,
encompasses large parts of the old city, including Triana, but 'La
Cartuja' generally refers to the northern lobe that was the site of Expo
92. Many modernistic buildings were constructed for the fair but
have failed to win the hearts of Sevillanos. A portion of the fair's
grounds is occupied by the **Isla Mágica*** amusement park, which
opened in 1997.

The most promising development in 'La Cartuja' is the **Centro
Andaluz de Arte Contemporáneo**** within the Conjunto Monumental
de la Cartuja, a 15th-century monastery that was one of many that
provided shelter to Columbus during his lifetime and held his remains
briefly in the early 16th century. When the monks were expelled in the
19th century, Englishman Charles Pickman converted the complex to a
porcelain factory that continued to operate until 1982. Now the
beautiful courtyards and Mudéjar chapels serve as galleries for changing
exhibitions of contemporary art.

Above
Bougainvillaea blazes in
the Casa Pilatos

**Museo de Bellas
Artes** € Pl. Museo 9;
tel: (95) 422–1829; open
Tue 1500–2000, Wed–Sat
0900–2000, Sun
0900–1415.

Museo de Bellas Artes✦✦✦

Housed in the former Convento de la Merced Calzada, so ancient that
it was renovated in 1602 and completely refurbished in 1992, Sevilla's
fine arts museum is second in Spain only to the Prado. The building
itself is one of the chief exhibits: the artwork is contained in 14
galleries arranged around three patios covered with extraordinary
16th- and 17th-century tiles of local manufacture. The masterpieces of
the museum are assembled in the old convent church in the middle of
the complex. Chief among them are a handful of delightful works by
Zurbarán, who could make even the flesh of saints and clerics seem
luminescent and sensual, a few Velázquez portraits, and an extensive
series of saints and Bible scenes by Sevilla's greatest master, Bartolomé
Esteban Murillo. The 19th-century rooms, with their effusive
romanticism and local subject matter, include depictions of society
ladies and of daily life in the cigar factory.

Right
The Plaza de América

Museo Arqueológico € Pl. de América; open Tue 1500–2000, Wed–Sat 0900–2000, Sun 0900–1400.

Museo de Artes y Costumbres Populares € Pl. de América; open Tue 1500–2000, Wed–Sat 0900–2000, Sun 0900–1400.

Museo Taurino € Pas. Cristóbal Colón; tel: (95) 422–4577; www.realmaestranza.com; open daily 0930–1900, days of bullfights 1000–1500. There is also a ticket office for corridas.

Parque María Luisa and its Plazas***

This extensive park system south of the cathedral owes much to noble largesse. The core gardens were donated to Sevilla in 1893 by the Duchess of Montpensier, and much of the surrounding park was the gift of Princess María Luisa de Borbón in 1914. This lush green oasis has a rich variety of trees, shrubs and flowers, but seems appropriately dominated by orange trees. The park and surrounding areas were built up as the site for the 1929 Ibero-American Exposition. Former colonies constructed stunning neo-Mudéjar buildings, many of which still serve as national consulates, and Spain went all out designing Plaza de España and Plaza de América as showcases. Alas, in 1929 the world plunged into depression and the fair was a flop. But the legacy of buildings and parkland has served Sevilla well.

Plaza de España, on the north-east side of the park, has been converted to government offices. This semicircular plaza, 200m in diameter, is an architectural extravagance that bends the Renaissance arcade, anchors it with Baroque towers and encrusts all the lower levels with *azulejo* tiles. Surrounded by a canal (rowing here is a popular family activity on Sundays) are 54 tiled enclosures depicting scenes from Spain's provinces.

The southeast flank of the park, **Plaza de América**, is filled with white pigeons and families on outings. On one side, the Renaissance-style **Museo Arqueológico** chronicles the succession of Andalucían cultures. The most stunning exhibit is the Tesoro Carambola, a collection of a Tartessian man's gold jewellery. Facing the museum is the former Palacio Mudéjar of the 1929 fair, now the **Museo de Artes y Costumbres Populares**. The museum is worth a visit just to see the old *feria* posters, flamenco costumes and *azulejos*.

Plaza de Toros de la Real Maestranza***

Sevilla's bullring is easily the world's most famous and quite possibly the most beautiful. The vast ochre and white structure near the river was completed in the last half of the 18th century for the Real Maestranza de Caballería (Royal Equestrian Society) and became Spain's leading venue for bullfighting in the early 19th century. Bizet made it world famous in his opera *Carmen*. In fact, a buxom bronze statue honouring the cigar roller stands across the street by the river. The immense ring seats 14,000 people and is generally full at every *corrida*. A box of honour for the royal family and the president of Spain sits at the top of the ring facing the gate from which the bulls are released. The 20-minute tour of the bullring and its associated museum bears a strong resemblance to official tours of old churches, with reverential viewing of faded costumes, dramatic oil paintings and the heads of bulls. One head, in fact, is of the cow 'Islera', whose offspring, 'Islero' gored Manolete to death in Linares in 1947, one of the most traumatic events of modern bullfighting. On close observation and a little reflection, the human

Opposite
The Alcázar

side of the god-like matadors emerges in the *enfermería*, where wounded matadors were treated, and the poignant chapel, where they prayed before the fights.

Reales Alcázares €
*tel: (95) 456–0040;
open in summer Tue–Sat
0930–2000; Sun
0930–1800; winter Tue–Sat
0930–1800, Sun
0930–1430.*

Several companies
including Sevirama (*tel:
(95) 456–0693*) and Seville
Tour (*tel: (95) 450–2099*)
offer **tours on open-air
buses** (€€) with stops at
major sites and reboarding
allowed for 24 hours.
Board at Torre del Oro.

Cruceros Turísticos
€€–€€€ *tel: (95)
456–1692.* One-hour
sightseeing cruises on the
Río Guadalquivir depart
from the dock below the
Torre del Oro every 30
minutes daily from
1130–2215. Day-long
cruises to Sanlúcar de
Barrameda depart at 0900;
call for dates.

**Teatro de la
Maestranza** *Pas.
Cristóbal Colón 22; tel: (95)
422–6573;
www.maestranza.com* is the
city's major performance
hall.

**Flamenco
performances** geared to
tourists include **El Arenal**
(*c/ Rodo 7; tel: (95)
421–6492*), **El Patio
Sevillano** (*Pas. Cristóbal
Colón 11–A; tel: (95)
422–2068*), **Los Gallos** (*Pl.
Santa Cruz s/n; tel: (95)
421–6981*) and **Sol Café**
(*c/Sol 5; tel: (95) 422–5165*).

Reales Alcázares✦✦✦

Since the King of Spain stays here when he visits Sevilla, the
Alcázar can claim to be the oldest palace in Europe still in use. The
original fort was constructed by the Moors in the 10th century, with
palaces added as the region prospered. After 1248, the Alcázar
became the primary residence of several Spanish monarchs, including
Fernando III, who recaptured Sevilla, and of his son, Alfonso X,
who constructed the Gothic palace now called the Salones de
Carlos V.

But Alfonso's grandson, Pedro I, had the greatest impact of all,
mustering an army of architects and artisans in 1364–6 to build the
Palacio de Don Pedro. Workers who had built the Palacio Nazaríes in
Granada a few years earlier were joined by Muslim and Jewish artisans
from Toledo and Sevilla to create one of the defining works of the
Mudéjar style, synthesising 400 years of Iberian Muslim architectural
tradition.

The Alcázar can be a confusing place, with its accretion of
architecture over several centuries and lack of a clear touring path.
While wandering aimlessly in awe is not a bad thing, renting one of
the headphone tours can bring order from chaos. Visitors enter
through the Patio del León, part of the garrison of the 11th-century
Moorish palace, which leads into the larger Patio de la Montería,

Right
Ancient Roman statue in
the Casa Pilatos

central to the entire complex. The courtyard serves as an anteroom to admire the façade of the Palacio de Don Pedro directly ahead. The most spectacular of the palace's public rooms, the Ambassadors' Hall, served as Pedro I's throne room. With its triple arches along the sides and elaborate interlaced dome with stalactite plaster carvings it was clearly made to impress.

The centre of the private quarters, the small Patio de las Muñecas, is adorned with filigree carving comparable to the Palacio Nazaries in Granada. The shell motif used throughout is an Arabic symbol for water, signifying wealth in a dry country. Most of the rooms of the private quarter remain reserved for the royal family.

On one side of the Patio de la Montería are two 15th-century palace additions: the Salón del Almirante, hung with Goya tapestries, and the Sala de Audiencias, which displays a model of Columbus' flagship, the *Santa María,* and the famous 16th-century altarpiece *Virgen de los Navigantes.* The opposite side of the Patio de la Montería opens on to the gardens of the Patio del Crucero, much favoured by Pedro I's mistress, María de Padilla; King Pedro lived in the Salones de Carlos V on the far side of the garden. Although the rooms have been extensively remodelled, they are noted for their wall tiles and tapestries. The Salones lead into the Alcázar's extensive gardens in both Renaissance and Romantic styles.

⚫ **Bienal de Flamenco** *tel: (95) 423–4465* held in even-numbered years in Sept is one of Spain's major festivals of the art.

Accommodation and food

Las Casas de la Judería €€€ *Callejón de Dos Hermanos 7; tel: (95) 441–5150, fax: (95) 442–2170; www.casasypalacios.com*. One of Sevilla's prettiest hotels, with rooms set around three classic courtyards, once incorporated into three palaces.

Hostería del Laurel €€ *Plaza de los Venerables 5; tel: (95) 422–0295, fax: (95) 421–0450*. Attractive 21-room hotel on small tree-lined square in the heart of Santa Cruz. Rooms are spotless and simply furnished.

Hotel Alfonso XIII €€€ *San Fernando 2; tel: (95) 491–7000; fax: (95) 491–7099; www.westin.com/hotelalfonso*. Neo-Mudéjar hotel built in 1928 to be the most luxurious in Europe. Countless tourists have a drink in the bar and fantasize about the guest rooms.

Hotel Doña María €€ *c/ Don Remondo 19: tel: (95) 422–4990; fax: (95) 421–9546*. Literally around the corner from the cathedral, yet quiet; unbeatable rooftop view of the cathedral and Giralda.

Hotel Los Seises €€–€€€ *c/ Segovias 6; tel: (95) 422–9495; fax: (95) 422–4332; www.hotellosseises.com*. The 43 rooms of this 16th-century archbishop's palace in Santa Cruz display many artistic flourishes.

Hotel Taberna del Alabardero €€–€€€ *c/ Zaragoza 20; tel: (95) 450–2721; www.tabernadelalabardero.com*. A mansion occupied by a noble family until 1990 has been converted to 10 unique bedrooms conveniently located for major sites. Great *tapas* bar (€) and restaurant (€€–€€€).

Egaña Oriza €€€ *c/ San Fernando 41; tel: (95) 422–7211*. Classic Spanish cuisine gets creative, elegant interpretation in a chic dining room. The attached bar offers great *tapas*.

Mesón Don Raimundo €€€ *c/ Argote de Molina 26; tel: (95) 422–3355*. This restaurant in a 14th-century Santa Cruz monastery emphasises Andalucían main dishes and Mozarabic desserts.

El Rinconcillo €–€€ *Pl. Terceros; tel: (95) 422–3183*. Sevilla's oldest tavern was established in 1670.

Río Grande €–€€ *c/ Betis 70; tel: (95) 427–8371*. One of the best restaurants on the Triana banks of the Río Guadalquivir.

Below
Torre del Oro

Casual outdoor dining is at its best in Barrio Santa Cruz in Pl. Catalina Ribera and the adjacent streets where c/ Santa María La Blanca meets Avda Menéndez Pelayo.

Horno San Buenaventura *Avda Constitución 16; tel: (95) 422–1819.* This bakery-deli is a good spot for sandwiches, pastries or a takeaway.

El Torno Pastelería de Conventos de Clausura *Pl. Cabildo s/n; no tel.* One-stop shopping for pastries.

Shopping

Allegro *c/ Dos de Mayo 38* has a wide selection of Spanish classical, popular and flamenco music on cassette and CD.

Cerámica Santa Ana *c/ San Jorge 31* is one of the largest of Triana's ceramics factories and will ship purchases.

Molino de Santa Cruz *c/ Cruces 7.* The place to pick up your extra-virgin olive oil, with a large selection available.

Le Portier Didier *c/ Ximénez de Enciso tel: (95) 421–4532.* Small shop in Santa Cruz selling fans, silk scarves and shawls, all handpainted.

Sol Sevilla *c/ García de Vinuesa 18.* The largest selection of flamenco, bullfighting and Sevilla posters, as well as a good choice of shawls, ceramics and T-shirts.

The **Thursday flea market** on c/ Feria dates from the 14th century. **Sun flea market** at Pl. Cabildo (coins and stamps), and pet market at Pl. Alfalfa.

Suggested tour

Total distance: About 5km.

Time: 2 days.

Day 1 Route: Begin at the **REALES ALCAZARES ❶**, then cross Pl. del Triunfo to the **CATHEDRAL ❷**. Between the two, fronting on Avda Constitución, is the **Archivo de Indias**, the library and repository of maps, documents and objects related to the Spanish colonisation of the Americas (currently closed for renovation). Proceed through Pl. del Triunfo up narrow c/ Romero Murube into **BARRIO DE SANTA CRUZ ❸**, using the tourist office map to navigate the maze of streets. Streets leading upwards and slightly to the right emerge at the **Jardines de Murillo***, a beautiful stretch of gardens marking the east side of the *barrio.* Turn right and stroll through the gardens to c/ San Fernando, noting on its far side the **Antigua Fábrica de Tabacos***, now part of the

⬢ Archivo de Indias
Pl. Triunfo; tel: (95) 421–1234. Closed for renovation at time of research. Contact tourist office for an update.

Torre del Oro € *On riverbank north of Puente San Telmo; tel: (95) 422–2419; open Tue–Fri 1000–1400, Sat–Sun 1100–1400.*

Hospital de la Caridad € *c/ Temprado s/n; tel: (95) 422–3232; open Mon–Sat 0900–1300 and 1530–1830; Sun 0900–1300.*

Itálica € *Santiponce; tel: (95) 599–6583; open in summer Tue–Sat 0900–2000; Sun 1000–1600 and winter Tue–Sat 0900–1700; Sun 1000–1600, closed holidays. Free with EU passport.*

university, where the fictional Carmen and her co-workers used to roll cigars on their thighs.

Continue one block along Avda del Cid to the traffic roundabout, Glorieta San Diego, and cross diagonally to the amazing stone-and-tile Plaza de España. This grand semicircle faces **PARQUE MARIA LUISA ❹**, a superb area for strolling through a succession of formal gardens in a southeasterly direction to reach **PLAZA DE AMERICA ❺**. From the plaza, exit on to Paseo de las Delicias and turn right, walking 1.3km past the park to turn right on to Avda Roma, which ends at the Puerta de Jerez on the back side of the Alcázar.

Day 2 Route: Begin below Puerta de Jerez at the Río Guadalquivir, a lively scene of boats and kayaks. **Torre del Oro✦**, a defensive tower built by the Moors in 1220, houses a small naval museum. Continue along Paseo Cristóbal Colón to the **PLAZA DE TOROS ❻**. Stroll through the streets of Arenal behind the bullring to the **Hospital de la Caridad✦✦**, built by Manuel de Mañara, reputedly a model for the fictional Don Juan, when he repented of his sins. The tiles on the façade depict San Jorge and Santiago, slayers of dragons and Moors respectively. Just a few hundred metres past the bullring, Puente Isabel II crosses the river into **BARRIO TRIANA ❼**.

Detour: Turn right and walk 2km to the contemporary art museum in the 15th-century La Cartuja monastery on **ISLA DE LA CARTUJA ❽**.

From Puente Isabel II, continue straight to c/ San Jacinto, Triana's main street, where every establishment, even the local police precinct, seems to be covered in tiles. Turn down c/ Alfarería, circling back to Pl. Callao to the district's leading ceramics factories. Cross the entrance to the bridge and veer left to pick up the riverside c/ Betis that leads to Pl. de Cuba. From here it is an inexpensive taxi ride to **CASA DE PILATOS ❾** at the northern edge of the **BARRIO DE SANTA CRUZ**. The surrounding streets are a delightful maze. Find your way three blocks to Pl. San Pedro.

Detour: San Pedro is the south end of **BARRIO DE MACARENA ❿** (*see page 164*). The Basilica lies 1.3km further north.

From Pl. San Pedro, proceed five blocks downhill to **CALLE SIERPES ⓫**, turning left to eventually wind up at the Ayuntamiento in Pl. San Francisco.

Also worth exploring

Itálica, just a few kilometres north of Sevilla off the N630, was founded in 206 BC as the first major Roman settlement outside Italy. Within 400 years it became a splendid city, the birthplace of Trajan and Hadrian. Much of Itálica still lies beneath the suburb of Santiponce, but a portion has been excavated, notably the amphitheatre, baths and some housing.

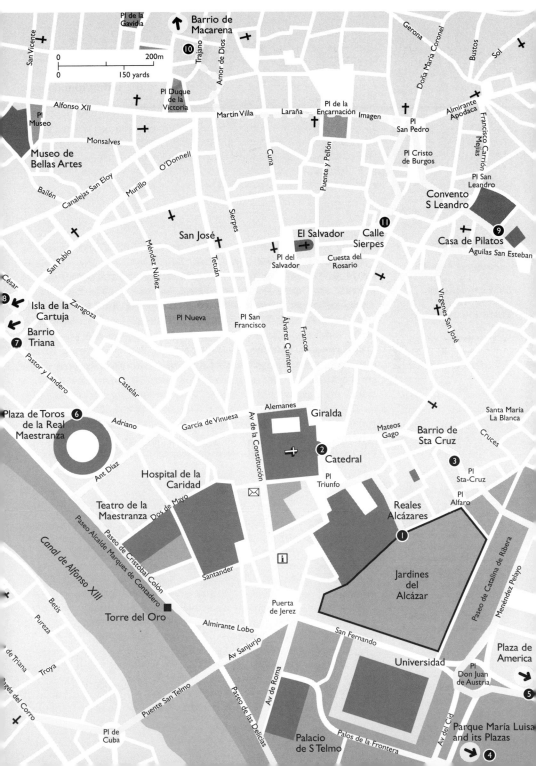

Ratings

Architecture ● ● ● ○ ○

History ● ● ● ○ ○

Museums ● ● ● ○ ○

Gastronomy ● ● ○ ○ ○

Scenery ● ● ○ ○ ○

Entertainment ● ○ ○ ○ ○

Nature and wildlife ● ○ ○ ○ ○

Shopping and crafts ● ○ ○ ○ ○

East of Sevilla

The achingly lonely and rolling fields of the *campiña* stretch to the horizon. Scorched in the intense Andalucían sun, they have produced prodigious quantities of olives and cereal crops since Roman days. Extensive archaeological excavations of Palaeolithic and Copper Age sites have revealed that human settlement is very old in this area. Wherever there is a rocky outcrop above the plain, one civilisation or another built a fortress that later grew into a city. With the exception of Carmona, the most Roman town in Andalucía, the communities remain monuments to a ducal elite who held the land and power close to their vests as the lords of Andalucía, rivals to Madrid. Churches and palaces in smaller towns are reaching the crossroads of decay where they will either be restored or fall to ruin, but the countryside retains the strange beauty of distant horizons.

CARMONA✦✦✦

ℹ️ Oficina de Turismo Arco de la Puerta de Sevilla s/n; tel: (95) 419–0955; www.turismo. carmona.org; open Mon–Sat 1000–1800, Sun 1000–1500.

📞 Azimut Turismo €€ tel: (95) 419–1721 offers 2-hr walking tours of the Roman, Moorish or Christian heritage of the city. The tourist office can make arrangements.

Commanding the fertile Guadalquivir valley, Carmona was founded by Carthaginians in the 3rd century BC and rose to prominence under the Romans, who named it *Carmo* when they took the town in AD 206. Five centuries later, the Moors preserved the name (in Arabic, 'Karmuna') and many traces of the Roman era. The **Necrópolis Romana✦✦✦**, on the west end of the city, is one of the most extensive Roman burial sites outside Italy. More than 250 tombs have been preserved and a well-marked walking path identifies different forms of burial. The ruins of a Roman amphitheatre stand nearby.

The old city is still contained within 4km of walls. Most visitors enter through the **Puerta de Sevilla✦**, also of Roman origin, although the tell-tale horseshoe arches demonstrate Moorish modifications. The gate forms part of the town's lower defensive wall. The Carthaginian fortification could not halt the Roman assault, but Romans and Moors

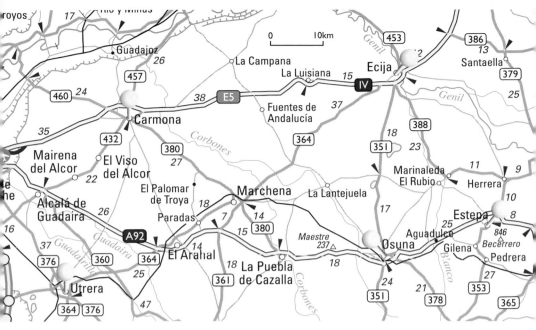

Necrópolis Romana € Avda Jorge Bonsor 9; tel: (95) 414–0811; open Tue–Fri 1000–1400; Sat–Sun 1600–1800; free with EU passport.

Alcázar de la Puerta de Sevilla € tel: (95) 419–0955; open Mon–Sat 1000–1800, Sun 0930–1500.

Prioral de Santa María c/ San José s/n; open Mon–Fri 1000–1400 and 1700–1900.

Museo de La Ciudad € c/ San Jose s/n; open in summer daily, 1000–1400 and 1830–2130; winter hours 1100–1900, closed Tue afternoons.

improved the **Alcázar de la Puerta de Sevilla** to make it one of the most complex defensive enclosures in Spain. An on-site map points out the exterior Roman moat, an interior patio to trap attackers and a gallery from which boiling liquids could be poured on enemies. Because they used different materials, Carthaginian, Roman and Moorish contributions remain distinct – the blending of eras and styles evident throughout the old city.

Carmona is small and easily explored by walking uphill from the Puerta de Sevilla. The town's main square, **Plaza San Fernando****, was laid out by the Romans and is surrounded by an attractive array of buildings, including the Renaissance **Casa del Cabildo*** and several cafés and restaurants. Off the plaza lies the 15th-century former **Convento de Santa Catalina***, its beautiful porticoed patio now serving as a central market.

Two blocks from the plaza, the **Prioral de Santa María*** is Carmona's main church. The blocky Gothic building replaced a mosque in the 15th century, but traces remain in the Patio de los Naranjos and the Mudéjar tower, which contains elements of the mosque's minaret. The nearby Casa Marqués de las Torres has a fanciful façade and is a good example of the noble mansions that share the streets alongside more modest whitewashed buildings. With its quiet courtyard and impressive stone staircase, the mansion houses the **Museo de La Ciudad****, where earnest displays chronicle the area from Palaeolithic to medieval times. The museum also explores aspects of modern and contemporary Carmona – even identifying more than 20 different forms of local bread.

Further uphill is the **Alcázar de Arriba***, constructed by the Moors and reworked by Pedro I, known as Pedro the Cruel. The craftsmen who created the Mudéjar splendour of Sevilla's Alcázar (*see page 174*) also contributed to Pedro's palace, but their work perished in the earthquakes of 1504 and 1755. All that remains are the impressive entrance gate and three towers, now marking the ceremonial entrance to the Parador de Carmona, built to evoke a Moorish palace. To the north of the parador, the **Puerta de Córdoba*** is undergoing long-overdue renovations. It serves both as a 'back door' to the highway and as access to valley hiking trails.

Accommodation and food in Carmona

Alcázar de la Reina €€ *Pl. Lasso 2; tel: (95) 419–6200; fax: (95) 414–0113; www.alcazardelareina.com*. This stylish hotel is the newest entry in Carmona's upscale lodging choices.

Casa de Carmona €€–€€€ *Pl. Lasso 1; tel: (95) 414–3300; fax: (95) 414–2889; www.casadecarmona.com*. Aristocratic palace with the highest standards of luxury and service. The elegant dining room offers menus at bargain prices (€–€€).

Parador de Carmona €€–€€€ *Alcázar s/n; tel: (95) 414–1010; fax: (95) 414–1712; www.parador.es*. Built in the Mudéjar style within the walls of an Arabic fortress, this may be the most beautiful *parador* in Andalucía.

Pensión Comercio € *Torre del Oro 56; tel: (95) 414–0018*. Modest lodging right inside the old city walls with a tranquil courtyard and good-value (€) restaurant. Cash only.

ECIJA**

Half-way between Sevilla and Córdoba, Ecija is perversely proud of its nickname as *la sartenilla de Andalucía,* or 'frying-pan of Andalucía', a title justified by a historic high temperature of 52 °C. Residents compensate for the extreme heat by closing many establishments at noon and rarely reopening until 1730 or 1800, if at all. Ecija thrived during the first two centuries AD as a producer of olive oil for the Roman empire, then languished under the Córdoban caliphate. Fernando II settled 200 families of Castilian nobility here promptly after taking the town in 1240, but it did not return to prosperity until the 17th and 18th centuries, when the olive groves were combined into vast estates. The families who benefited from this 'land reform' grew wealthy, building grand mansions and endowing the town with churches and convents. The city today has a faded baroque look, as much of it was rebuilt at great expense following the 1755 earthquake.

During Franco's era, tensions between haves and have-nots led to the establishment of a major army barracks in the beautiful Palacio de

Dulces (sweets) are available from *retornos* at the Carmelite Convento de las Teresas *c/ del Conde s/n* and the Franciscan Convento de las Marroquíes *c/ Secretario Armesto 2* as well as in the shop Yemas El Ecijano *c/ Cintería 2*.

Benamelí. While the army retains a strong presence in Ecija, the palace now contains the city's excellent **Museo Histórico✦✦✦**. The reception room, which doubles as the tourist office, opens onto the fine art gallery. The rooms off the two Renaissance courtyards are arranged according to historical periods. The Roman and 'proto-historic' rooms have the finest exhibitions, including a 2nd-century AD Roman mosaic of Dirce being dragged by a bull (formerly in the town hall) and some extraordinary gold jewellery dating from approximately 2000–1000 BC.

Ecija's heart, the Pl. de España, was recently torn up for repairs and stands, alas, walled off with concrete blocks, somewhat spoiling the centre of town. The **Iglesia de Santa María✦** off the plaza behind the *ayuntamiento* has an extraordinary altarpiece in the side chapel of La Virgen del Rosario as well as several side altars with sculptures in the style of (but not by) Pedro Roldán. The **Iglesia de Santiago✦**, a few blocks south off c/ Calla, has a tortured Roldán crucifixion as well as a tearful Virgen de los Dolores.

While the Palacio de Benamelí offers the best chance to appreciate Ecija's Baroque noble homes, two worth viewing from the outside are the painted, curved façade of **Palacio de Peñaflor✦**, which runs along c/ Castellar, and the 16th-century **Palacio de Valdehermoso✦**, with its salvaged Roman pillars and Plateresque façade. Peñaflor has been restored as a project to train young artisans in historic restoration. Contact the tourist office if you are interested in a tour.

Accommodation and food in Ecija

Hotel Ciudad del Sol € *c/ Miguel Cervantes 48; tel: (95) 483–0300; fax: (95) 483–5879; www.hotelpirula.com.* Modest lodgings near town centre.

La Reja *c/ Garcilópez 1; tel: (95) 483–3012* off Pl. España is one of many colourful bars offering sherry from the barrel and the local baked codfish cakes. *Closed Sun.*

Restaurante Casa Herrera €–€€ *Pl. España 27; tel: (95) 483–0008.* Even the olive-oil aristocracy couldn't have asked for more in this excellent eatery serving traditional *campiña* dishes.

ESTEPA✦

Once the Roman capital of the wheat and olive plains, Estepa was briefly an important frontier between Christians and Moors and enjoyed a short-lived surge of wealth in the 18th century. It retains some extraordinary Baroque-era churches, all located directly uphill from the Pl. del Carmen. Follow signs to the *ayuntamiento* and walk up the narrow passage across the plaza. Post 18th-century Estepa was nearly destroyed in recent floods and is still under reconstruction.

ⓘ Oficino de Turismo
*Plaza del Carmen; tel:
(95) 591–2771.* The
ayuntamiento can also
provide maps of the town,
and the Casa de la Cultura
*c/ Saladillo 12; tel: (95)
591–2717* offers a local
booklet highlighting the
sights.

Above
Estepa's baroque
Iglesia del Carmen

Accommodation and food in Estepa

Rooms are scarce, as the once-bustling thoroughfare of Avda de
Andalucía has been renewed and many older buildings have been
demolished. The **Hostal El Balcón de Andalucía €** *Avda Andalucía 23;
tel: (95) 591–2680* provides simple but clean rooms with good views
over the agricultural valley. The **Casino Cultural de Estepa** *c/ Mesones
36; tel: (95) 591–2961* is a good place to try *salmorejo,* a thick, cold
tomato soup that is a local speciality.

Osuna✤

ⓘ Oficina de Turismo
*Ayuntamiento, Pl.
Mayor; tel: (95) 481–2211.*

ⓒ Hotel Villa Ducal
*€–€€ A334 km88;
tel: (95) 582–0272; fax:
(95) 582–0180* along the
Sevilla–Málaga highway has
clean, quiet rooms.

Right
Osuna

In the 16th and 17th centuries, the Dukes of Osuna maintained an iron grip on the olive oil lands of the plains east of Sevilla, and nearly four centuries later Osuna still feels the effect of their domination. Many **Baroque mansions✤** line the narrow streets off c/ Carrera, where *tapas* **bars** and **cafeterías** offer the best casual dining. But the main attraction of the town is the massive Renaissance **Colegiata de Santa María de la Asunción✤✤** (*€ Pl. Colegiata s/n; tel: 95 481–0444; open Tue–Sun 1000–1330 and 1530–1830*), which stands high above the town in the spot usually occupied by a ruined Moorish fortress. The *Crucifixión* painting by José de Ribera is its true treasure. The guided tour concludes in the adjacent pantheon which holds the subterranean tombs of the Dukes of Osuna.

Utrera✤

ⓘ Oficina de Turismo
*c/ Rodrigo Caro 3; tel:
(95) 586–0931 fax: (95)
586–2056; www.utrera.org*

Utrera is famed for its green olives and the aroma of rich, green oil permeates the air. Often shunned for its industrial outskirts, the centre of the city has a well-heeled grace enhanced by lavish tilework in every doorway and dozens of bronze statues throughout the city honouring famous flamenco singers, including native son Enrique Montoya. The ruined Moorish fortress in the middle of town is the centrepiece of a beautiful park complex. Each year, during the last weekend in June, **Potaje Gitano** (*tel: (95) 586–0931*), the flamenco-singing festival, is held in these grounds.

Accommodation and food in Utrera

Hostal Las Delicias *€ c/ Abate Marchena 2; tel: (95) 486–1012*. Simple clean accommodation with a small restaurant in the centre of town.

Hotel R. Don Clemente *€ Vía Marciala 24; tel: (95) 586–2504*. Modest hotel convenient for the main road, yet within walking distance of the town centre.

Suggested tour

Iglesia San Juan Bautista c/ San Juan s/n, Marchena; no tel; open only after 2000 daily mass. (Mass is held in the evenings here because of the heat.)

Total distance: 163km.

Time: 6–8 hours.

Links: This tour connects to Sevilla (*see pages 164–79*) from Carmona, and to Córdoba (*see pages 188–201*) from Ecija.

Route: Leave **CARMONA ❶** (30km east of Sevilla on the N-IV) by the Puerta de Córdoba.

Follow the road through the gate 2km to the N-IV *autovía*, which leads 53km east through fields that alternate between grains and sunflowers to **ECIJA ❷**. South of town is the Estepa road, which begins as the bumpy A388 for 24km before switching to the narrower but smoother SE735 for the 14km drive through olive groves to **ESTEPA ❸**, the tiny city on a big hill.

At Estepa, drive west for 24km to **OSUNA ❹**, then another 19km west to the exit for the A380 northwest to **Marchena✶**, where the museum of the **Iglesia de San Juan Bautista✶** holds nine exquisite Zurbarán paintings. The A380 continues for 27km to return to Carmona.

Also worth exploring

El Cortijo de Arenales *Morón de la Frontera, tel: (95) 595–7048.* Count de la Maza's bull-breeding farm can be visited by appointment to see the traditional day-to-day activities of a functioning *ganadería*.

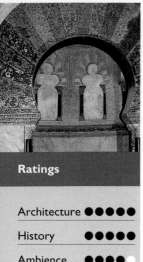

Córdoba

Ratings

Architecture ●●●●●

History ●●●●●

Ambience ●●●●○

Museums ●●●●○

Shopping
and crafts ●●●●○

Gastronomy ●●●○○

Parks
and gardens ●●○○○

Entertainment
●●○○○

Córdoba reached its apogee in the 10th and 11th centuries as the fabled capital of western Islam, a cosmopolitan centre of art, science and scholarship that ranked among the great cities of the world. Nearly a millennium later, the bare bones of that eminence remain in the largest mosque and most intact medieval Arabic city layout in Europe. Curiously, Córdoba's lure is less about monuments than about the texture of a community that took form 1000 years ago. Today the padding of trainers on the cobblestones echoes the long-ago shuffle of sandals as the inhabitants scurried through the streets on their way to market and to prayer. Almost every town in Andalucía has a *casco antiguo*, but none so extensive as Córdoba's warren, where getting lost is the surest way to find the beating heart of an ancient world.

Getting there and getting around

ⓘ Oficina de Turismo
c/ Torrijos 10; tel: (95) 747–1235; fax: (95) 749–1778; e-mail: otcordoba@andalucia.com; www.andalucia.org; open Mon–Fri 0930–1900; Sat 1000–1900; Sun 1000–1400.

Arriving and departing
The N-IV/E-5 autovía links Córdoba to Sevilla on the west and La Mancha to the northeast. The high-speed Madrid–Sevilla AVE train serves Córdoba's main railway station on Avda de América on the north side of town, about a 20-min walk from the old city.

Parking
Limited on-street parking is available outside the walls of the old city, including along Parque de la Victoria or in the parking lot of El Corte Inglés on Avda Ronda Tejares. Most hotels have parking.

Getting around
Guided walking tours of the Judería (€€€) led by Visión Córdoba depart from the Triunfo de San Rafael next to La Mezquita. The same

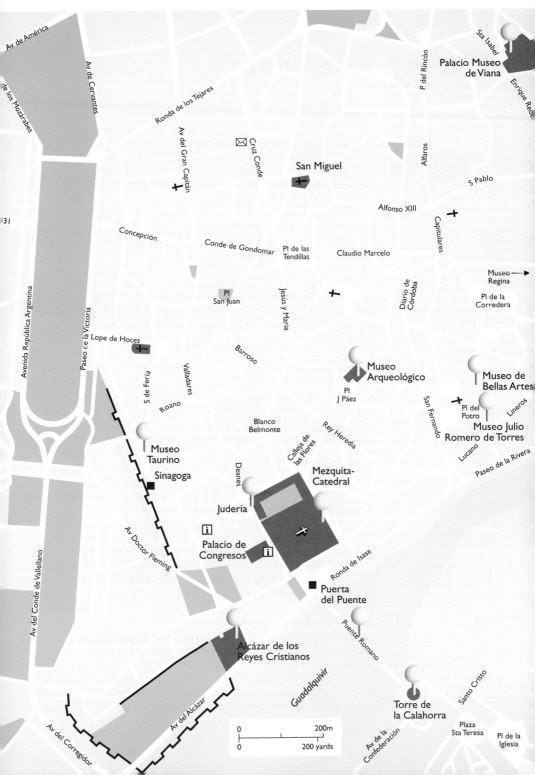

Av de América

Av de Cervantes

de los Mozárabes

Avenida República Argentina

Paseo de la Victoria

Ronda de los Tejares

Av del Gran Capitán

Cruz Conde

San Miguel

P del Rincón

Palacio Museo
de Viana

Sta Isabel

Enrique Redel

Alfaros

S Pablo

Alfonso XIII

Capitulares

Concepción

Conde de Gondomar

Pl de las
Tendillas

Claudio Marcelo

Diario de
Córdoba

Museo →
Regina

Pl de la
Corredera

Pl
San Juan

Jesús y María

Pl
J Páez

Museo
Arqueológico

Museo de
Bellas Artes

Lineros

Pl del
Potro

Museo Julio
Romero de Torres

Lucano

31

Lope de Hoces

Barroso

Valladares

Roano

S de Feria

San Fernando

Paseo de la Rivera

Museo
Taurino

Sinagoga

Blanco
Belmonte

Calleja de
las Flores

Rey Heredia

Deanes

Mezquita-
Catedral

Av del Conde de Vallellano

Av Doctor Fleming

Judería

Palacio de
Congresos

Ronda de Isasa

Puerta
del Puente

Puente Romano

Alcázar de los
Reyes Cristianos

Guadalquivir

Torre de
la Calahorra

Santo Cristo

Plaza
Sta Teresa

Pl de la
Iglesia

Av del Conde de Vallellano

Av del Alcázar

Av del Corregidor

Av de la
Confederación

0   200m

0   200 yards

Alcázar de los Reyes Cristianos €
Campo Santo de los Mártires; open Tue–Sat 1000–1400 and 1830–2030, Sun 0930–1430.

Sinagoga € *c/ Judíos s/n; open Tue–Sat 1000–1330 and 1530–1730, Sun 1000–1330.*

The Judería is full of shops, including the **Zoco** at c/ Judios s/n, almost opposite the Sinagoga, which has small studios for local artisans, specialising in silver jewellery.

company also provides transport and guided tours of Medina Azahara (€€€). *Tel: (957) 23–1734.*

Sights

Alcázar de los Reyes Cristianos♦♦

When Alfonso X took Córdoba in 1236, he rebuilt the Moorish fortifications on the banks of the Río Guadalquivir west of the mosque as his own palace-fortress. Fernando and Isabela held the last Moorish king, Boabdil, prisoner here and received Columbus prior to his first exploratory voyage. The Inquisition occupied the Alcázar from 1490 to 1821 and it served as a prison into the Franco years. The building has long been under renovation, and aerial views of the city and river from the ramparts are now out of bounds. It's worth a quick walk-through to see the Roman mosaics mounted in the throne room and to examine the Moorish baths. Serene Moorish-style gardens spread out below the fortress in broad terraces of bedded flowers and bitter oranges, punctuated by long, rectangular ponds. Statues at the centre commemorate Columbus's historic audience with Fernando and Isabela.

Judería (Old Quarter)♦♦♦

Little altered since the 13th century, Córdoba's 13km² old city tells a beguiling tale. The occasional moped may speed around the corner and a few residents and many taxi drivers thread their cars through the throngs walking the narrow passageways, but once the engine noise dies, the streets revert to the Middle Ages. The ancient walls have been whitewashed so often that every corner has become a curve. The only sharp lines visible are on wrought-iron grates dividing private courtyards from the street. Although usually called the Judería, or Jewish quarter, the district housed Jews, Christians and Muslims in roughly equal numbers a millennium ago.

Most visitors approach the old quarter via La Mezquita, but the street maze makes more sense by entering at the northeast corner through the **Puerta de Almodóvar♦** and turning right on c/ Judíos, which leads to the only medieval synagogue left in Andalucía. The barren and tiny **Sinagoga♦** is at its best filled with tourists, whose boisterous tones are suddenly silenced by reverence when they enter. A nearby statue pays homage to the great Jewish philosopher **Moisés Maimónides♦**, born here in 1135.

The Judería's charms can be overwhelmed by the bustle of crowds on the south side near La Mezquita, but even a few streets north of the mosque it reverts to a wayfarer's delight. Doorways stand open to reveal elaborately tiled entries, small markets are marked with barrels of olives and mounds of pistachios. **Calleja de las Flores♦** to the northeast of the mosque is celebrated as a picturesque alley of whitewashed walls covered with hanging baskets of flowers, but in truth the same can be said of most residential streets in the district. Flower fever reaches its peak in May during the *Concurso de Patios*, Córdoba's famous Patio Festival (*see box on page 200*).

Below
The Alcázar

La Mezquita✦✦✦

Córdoba's mosque demonstrates the inescapable stamp of Moorish culture on the city, even after seven centuries of Christian rule. Impressive from the exterior only for its size – 129m by 179m – inside it retains the ascetic spirituality of a desert people. A forest of red and white arches reaches into the distance like billowing tents at a great oasis, evoking the gathering of the people in worship of their god. The mosque could hold 40,000 worshippers facing Mecca. It requires some imagination to see the arcades flooded with light from open portals, as the arched doors have been sealed for centuries, producing a cadaverous gloom characteristic of Christian cathedrals. Improved modern lighting, particularly in the area of the glorious *mihrab* (prayer niche), helps compensate.

Museo Arqueológico € Pl. Jerónimo Páez 7; open Tue 1500–2000, Wed–Sat 0900–2000, Sun 0900–1500.

Construction of the mosque began during the reign of Abd al-Rahman (756–88) on the site of a Visigothic church that had been built, in turn, over a Roman temple. The builders used the stone, columns and even capitals from preceding structures, topping them with supporting pilasters for the arches of white stone and red brick. The initial construction phase includes the core of 11 naves. Subsequent additions in the 9th–11th centuries roughly doubled the size of the mosque, making it the second largest of its time in the Islamic world and the grandest of western Islam.

Wracked with political dissent and isolated from Damascus, Córdoba returned to Christian control in 1236. But even the early Christian kings, so hostile to Islam, were respectful in their conversion of La Mezquita. A small chapel built by Mudéjar craftsmen in a complementary style – **Capilla de Villaviciosa*** – was added in 1371. The chief architectural desecration occurred in 1523 when Carlos V permitted the church to construct the **Capilla Real*** and the **Catedral**** in full-blown, gaudy Spanish baroque style in the middle of one of the most beautiful and simple buildings on earth. Even the king was appalled when he saw the results and chided the archbishop for ruining a unique work of art. Still, it is worth having a look at the cathedral's 18th-century carved mahogany choir stalls.

The Mezquita is inevitably crowded with visitors, yet the **Patio de los Naranjos**** on the north side always remains a retreat from the hubbub. Originally the area of ritual ablutions before prayer, the patio's fountains are now purely decorative. Yet the sound of water, the shade of orange trees and the rhythmic and repetitive patterning of the gardens still work their magic of bringing the swirl of the world to a contemplative halt.

Museo Arqueológico**

Córdoba has a long past to excavate. It seems as if every time the city tries to create underground parking, Roman ruins are revealed and the car park is put on hold. The museum's collections, set in a delightful Renaissance mansion with Moorish echoes, are predictably weak in pre-Roman finds and overloaded with weathered Roman statuary and all manner of stone and ceramic items from the Moorish days. Roman mosaics cover many walls. Because so many samples of Roman and Moorish architectural details remain in Córdoba, the museum is able to illustrate the evolution of styles over the centuries when the city was Roman, then Moorish. Even a few Visigothic items creep in to reflect the brief interregnum between the collapse of Rome and the arrival of the Moors. Pedantic labelling is something of an irritation, but because so many items either recall everyday life in Córdoba (like the ceramic well cylinders still used as pots for patio trees) or are images of animals, kings and gods, they have a natural appeal that extends beyond their scholarly significance.

Museo de Bellas Artes € Pl. Potro 1; open Tue 1500–2000, Wed–Sat 0900–2000, Sun 0900–1500. Free with EU passport.

Museo Julio Romero de Torres € Pl. Potro 2; open Tue–Sat 1000–1400 and 1630–1830; Sun 0930–1430; Fri free with EU passport.

Museo Taurino € Pl. Maimónides 5; open Tue–Sat 1000–1400 and 1630–1830; Sun 0930–1430; Tue free with EU passport.

Palacio Museo de Viana € Rejas Don Gome 2; open Mon–Fri 1000–1300 and 1600–1800; Sat 1000–1300.

Museo Regina € Pl. Luís Venegas 1; open Mon–Sat 1000–1500 and 1700–2000.

Museo de Bellas Artes*

The religious paintings hail from many inactive convents and monasteries. A handful of excellent paintings dot the modern galleries, but 'modern' is more a matter of era than style. Don't expect a Picasso, Miró or Dalí among them; Córdobans preferred romantic naturalism. The building, the former Hospital de la Caridad, outshines the work on its walls and the former chapel, with its Mudéjar ceiling, is the best work in the place.

Museo Julio Romero de Torres*

One of the better 'modern' paintings in the Museo de Bellas Artes is a moody Julio Romero de Torres depicting the aftermath of a love affair gone bad. At his best, Romero de Torres was a colourful and sensuous painter but his fixation with painting seductive nudes and semi-nudes seems sadly obsessive in the aggregate.

Museo Regina**

Spain's sole museum devoted to the history of jewellery. Watch craftsmen at work creating the delicate silver filigree pieces for which the city is famed. During construction, Roman and Moorish archaeological remains were found (nothing unusual here!) which are on view on the ground floor.

Museo Taurino***

Córdobans are passionate about bullfighting and the city has produced some of Spain's most famous matadors, including Manolete and El Cordobés. Most galleries concentrate on the careers of individual matadors, displaying costumes, posters, photographs and other memorabilia. Many mounted bulls' heads adorn the walls, but despite the 'trophies', the museum captures much of the grace and daring of the inescapably brutal spectacle. Visitors are left with the contradictory images of a capped-tooth, tow-headed, grinning El Cordobés (possibly the greatest showman of the modern era) and the sombre marble sculpture of Manolete lying in state. Even foes of bullfighting should visit for the insight into the Spanish psyche.

Palacio Museo de Viana**

The rooms of this magnificent 15th-century villa chronicle the noble lifestyle of the various marquesses of Viana, with the rooms preserved as they were when the last petty nobles lived here. But the 14 courtyards constitute a spectacular overview of Córdoban patio gardening, with each garden constructed to highlight certain plants or gardening techniques. Covered in climbing English ivy and roses, the Gate Courtyard could almost be northern European. While the Madame Courtyard is indisputably Mediterranean with a ring of cypresses shaped into a crown and walls draped with jasmine, bougainvillaea, fairy roses and espaliered mandarin orange trees.

Opposite
A Córdoban patio

Torre de la Calahorra € *Puente Romano; open May–Sept daily 1000–1400 and 1630–2030, Oct–Apr daily 1000–1800.*

Gran Teatro *Avda Gran Capitán 3; tel: (95) 748–0237; www.teatrocordoba.com* is the main performance hall for music, dance and theatre.

Tablao Cardenal *c/ Torrijos 10; tel: (95) 748–3320* and **Mesón La Bulería** *c/ Pedro López 3; tel: (95) 748–3839* present flamenco shows almost every evening from 2200.

Plaza de la Califas bullring is located at *Avda Gran Vía del Parque; tel: (95) 741–4999.*

Río Guadalquivir*

The once-mighty Guadalquivir is now a broad, marshy river as it flows through Córdoba, though it was still navigable by sea-going vessels as recently as the time of Columbus. The 16-arch **Puente Romano*** that spans it between the triumphal arch and the Torre de Calahorra was constructed during the reign of Julius Caesar, first restored in the 8th century and repaired many times since. It does not advertise its antiquity, since many modern bridges in Andalucía are constructed with the same time-honoured Roman techniques. The river's flow was much swifter during the Moorish era, and several **water wheels*** lined the banks to power mills and provide the city with water. One has been restored in picturesque fashion just below the Alcázar.

Torre de la Calahorra***

Billing itself as the 'museum of life in al-Andalus', the Torre should be every first-time visitor's initial stop in Córdoba. The 90-minute delay before moving along to the more crowded Mezquita is amply repaid with perspective on the city during its 11th-century heyday. Each set of exhibits is keyed with a narration that plays over headsets, available in several languages. The history of Córdoba is painted in rosy hues: a city where Christians, Jews and Muslims lived together in harmony and produced wonders of art and science that Europe would not see

Semana Santa
tel: (95) 747–1235
is celebrated with
processions from Palm
Sunday to Good Friday.

Concurso de Patios
tel: (95) 747–1235.
May event allows visitors
to enter many of the
city's traditional patios
and meet their owners,
who compete for prizes
in a number of categories.

Feria de Mayo
tel: (95) 747–1235.
Ten-day celebration
includes the city's most
important bullfights.

Below
The gardens of the Alcázar

again for another five centuries. Be patient with the initial room, which spotlights the Jewish philosopher Maimónides and his Muslim counterpart Averröes, before moving on to the more sectarian figures of the lawgivers and religious zealots Al-Arabi and King Alfonso X. More interesting are the rooms with models of parts of the city or typical houses, shops and workshops. They are set in the context of the modern Córdoban landscape, revealing the continuity of past and present.

The rooms ascend to the height of the tower, which gives a splendid long view of the Puente Romano and the fabled city. A poignant room that attempts to recount the scientific accomplishments of Córdoba can invoke a deep sadness at the learning that perished in sectarian warfare. By the end of the 11th century, for example, Córdoban scholars had produced a sufficient critique of Ptolemy's astronomy to predict lunar and solar eclipses and produce a stunning globe of the earth – perhaps not as accurate as one might wish for exploration, but anticipating Copernicus by 500 years. Alas, Córdoba's science was rejected by mainstream Islam as well as by most of Christianity. Some of the accomplishments – algebra, for example, and the preservation of ancient Greek mathematics – survived in isolated European Christian monasteries whose scholars had studied in Córdoba.

Accommodation and food

Campamento Municipal € *Avda Brillante 50; tel: (95) 727–8481; fax: (95) 728–2165; www.campingelbrillante.com.* Campsite on the outskirts of the city.

Hotel-Bar-Restaurante El Triunfo € *c/ Corregidor Luis de la Cerda 79; tel: (95) 747–5500; fax: (95) 748–6850; www.htriunfo.com.* This older, traditional hotel with 70 rooms is just outside the walls of the old city.

Hotel González €–€€ *c/ Manríquez 3; tel: (95) 747–9819; fax: (95) 748–6187; e-mail: hotelgonzalez@wanadoo.es.* Sixteen rooms have been carved out of a restored 16th-century palace within the old city walls.

Hotel & Hostel Maestro €–€€ *c/ Cardenal Herrero 6; tel: (95) 747–2410; fax: (95) 747–5395.* Side-by-side choice of hotel and hostel with little difference between the two, aside from price and size of rooms. Both have typical Córdoban patios with pots, plants and plates.

Hotel Maimónides €€€ *c/ Torrijos 4; tel: (95) 747–1500; fax: (95) 748–3803; e-mail: maimonides@arrakis.es; www.hotel-maimonides.es.* Situated across the street from La Mezquita, this hotel is comfortably luxurious.

Parador de la Arruzafa €€–€€€ *Avda Arruzafa s/n; tel: (95) 727–5900; fax: (95) 728–0409; e-mail: cordoba@parador.es; www.parador.es.* Built on the site of a summer palace of Abderraman I, the peaceful gardens and cool breezes are a respite from the city, about 3km away. The modern building and furnishings could do with some updating. The restaurant offers a copious buffet spread for lunch and dinner (€€€).

Los Patios € *c/ Cardenal Herrero 18; tel: (95) 747–8340.* Hidden shady patio opposite La Mezquita, with a good restaurant specialising in meat and fish dishes; part of the hotel of the same name.

Almudaina €€ *Jardines de los Santos Mártires 1; tel: (95) 747–4342.* Quiet and elegant restaurant just outside the city walls, with a few Arabic specialities on the menu.

El Churrasco €€ *c/ Romero 16; tel: (95) 729–0819.* Restaurant with bustling, traditional patio and attractive dining rooms, specialising in grilled meats.

Restaurante Vallina €€€ *c/ Corregidor Luis de la Cerda 83; tel: (95) 749–8750.* The building dates back an awesome 1600 years, with Roman columns to prove it. Meat dishes are the speciality, with steaks cooked on a griddle at the table.

Suggested tour

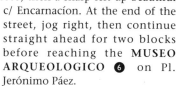

Total distance: 2.5km, 5km with detour.

Time: All day with brief stops, two days for more leisurely sightseeing.

Route: Begin at the **TORRE DE LA CALAHORRA** ❶ for a literal and figurative overview of Córdoba. Cross the **RIO GUADALQUIVIR** ❷ on the Puente Romano, stop for a look at the waterwheel and cross the street to the **ALCAZAR DE LOS REYES CRISTIANOS** ❸, lingering in the tranquillity of the gardens.

Enter the old city via the **Puerta del Puente**✳ arch and walk north up c/ Torrijos to the walled gardens behind **LA MEZQUITA** ❹, where the ticket window faces the mosque across the Patio de los Naranjos. After seeing the mosque and cathedral, proceed from the northwest corner of the complex along c/ Medina y Corella one block into Pl. Levi. Cross the plaza, turn right on to c/ Tomás Conde and continue to Pl. Maimónides, where the **Sinagoga**✳, **MUSEO TAURINO** ❺ and the old shopping bazaar of the **Zoco**✳ are all found. Behind the plaza, c/ Judíos rises to the **Puerta de Almodóvar**✳.

Turn right on to c/ Fernández and walk across Pl. Angel Torres then turn right again and head back towards the tower of La Mezquita. Turn left on to c/ Luque and enter Pl. Benavente. The picturesque **Calleja de las Flores**✳ terminates in the plaza. Take the second right (downhill) off the plaza on to c/ Bosco, then a sharp left up beautiful c/ Encarnación. At the end of the street, jog right, then continue straight ahead for two blocks before reaching the **MUSEO ARQUEOLOGICO** ❻ on Pl. Jerónimo Páez.

From the front of the museum, turn left on c/ Julio Romero de Torres and follow it downhill southeast around a dogleg to c/ San Fernando. Turn right, then left on c/ Romero Barro to enter Pl. Potro, where Córdoba's art museums are located. The plaza, which takes its name from the stone colt atop its central fountain, was at its height in the late 16th century, when Miguel de Cervantes lived on a nearby street. In *Don Quixote* he mentions the plaza and the inn, **Posada del Potro**✳, on its western side, now an art gallery.

Modern Córdoba north of the city walls has a **lively shopping and business district**✳. The one-time glamour of Pl. Tendillas has faded, but it has been replaced by newer shops on the pedestrian section of Avda del Gran Capitán.

Below
Córdoba's Patio Festival

Medina Azahara €
*Carretera Palma del Río
km 8; open May–Sept:
Tue–Sat 1000–1400 and
1800–2030, Sun
1000–1400; Oct–Apr:
Tue–Sat 1000–1400 and
1600–1800, and Sun
1000–1400. Free with EU
passport. Follow Avda
Medina Azahara out of the
city as it becomes A431. In
4km turn right and continue
3km to the site.*

Detour: Taxis usually wait at the bottom of the square. Save an uninteresting 1.5km walk and hire one to visit the **PALACIO MUSEO DE VIANA** ❼.

Also worth exploring

The palatial city of Medina Azahara**, about 7km northwest, was built during Córdoba's golden age, but enjoyed only fleeting glory. Caliph Abd al-Rahman III ordered construction to begin in 936 and spared no expense in creating a showpiece palace that was destroyed 74 years later by the Berbers and further plundered over the centuries for building materials.

Both ruins and excavations hint at the complexity of the site, with its palace buildings and reception rooms, numerous mosques, markets, baths, barracks for the royal guards, weapons factories, gardens, zoo and aviary cages, not to mention the many homes of those who kept this small city running. The fraction of the site that has been excavated is more than enough to evoke the melancholic spirit of a lost time and place.

The substantially reconstructed Salón de Abd al-Rahman III serves as a monument to the visionary caliph. It features elegant horseshoe arches and detailed marble carvings with naturalistic images, including a tree-of-life design. Accounts of palace life suggest that visitors were impressed with such theatrical flourishes as crystals creating rainbows in one room and a bowl of mercury reflecting light in another. Today the salon impresses with its mute artistry.

Córdoba's Patio Festival

The central patios so typical of Córdoban architecture always intrigue visitors. Who can resist peeping in to catch a glimpse of colour or hear the burble of a small fountain? For two weeks each May, about 40 of these domestic retreats open for evening visits in the Concurso de Patios, 'a way to really see the old Córdoba', as one young Córdoban put it. Householders virtually bury their patios in flowering plants – geraniums, or *gitanillas*, are the most popular. They hang from baskets, overflow planters and sprout from colour-co-ordinated pots along whitewashed walls. Most patios in the competition lie outside the old quarter but still within a maze of narrow streets. The tourist office map helps, but the quest invariably leads to wrong turns and a satisfying meander through residential Córdoba that reveals more of the texture of daily life than any cut-and-dried itinerary.

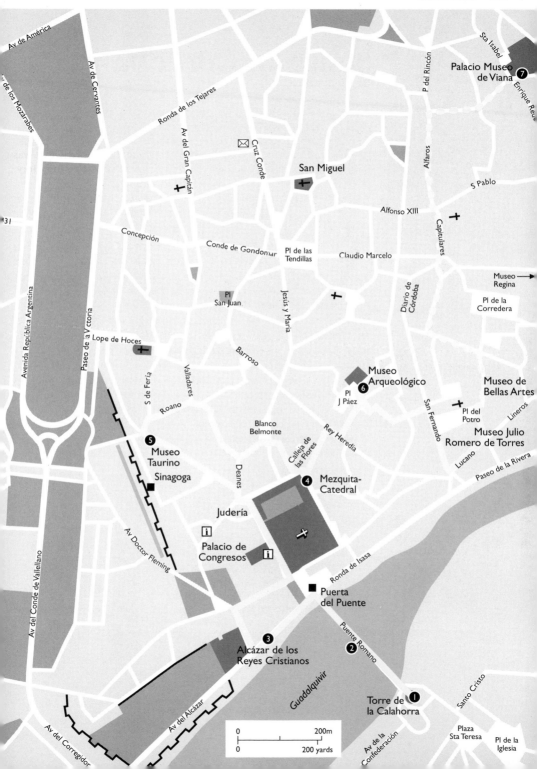

South of Córdoba

Ratings

Outdoor activities	●●●●○
Architecture	●●●○○
Gastronomy	●●●○○
Nature and wildlife	●●●○○
History	●●○○○
Shopping and crafts	●●○○○
Entertainment	●○○○○
Museums	●○○○○

The rolling hills and small river valleys southeast of Córdoba en route to Granada are sometimes identified as the 'Route of the Caliphate' because the area was the main trade path between the two Moorish capitals. Heavily contested between Christians and Moors for nearly three centuries after the fall of Córdoba, the towns were invariably fortified and fortresses and castles virtually litter the landscape. But medieval history takes a back seat here to the pleasures of the countryside, for the lowlands are lush with Pedro Ximénez vines that produce a heady sherry-like wine and the hills are covered in olives from which Spain's finest oil is pressed. Although the area offers little in the way of formal attractions, there is good hiking in the Parque Natural Sierras Subbéticas and the towns themselves make interesting diversions to break up the drive between Córdoba and Granada.

BAENA❖

ℹ Oficina de Turismo
Pl. de la Constitucion 13; tel: (95) 767–1946; fax: (95) 767–1108; open Tue–Wed 1000–1300, Thur–Fri 1700–2000, Sat–Sun 1200–1400.

🏠 Nuñez de Prado *c/ Cervantes 15; tel: (95) 767–0141. Open Mon–Fri 0900–1400 and 1600–1930.*

Since its founding by the Romans, Baena has been celebrated for its fine olive oil. The town boasts its own *denominación de origen* and a regulatory board that oversees production. The best oil, with only 0.2 per cent residual acidity, can be found in gourmet stores throughout Spain, and the less exquisite mere virgin olive oil is held in immense storage tanks at the edge of town. This green gold has made Baena reasonably prosperous. The old town high on the hill includes a **castle**❖ that began as a

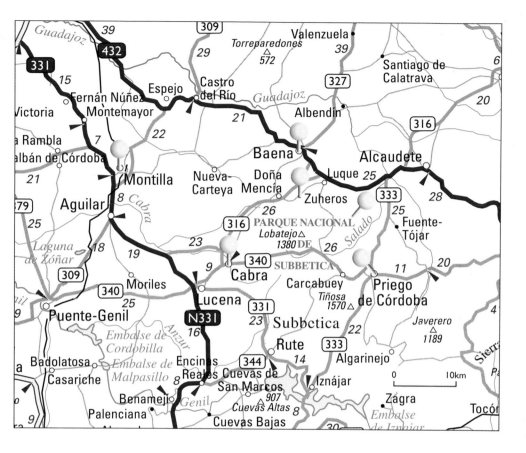

9th-century Moorish fortress and became the palace of the Dukes of Baena in the 16th century. Pl. de la Constitución is surrounded by handsome buildings, including the old arcaded **almacén**, an olive warehouse that now houses the cultural centre. During November it's worth visiting the **Nuñez de Prado◆** olive mill to watch the production of free-run oil, which requires no less than 11kg of olives to produce a single litre of oil.

Accommodation and food in Baena

Hostal Rincón € *c/ Llano del Rincón 13; tel: (95) 767–0223.* No-frills small hostal with en-suite rooms over a popular local restaurant and bar.

Mesón Casa del Monte € *Pl. de la Constitución; tel: (95) 767–1675.* Dine under a stone-vaulted ceiling at this superb restaurant dishing up traditional fare in this atmospheric central plaza.

CABRA*

ⓘ Oficina de Turismo
c/ Santa Rosalía 2;
tel: (95) 752–0110;
www.cabra.net; open Mon–Fri
1000–1300, Sat
1100–1300.

ⓘ Museo
Arqueológico
Municipal € *Casa de*
Cultura, c/ Martín Belda 25;
tel: (95) 752–0110.
www.cabra.net; open Mon–Fri
1000–1400 and
1800–2100.

◔ Danza de las
Mudanzas *tel: (95)*
752–0110. Traditional
dances celebrate the
conclusion of the olive
harvest in mid-November.

Like its namesake, the goat, Cabra perches on dry hills overlooking valleys of olive groves and wheat fields. Inhabited since Neolithic times, it assumed its current shape under the Moors, who left behind the maze of narrow streets later embellished with Baroque architecture. The castle at the head of the town is a Christian reconstruction of a Moorish fort, and the adjacent **Iglesia de la Asunción*** was built over the mosque. This Baroque country gem features striking barley-sugar columns on the portal and a fine altar of red and black jasper. Cabra's long past is encapsulated at the **Museo Arqueológico Municipal*** in the Casa de Cultura. Although some of the best finds have been spirited off to Córdoba and Madrid, the museum chronicles the prehistory of the area to the Roman conquest in AD50, then steps through time with Visigothic and Moorish artefacts.

Accommodation and food in Cabra

Hostal San José € *Avda Fuente del Río 12; tel: (95) 752–0368.* Good-value, basic accommodation offering small comfortable rooms with en-suite facilities.

Mesón del Vizconde € *c/ Martín Belda 16; tel: (95) 752–1702.* Cabranos are especially fond of fish, which they prepare with sauces and oils using local herbs and seasonings. Vizconde is the town's premier fish restaurant, and the sea bass with fennel sauce is a winner.

Below
Cabra

MONTILLA✧

ℹ️ Oficina de Turismo
c/ Capitán Alonso
Vargas 3; tel: (95) 765–
2462; fax: (95) 765–7933;
www.turismomontilla.com;
open Mon–Fri 1000–1500 in
summer, 1000–1400 and
1630–1900 in winter.

🛒 Tonelería Durán
Avda Andalucía 12 sells
a wide variety of local
montillas.

**🍴 Hotel-Restaurante
Alfar €** Carretera
Córdoba–Málaga km 14;
tel: (95) 765–1120;
fax: (95) 765–1120;
www.hotelalfar.com.
Attractive complex 6.5km
south of town has a pool –
and a discotheque.

A sprawling industrial town close to Córdoba, Montilla is the main centre for the production of Montilla–Moriles wines. Fermented in the presence of oxygen using a thick *flor* of sherry yeast, Montilla wines resemble some of the lesser sherries. Only the rugged red Pedro Ximénez grape (reserved elsewhere for sweet dessert wines) can tolerate the intense heat of the Córdoban *campiña*, where it produces elevated sugar levels that ferment out to 16 per cent alcohol. As a result, Montilla producers do not fortify their wines, although they do age them in *soleras*, the sequence of oak barrels also used in sherry country. The fermentation chambers are pretty earthenware urns called *tinajas* with their pointed ends dug into the ground. The powerful corporate Alvear now dominates Montilla production, and offers **bodega tours✧** at its original 18th-century compound (€ *Avda María Auxiliadora 1; tel: (95) 766–4014; open Mon–Fri 0830–1330 and 1500–1830*). Call for times of tours and tastings. At the edge of town along Avda Andalucía several manufacturers also sell planters, wine racks and other objects made from wine barrels.

PARQUE NATURAL SIERRAS SUBBETICAS✧✧

**ℹ️ Parque Natural
Sierras Subbéticas,**
Centro de Visitantes,
Carretera A340, km 57,
Cabra; tel: (95) 733–4063.
Information centre for the
Sierras Subbéticas is just
outside Cabra and keeps
irregular hours.

**Centro de Visitantes
'Santa Rita'** Carretera
A340 km57, Cabra; tel:
(95) 733– 4034. With
informational exhibits on
the ecology of the park, this
centre has a good standard
park map and a sketchy but
useful brochure outlining
the network of hiking trails.

With an area of more than 31km², this semi-mountainous region was declared a natural park in 1988. The park is bounded by the towns of Cabra on the west, Zuheros and Luque on the north, Priego de Córdoba on the east and Rute on the southwest. Several small villages lie within the park, but its chief attractions are the cross-country hiking paths, unusually well-developed for Andalucía. One of the most popular walks is the climb to the **Ermita de la Virgen de la Sierra✧** east of Cabra. Several pilgrimages are made to this shrine throughout the year, the largest and most colourful of which is the Romería de los Gitanos in the third week of June. The easy route departs from the C336, 5km east of Cabra, climbing a moderately steep 3.5km trail to the hermitage. The more interesting but longer route departs from Zuheros on the A340 at km19.5 and roughly follows the Río Bailon valley for 7.5km to La Nava before beginning the 1.5km uphill walk to the *ermita*.

PRIEGO DE CORDOBA✧✧

In this Moorish area between Córdoba and Granada, Priego stands out as quintessentially baroque, since it flourished in the 18th century as a

Oficina de Turismo
*c/ Río 33; tel: (95)
770–0625; open Tue–Wed
1000–1300, Thur–Fri
1700–2000, Sat–Sun
1200–1400. Provides town
map with detailed listings of
Priego's striking churches,
which are usually open
1100–1300 and
1830–2100.*

centre for the production of silk textiles. That surge of wealth led to an ecclesiastical building boom manifest in the fine reconstruction of the 16th-century **Parroquia de Nuestra Señora de la Asunción**❖. While the original structure is Gothic-Mudéjar, the interior is encrusted with baroque detail. The *sagrario* chapel, declared a national monument in 1932, is one of the supreme achievements of Spanish baroque. The church fronts on lovely modern gardens flanked by the often-reformed and now private **Moorish castle**❖. Behind the church stands the old Moorish quarter of the city, **Barrio de la Villa**❖, a classic labyrinth of narrow streets, white houses and potted geraniums circled by the pretty **Calle Real**❖. One street away is the **Balcón del Adarve**❖, with striking views over the cliff where the *barrio* perches.

Down in the busy town centre, two impressive structures face each other across Pl. de la Constitución: the Baroque *ayuntamiento*❖ (town hall) and the Rococo **Colegio de Nuestra Señora de las Angustias**❖. Heading south from the centre, c/ Río leads to the Oficina de Turismo, which occupies the birthplace of **Niceto Alcalá Zamora**❖, the first president of the Spanish Republic (1931–6). The street leads to a pleasant park around the often over-hyped **Fuente del Rey**❖. Embellished many times since its 16th-century construction, this 180-jet pool with multiple basins features several statues that are stone metaphors of royal power.

Accommodation and food in Priego de Córdoba

El Alijibe € *c/ Abad Palomino 7; tel: (95) 770–1856.* Cosy informal *tapas* bar and restaurant with some unusual local specialities.

Hotel Río Piscina € *Carretera Monturque-Alcalá km44; tel: (95) 770–0186; fax: (95) 770–0638.* Modern 47-room hotel with pool, on the south edge of town.

Villa Turística de Priego €€ *Aldea Sagrilla; tel: (95) 770–3503; fax: (95) 770–3573; www.villaturisticadepriego.com.* Tourist village in typical Andalucían style 7km west of Priego offering self-catering units and several dining options.

ZUHEROS❖

Zuheros is a mountain-top town, with no less than three *miradors* providing spectacular views of the surrounding valleys. The upper level of this steep little town is capped, of course, by ruins of a **Moorish castle**❖, which face the main church. Zuheros functions as the trailhead for several outstanding hikes in the Sierras Subbéticas. About 1km above the town centre is the entry point for the **Cueva de los Murciélagos**❖ or 'Cave of the Bats' *(follow signs; tel: (95) 769–4545;*

open Sat, Sun and holidays 1 Apr–30 Sept 1100–1930; 1 Oct–31 Mar 1100–1730; open Mon–Fri for unguided visits: call for opening hours). Visits are limited to 150 people per day (reservations are required) to protect the sensitive archaeological excavations that have pushed back the horizon of the Spanish Neolithic period by two millennia. The fragile cave paintings, which include some unusual representations of mountain goats, are the highlight, although some of the chambers are also noted for their impressive stalactites and stalagmites.

Suggested tour

Total distance: 248km.

Time: One long day.

Links: This route links to Córdoba (*see pages 188–201*) in the north, and Granada (*see pages 232–45*) in the south.

Route: This route is rarely followed in this circular fashion, as it represents two alternatives for journeys between Córdoba and Granada. From Córdoba follow the N-IV toward Sevilla, turning south in 20km on the A331 towards Málaga. Proceed 28km through an introduction to the mixed countryside of this route – olives on the hilly east side of the road, grapes and wheat on the lowland west side – to the turn-off for **MONTILLA ❶**. The A331 continues south for another 9km, passing through the outskirts of **Aguilar de la**

Oficina de Turismo
*c/ Horno 50; tel: (95)
769–4545; open in summer
0900–1400 and
1700–1900; in winter
1000–1400 and
1600–1800.*

**Hotel-Restaurante
Zuhayra €**
*c/ Mirador 10;
tel: (95) 769–4693;
fax: (95) 769–4702;
www.zuheros.com.* The
town's only hotel fits its
setting well and has a good
restaurant (€).

Frontera✦, where little has happened since the 889 revolt of Muslim converts to Christianity under Omar ibn Hafsun. Aguilar has very picturesque castle ruins. In another 18km, turn on to the A430 east (marked C336 on some maps and signs) to enter the **PARQUE NATURAL SIERRAS SUBBETICAS ❷**, pausing in 4km at the Santa Rita visitor centre. The turn-off to visit **CABRA ❸** comes up quickly. The highway changes number to A340 here and begins to climb into the low hills of the Subbética as vineyards give way almost entirely to olive groves. In 24km, stop at **Agrícola Virgen del Castillo**✦, the roadside store of an olive growers' cooperative, to sample the delicious local oil. This is olive country, pure and simple, and as the road

Right
Olive country
in the Subbeticas

Right
One of Priego's
many baroque churches

narrows when it approaches **PRIEGO DE CORDOBA** ❹ in 10km, you could be delayed by heavily laden olive-oil tankers straining to crest the hills. In fact, the air in Priego is permeated with the sweet scent of fresh olive oil.

The conventional route here is to remain on the A340 for 24km and turn south on the N342 for the 54km drive into Granada. But to circle back to Córdoba, leave Priego on the A333, following signs towards Jaén (*see page 224*). The winding road passes through beautiful high country of gnarled olive trees for 20km to connect to the N432, where a left turn leads 11km northwest to **BAENA** ❺, home of Spain's most celebrated oil. From Baena, the N432 continues another 62km back to Córdoba, passing through the pretty little villages of **Espejo◦**, lorded over by a Gothic-Mudéjar castle, and **Castro del Río◦**, whose woodcarvers are renowned for their furniture and statues of olive wood.

Also worth exploring

The town of **Rute**, about 30km south of Cabra, is famed for its production of potent *anís,* an aniseed-flavoured eau-de-vie made with mountain spring water. About 20 small *bodegas* in the town offer samples of both the ferocious *anís seco* (55% alcohol) and the syrupy *anís dulce* (35%). The **Museo de Anís** on the main square charges no admission, making its profits instead on the sale of products. (*Pl Principal; no tel; open daily 1000–1400, 1700–1900.*)

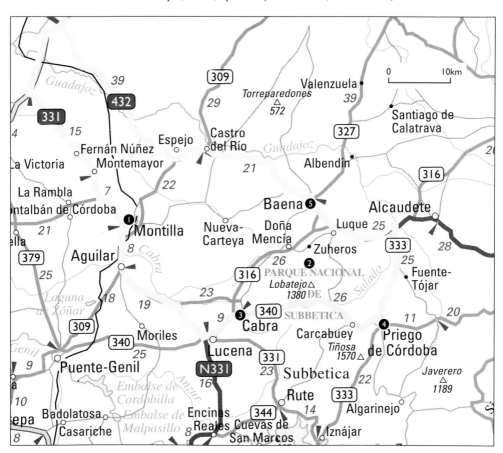

Renaissance cities

Architecture ●●●●●

Nature and
wildlife ●●●●○

Outdoor
activities ●●●●○

Gastronomy ●●●○○

History ●●●○○

Museums ●●●○○

Shopping and
crafts ●●●○○

Entertainment
●○○○○

The rich orchards of the central Jaén countryside produce about 10 per cent of the world's supply of olive oil. The 16th-century nobility who grew wealthy on this green gold moved in high circles of the Spanish court, gaining a worldly sophistication and cosmopolitan taste in architecture uncommon among country lords. Employing the genius of local architect Andrés de Vandelvira, they commissioned the greatest concentration of fine Renaissance buildings in all of Spain, and rebuilt the streets of Jaén, Baeza and Ubeda to accommodate them. As a result, the Renaissance cities feel unlike any others in Andalucía – full of light, proportion and crisp rectangularity. Yet the rolling groves of olives suddenly give way to dense forest just east of the cities, where the mountains of the rugged Sierra de Cazorla are home to the largest natural park in Spain.

BAEZA✦✦✦

ℹ **Oficina de Turismo**
*Pl. del Pópulo s/n; tel:
(95) 374–0444; e-mail:
otbaeza@andalucia.org;
www.andalucia.org; open
Mon–Fri 0900–1400 and
1700–1900, Sat 1000–
1300 and 1700–1900, and
Sun 1000–1300.*

Baeza is the smallest and possibly brightest gem of the Renaissance triangle, a small city that flourished as the seat of one of Spain's first universities. The heart of the modern town is **Plaza de España✦**, which stands at the head of **Paseo de la Constitución✦**, a green park flanked by shops and offices. The plaza's highlight, the **Torre de los Aliatares✦**, is one of the few reminders that Baeza flourished in Moorish times as a bazaar town for the region. At the foot of the paseo, **Fuente de los Leones✦** is the centrepiece of Pl. del Pópulo. The sculptures on the fountain – four lions and a regal woman – are nearly eroded away, which is not surprising since they were perhaps 10 centuries old when they were assembled into a fountain. Unearthed 15km west of town in the Iberian village of Cástulo, they predate even the Roman occupation of the area. Steps behind the fountain lead up

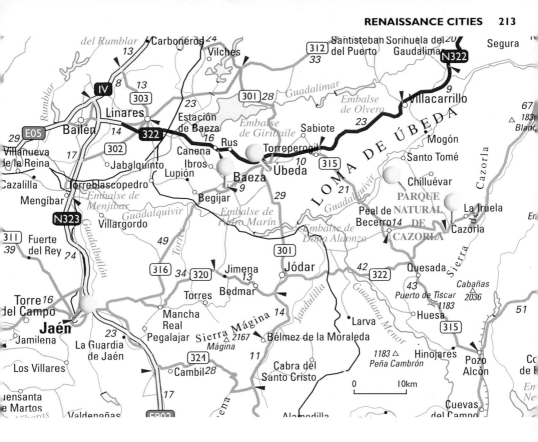

P On-street parking is generally free and generally unavailable. There is an ample and inexpensive underground car park on c/ Barreras, just behind the Torre de los Aliatares and another in c/ Compañia.

Pópulo *Pl. Leones 1; tel: (95) 374-4370.* This delightful shop sells local olive oil, honey and pollen as well as ceramics and some choice antiques, including 17th-century church music bound in vellum. Operator Sebastián Moreno also gives advice on touring, arranges mountain stays and gives out maps when the regular tourist office is closed.

to the 'Zona Monumental', the area between the original university and the town's cathedral.

With the exception of the Moorish-Gothic **Iglesia de Santa Cruz+**, a 13th-century church adapted from a mosque, the Zona Monumental is dominated by Renaissance architecture, mostly designed by Andrés de Vandelvira and executed in large limestone blocks. Starting literally from the top, the **Catedral de Santa María++** underwent a 16th-century reconstruction that obscured the 13th–14th century Mudéjar features. Despite the Plateresque façade of the main entrance, the low profile of the building gives away its Gothic origins. The altar screen on the old choir is perhaps the finest work of Maestro Bartolomé, the 16th-century Jaén genius of sculpture in wrought iron. In front of the church stands the striking 16th-century **Fuente de Santa María+** in the style of a Roman triumphal arch, something of a self-tribute by the nobleman who commissioned it. Downhill on the left is the **Antigua Universidad+**, built shortly after Baeza became one of the first towns to fall to Fernando III in 1227. It now houses a high school. The reddish-brown graffiti derives from the curious tradition of students painting their names on the building with bull's blood as a rite of graduation. One of the rooms is modestly famous as the classroom where the great poet Antonio Machado taught French between 1914 and 1919.

Additional examples of Renaissance architecture abound in Baeza, though not in such concentrations. One street west of Paseo de la Constitución, the **ayuntamiento**◦ on c/ Benavides occupies nearly a half block with an imposing Plateresque façade. At the end of this street, on c/ San Francisco, is the city's fresh food market, named after the adjacent ruins of the **Convento de San Francisco**◦. By all accounts, Vandelvira considered the chapel here his greatest masterpiece. Badly damaged in the 1755 earthquake and sacked by Napoleon's troops, parts of it have been restored in the last decade, revealing a carved limestone wall where Renaissance proportions are stretched to their limits by ornamental detail that verges on the baroque.

Accommodation and food in Baeza

Hotel Baeza €€ *c/ Concepcíon 3; tel: (95) 374–8130; fax: (95) 374–2915.* Set in a capacious old hospital with beautiful central patio, the small rooms feature all the essential modern comforts, especially air conditioning.

Many fine and venerable **tapas** bars around Pl. de España serve a broad selection of meat delicacies along with the usual sardines and potato omelettes.

Below
Baeza

CAZORLA✣

ℹ Oficina Municipal de Turismo c/ Pas. del Santo Cristo s/n (in the Casa de Cultura by the park); tel: (95) 371–0102; www.ayto-cazorla.es. Contrary to all the signs, this office is tucked away above the town centre. Other offices advertising 'información turística' are either map shops or guide services offering park excursions.

🅿 The best parking is on the square in front of the mercado de abastos below Pl. de la Constitución. Parking is banned here Sat–Mon, forcing visitors to vie for the rare on-street spaces.

Nestled beneath the *Peña de los Halcones*, or 'Falcons' Peak', Cazorla serves primarily as base camp for excursions into the adjacent natural park. But it is worth spending an hour or two seeing the town. From the main Pl. de la Constitución, c/ Dr Muñoz rises 150m to the oval Renaissance square of **Plaza Corredera✣**, dominated by a 17th-century convent converted to the *ayuntamiento* (town hall). A short distance south via c/ Gómez Calderón, the immense ruins of the **Iglesia de Santa María✣**, designed by Andrés de Vandelvira and destroyed by Napoleon's troops, serve as an outdoor concert and theatrical venue. Above the **Plaza Santa María✣** stands the **Castillo de la Yedra✣** which combines Roman, Moorish and Castilian architecture.

Accommodation and food in Cazorla

Camping Cortijo San Isicio € *Camino de San Isicio s/n; tel: (95) 372–1280; open 1 Mar–1 Nov.*

Hotel Guadalquivir € *c/ Nueva 6; tel: (95) 372–0268; fax: (95) 372–0696.* In keeping with Cazorla's role as a gateway to what passes for wilderness, the furnishings of this crisp new hotel in an ancient building incline toward rustic pine.

Juan Carlos €–€€ *Pl. Consuelo Mendieta 2; tel: (95) 372–1201.* Popular with locals, the menu includes a predominance of game dishes, as well as some surprisingly innovative starters.

Mesón Don Chema *c/ Escaleras del Mercado 2; tel: (95) 372–0607.* Just off Pl. de la Constitución, Don Chema favours the best buys of the day at the adjacent produce market and the freshest-cut meat from the community butcher 50m away.

Villa Turística de Cazorla €€ *c/ Ladera de San Isicio s/n; tel: (95) 371–0100; fax: (95) 371–0152; www.ayto-cazorla.es.* One of the first 'tourist villages', this community outside the town has 32 villas with central meeting rooms, restaurant, game rooms, gardens and pool. All units boast complete small kitchens. An excellent base for a week of hiking different routes in the Parque Natural de Cazorla.

JAEN✣✣

Settled by the Romans and expanded by the Moors as a convenient stopover for caravan routes, Jaén came into its own after Fernando III wrested the city from the Córdoban caliphate in 1246 and made it the seat of a Catholic bishopric. Conveniently bypassed by the modern *autovías* and too diffuse to appeal to bus-tour organisers, Jaén does not

ⓘ **Oficina de Turismo Palacio**
Condestable c/ Maestra 18; tel: (95) 324–2624; www.andalucia.org: www.aytojaen.es; open summer Mon–Fri 1000–2000 and Sat–Sun 1000–1300; winter Mon–Fri 1000–1900 and Sat–Sun 1000–1300. Provides information on the city.

Oficina de Turismo Junta de Andalucía c/ Arquitecto Berges 1; tel: (95) 322–2727 provides information for the entire region.

ⓟ The underground car park at Parque Victoria is within walking distance of all in-city sights.

◌ A Thur morning flea market is held at the Recinto Ferial on Avda Granada.

◑ Jaén's major celebrations are **Semana Santa** (Holy Week) and the **Feria de San Lucas**, a nine-day event in Oct.

usually appear on tourist itineraries. Nonetheless, it has two first-rate cultural landmarks and several smaller attractions within the city as well as an impressive hilltop castle above.

The **Catedral**✦✦✦ (Pl. Santa María; tel: (95) 323–4233; open summer Mon–Fri 0830–1300 and 1700–2000; Sat–Sun 0900–1300; winter Mon–Fri 0830–1300 and Sat–Sun 0900–1300 and 1700–1900), begun in 1492 and finished in the 18th century, is largely based on the design of Andrés de Vandelvira and is his greatest work. Despite the interior gloom, the cathedral represents the apogee of a highly regional style based on Vandelvira's application of Renaissance proportions to his training as a Gothic stonemason and his penchant for decorative detail. The cathedral is all the more impressive thanks to the extraordinary carvings and statuary on the main façade by Pedro Roldán.

The extensive and sumptuous **Baños Arabes**✦✦✦ might be called the 'mosque of water', for their grace and ingenuity seems an act of worship in stone. The largest Arab baths remaining in Spain, they were originally constructed in the 11th and 12th centuries and were famous throughout al-Andalus. They fell into disuse after the reconquest and in the 14th century housed a tannery. In the 16th century, the viceroy of Peru constructed his palace on the site, filling the subterranean structures with dirt until they were rediscovered in 1913. Excavated, restored and reopened in 1984, they are part of a museum complex in the **Centro Cultural Palacio de Villardompardo** (Pl. Santa Luisa Marillac; open Tue–Sat 0900–2000, Sun 0930–1430). A single free admission also routes visitors through the **Museo de Arte Naif**✦ and the **Museo de Artes y Costumbres Populares**✦. The 'naïve' art is repetitious, full of artists' donations with little curation. The folk arts museum, by contrast, does a commendable job representing the cultural traditions of the area. The best salons contain samples of ceramic styles from several parts of Jaén province and of traditional, mostly 19th-century clothing.

Like all Spanish cities, Jaén is dotted with churches, but none older than the **Iglesia La Magdalena**✦ (c/ Magdalena Baja; tel: (95) 319–0309; open daily 1800–2000). It is definitely worth walking a few blocks past the museums to see the wonderful 13th-century bas-relief of Mary Magdalene wringing her hair. It is a rare case of respectful conversion of a small mosque into a small church.

The archaeological sections of the **Museo Provincial**✦✦ (€ Paseo Estación 27; tel: (95) 325–0600; open Tue 1500–2000, Wed–Sat 0900–2000, Sun 0900–1500) are extraordinary, from the Greco-Iberian statuary and ceramics to Moorish pots and architectural details. The Roman period is well-represented, with highlights being a large collection of coins minted from local silver and a startling 4th-century marble Christian sarcophagus carved with the temptations of Christ. The fine arts museum contains a few well-displayed medieval paintings and religious carvings.

Jaén is capped by the **Castillo de Santa Catalina**⁺⁺ *(tel: (95) 312–0733; open summer Tue–Sun 1000–1400 and 1700–2100; rest of the year Tue–Sun 1000–1400 and 1530–1930)*, constructed in the 13th century by Ibn al-Ahmar and hastily modified to look more 'Christian' by Fernando III, who named it after the saint's day of his victory at Jaén. A *parador* occupies part of the castle's original confines. A walkway along the walls facing the city provides a stunning view of the surrounding countryside: the toy-like structures of Jaén at the foot of the mountain and rolling hills of olive trees all the way to the horizon.

Accommodation and food in Jaén

Hotel Condestable Iranzo €–€€ *Pas. Estación 32; tel: (95) 322–2800; fax: (95) 322–2800; www.iranzotel.com.* Modern hotel across from Parque Victoria that lowers its rates substantially at weekends.

Parador de Jaén €€–€€€ *Castillo de Santa Catalina; tel: (95) 323–0000; www.parador.es.* Sturdy stone hotel built within the castle walls blending medieval atmosphere with modern comforts. El Cid would not have felt out of place here, especially in the soaring dining room modelled on a medieval manor hall.

The best casual dining is in the **cafés** and ***tapas* bars** on c/ Nueva near Pl. de la Constitución and c/ Arco del Consuelo near the cathedral.

PARQUE NATURAL SIERRA DE CAZORLA❖❖

ⓘ **Cazorla's Oficina Municipal de Turismo** c/ Pas. del Santo Cristo s/n (in the Casa de Cultura by the park); tel: (95) 371–0102 is the best bet for maps and detailed park information. Official park visitors' centres are also located in **Siles** tel: (95) 349–1143 and at **Torre del Vinagre** Carretera del Tranco km18; tel: (95) 371–3040.

🚶 A variety of entrepreneurs offer 4x4 and guided walking tours in the park, but the most established and sanctioned of the group is **Quercus** c/ Juan Domingo 2, Cazorla; tel: (95) 372–0115.

The largest natural park in Spain, Cazorla attracts both casual drivers who enjoy mountain roads punctuated by occasional villages, a substantial contingent of back-country travellers who are happiest when hiking steep terrain through some of Europe's densest forest. The tourist associations are of only moderate help for serious hikers, as the general maps are extremely vague on trails and access roads; it is therefore necessary to purchase detailed topographic maps before venturing much out of sight of paved roads. Given that overnight camping and campfires are forbidden within the park, much of it remains truly natural because no one can get to it. Several villages, however, can provide a base for exploration.

For penetrating the wilder, more dramatic stretches it is best to book a 4x4 excursion, which may be combined with hunting, fishing or rock-climbing. But to get a taste of the park's potential, a good compromise is to drive from the village of Cazorla through La Iruela, turn right on leaving town and follow signs along a twisting mountain road towards Vadillo to the **Puente de las Herrerías**❖. Here there are panoramic views of some of the greatest limestone massifs in the southern end of the park. The route switches to a footpath along the edge of a deep gorge, high above the Río Guadalquivir, leading to a series of striking waterfalls, including **Salto de Linarejos**. The return trip is an easy, two-hour walk.

Accommodation and food in the Parque Natural de Cazorla

Camping Cortijo tel: (95) 372–1280. Family orientated camping 4km from the centre of the village.

Camping Río de Molinos € Carretera Acebas km1 Siles; tel: (95) 349–1003; www.riodemolinos.com. Rustic camping with limited amenities.

Hotel de Montaña Riogazas € Carretera de La Iruela al Chorro km4.5, Cazorla; tel: (95) 312–4035; fax: (95) 371–0068. Located just 7km from Cazorla centre near the park's access control gate, Riogazas strikes an excellent balance between hotel comfort and hunting-lodge rusticity.

Parador Nacional de Cazorla €€ Carretera de Sacejo s/n, Parque de Cazorla; tel: (95) 372–7075; fax: (95) 372–7077; www.parador.es. The parador has successfully adapted its functional modern architecture to create an interior that evokes the feeling of a hunting lodge fit for a duke. Set within the park, it has fabulous views.

UBEDA✦✦✦

ℹ **Oficina de Turismo Junta de Andalucía**
Palacio del Marqués del Contadero 4; tel: (95) 375–0897; fax: (95) 379–2670; e-mail: otubeda@andalucia.org; www.andalucia.org

🅿 Follow signs to 'Zona Monumental'. Parking is strictly prohibited on the main plaza but small pockets of free parking are available on side streets.

Fernando and Isabela ordered the walls of Ubeda demolished to quell the squabbling among the noble families who had become established in this olive oil countryside after the reconquest. A few vestiges remain: the Moorish **Puerta del Losal✦**, with its double horseshoe arch, and the Christian **Puerta de Granada✦** where the horse troughs are still in use. The royal plan worked. The nobility stopped fighting and started building, trying to outshine each other with palaces and churches. Their designer of choice was Andrés de Vandelvira, who had a hand in many of the 14 churches and two dozen or so palaces that make Ubeda an open-air museum of Renaissance architecture. The city has mounted informational posts in Spanish and English adjacent to most of the important structures.

Some of the finest buildings are concentrated in the **Plaza Vázquez de Molina✦✦✦**, often called Plaza Monumental and considered one of Spain's most graceful and stately architectural districts. The plaza also contains a statue of Vandelvira, making the area something of a homage to the man who defined a style.

Although few of the buildings are open to the public, their façades alone tell the evolution of Ubeda's Renaissance. The **Palacio del Marqués de Mancera✦** was already old-fashioned when it was built at the end of the 16th century as a late-medieval 'tower house', reminiscent of the fortified homes of the warring nobility. The less anxious Renaissance style is epitomised in the **Parador de Condestable Dávalos✦**, a noble mansion converted to a state-run hotel, and the **Palacio de las Cadenas✦**, commissioned as a palace but used as a convent and now housing the town hall. Visitors can look into the courtyards which reveal graceful proportions and restrained décor.

Right
Ubeda's Plaza Monumental, with the Parador on the left

① Capilla del Salvador € Pl.
Vázquez de Molina s/n; open
Mon–Sat 1000–1400 and
1700–1930; Sun
1045–1400 and
1630–1930.

Museo de Ubeda € c/
Cervantes 6; open Tue
1500–2000, Wed–Sat
0900–2000, Sun
0900–1500.

Hospital de Santiago
Avda Cristo Rey s/n; open
Mon–Sat 0800–1500 and
1530–2200.

**Museo de San Juan de
la Cruz** tel: (95)
375–0615; open Tue–Sun
1100–1300 and
1700–1900.

Ⓐ Alfarería Góngora
c/ Cuesta de la Merced
32 and **Alfarería Paco
Tito e Hijo** c/ Valencia 22
are two family-run
establishments that carry
on Ubeda's ceramics
tradition.

**Ⓕ Festival
Internacional de
Música y Danza** tel: (95)
375–0897. One of the
largest festivals of its kind
features classical and
chamber music, opera,
jazz and flamenco
performances in the city's
palaces and plazas.

Fiestas de San Miguel
tel: (95) 375–0897.
Concerts, parades and
corridas occur from late
Sept to early Oct.

Opposite
Ubeda's Capilla
del Salvador

The Palacio de las Cadenas is the handiwork of Vandelvira, as is the the **Capilla del Salvador**∗∗ on the east end of the plaza. This church fuses Vandelvira's artistry with the power and ego of its patron, Francisco de los Cobos, often identified as the Spanish prototype of the Renaissance courtier. Scholars still debate the complex iconography – half Christian, half pagan – of the façade with its allusions to death, wealth, family honour and a possibly blasphemous equation of de los Cobos with Christ the Saviour. Easier to distinguish is the powerful figure of Santiago the Moorslayer over the north door. Along with lions (the local nobles were called the 'lions of Ubeda'), the Santiago motif appears with great frequency throughout the city. Other architects produced plans for parts of the Capilla, but Vandelvira alone executed the arched sacristy, whose simple purity contrasts with the baroque retable on the main altar.

The Plaza Monumental is the heart of Renaissance Ubeda, but it is worth exploring other streets where the great limestone-block Renaissance mansions are sandwiched between the more typical whitewashed Andalucían houses.

Plaza del 1° de Mayo∗, now a tranquil tree-lined square with a charming bandstand, once flared with the fires of the auto-da-fé in the days of the Inquisition. Following c/ Cervantes from the square leads to the **Museo de Ubeda**∗ in the 14th-century Casa Mudéjar with a simple patio and pointed arches. The museum relates the region's history. Exhibits include fragments from a Roman funerary structure, including expressive heads of a man and woman, found in a farmyard in 1965. Roman ceramics trace the local industry back to the 2nd century AD, noting that the local clay with an admixture of 10 per cent iron oxide and 2 per cent lime is very plastic and takes on a red hue when fired.

Head back to the Plaza and continue along c/ San Juan de la Cruz where you will find the **Museo de San Juan de la Cruz**∗, the former home of the diminutive friar. This museum offers a fascinating glimpse into the life of the poet and mystic. The cell where he died may also be viewed. Ubeda's pottery, which has Moorish curves and decorative influences, is famed for its distinctive green glaze, detailed carving and dramatic geometric patterns. The best place to view pottery are the workshops (alfarerías) concentrated along c/ Cuesta de la Merced and c/ Valencia.

Vandelvira's other major Ubeda masterwork is the **Hospital de Santiago**∗∗, located several blocks from Pl. Andalucía via the shopping district streets of c/ Mesones and Carrera Obsipo Cobos. Locals proudly point out that one of the two towers was recently restored to its original glazed ceramic tile roof in blue, red, yellow and green. The airy interior courtyard makes a grand entry to the chapel behind, damaged during the Civil War but restored for use as a concert hall. Everything about the building bespeaks grandeur without hubris, from the impressive stairways to the frescos and the ornate ceiling. Appropriately, the entire

Above
Green-glazed pottery
in Ubeda

building now serves as a cultural centre. A small self-service café is set into the stone walls in one corner – open during business hours and evenings until half an hour after performances.

Accommodation and food in Ubeda

Palacio de la Rambla €€ *Pl. Marqués 1; tel: (95) 375–0196*. The current Marquesa lets out eight guest rooms in this 16th-century palace filled with antiques. Price includes breakfast.

Parador Condestable Dávalos €€ *Pl. Vázquez Molina s/n; tel: (95) 375–0345; fax: (95) 375–1259; e-mail: ubeda@parador.es; www.parador.es*. This *parador* set in a 16th-century Renaissance palace also has a courtyard café, taberna and elegant restaurant with a very reasonable *menú del día* at lunch. The massive stone staircase is impressive, but alas there is no lift.

Parador Restaurante Nacional del Condestable Dávalos €€–€€€ *tel: (95) 375–0345*. Sixteenth-century palace, recently refurbished, the parador restaurant is renowned for its traditional cuisine, such as partridge with plums and stewed kid with pine nuts.

Mesón-Restaurante Navarro €–€€ *Pl. Ayuntamiento 2; tel: (95) 379–0638*. A restaurant with a few tables in the plaza, with a fairly ambitious *menú del día*.

Restaurante El Seco €–€€ *c/ Corazón de Jesús 8; tel: (95) 375–1452*. A local restaurant with a welcoming atmosphere, open for lunch only except for Fri and Sat evenings.

Pl. Andalucía and the surrounding streets just outside the city walls have a concentration of casual cafés with inexpensive menus and combination dishes.

Suggested tour

Total distance: 57km, 147km with detour.

Time: Less than half a day to drive, but 3–4 days to see the sights.

Links: This route connects to the Jaén's High Country (*see pages 224–31*) at Ubeda, and to Granada (*see pages 232–45*) at Jaén.

Route: To set the tone of Renaissance pace and grace, spend a day exploring **UBEDA ❶**, where Vandelvira's most classic buildings stand in close proximity.

Detour: Visit the **PARQUE NATURAL SIERRA DE CAZORLA ❷** by driving east on the N322 for 10km, turning southeast for 23km on the A315, then due east for 12km to **CAZORLA ❸**. The town serves as a departure point for northern, southern and central routes in the park. Retrace the roads back to Ubeda.

Leave Ubeda early in the morning, drive 9km west on the A316 to **BAEZA ❹**. After spending the morning in Baeza, continue 48km west on the A316 to **JAEN ❺**, where the major museums remain open in the afternoons. If space is available, spend the night at the *parador* next to the castle.

Also worth exploring

A little more than 50km southwest of Jaén via twisting mountain roads, **Alacalá de la Real** was founded by the first wave of Moorish invaders in 713 and changed hands many times over the centuries. Its hilltop fortress, with six Christian and nine Moorish towers, and local archaeological museum are essential for history buffs.

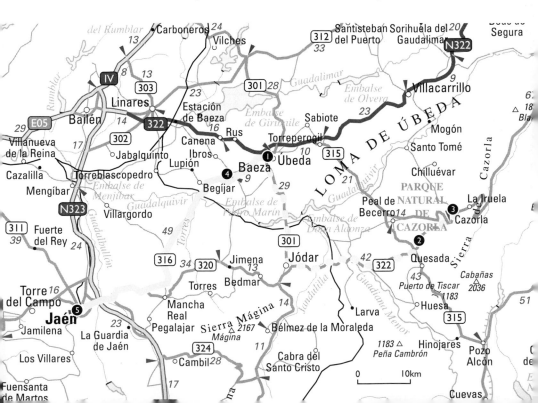

Jaén's high country

Mountainous northern Jaén province is ultimately defined by its history as the frontier between Andalucía and the rest of Europe: the crossroads of conquering armies from the Greeks and Romans to the Moors and the Spanish kings. Most travellers passing through are still in too great a rush to get somewhere else – Madrid if heading north, Córdoba or Sevilla if heading south – to heed the rugged mountain scenery or the olive-growing towns that line the ancient crease followed by the N-IV autovía. Jaén's mountain towns offer surprising diversity, from handsome Renaissance architecture to one of Spain's most sacred medieval shrines. The communities are known for their ceramics, both industrial and artistic, and northern Jaén's vast forested nature preserves are home to some of southern Europe's last large predators. Bullfighting is also strong here, with many breeding farms and Spain's most notorious bullring.

ANDUJAR✦✦

ⓘ Oficina de Turismo
Pl. Santa María s/n; tel:
(95) 350–4959; e-mail:
turismo@ayto-andujar.es

Ⓦ Turismo Verde
c/ Jorge Guillén 21; tel:
(95) 354–9030 arrange
guided photographic tours
in all-terrain vehicles,
walking and horse-riding
tours, fishing excursions
and rock-climbing in the
Parque Natural Sierra
de Andújar.

Set in an ancient valley, Andújar is one of the very few cities of Moorish origin not constructed on a hillside. Although most people make Andújar a base for exploring the adjacent park, the flat urban layout makes for pleasant walking around its broad plazas and through the maze of medieval streets. Like larger cities to the southeast, Andújar flourished in the 17th and 18th centuries, and its best domestic and civil architecture is Renaissance in style. The central plaza, officially Pl. de España but known locally as Pl. de la Merced, is dominated by the late 17th- and early 18th-century **Casa de Comedias✦**, a theatre converted into the *ayuntamiento* and currently closed for renovation. Open-air comedic productions are still held in the square. C/ La Feria leads from the front of the *ayuntamiento* towards the right, curving into Pl. Santa María, where the supremely

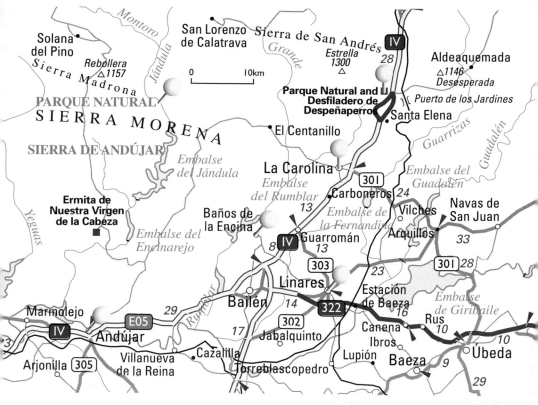

⬤ **Romería de la
Virgen de la
Cabeza** *last Thur–Sun of
Apr.* Pilgrims on horse and
on foot hauling ox-carts
leave Andújar for the
mountain hermitage 32km
away in the Parque Natural
Sierra de Andújar.

organised tourist office occupies **La Torre del Reloj***, built in the 16th
century as a tribute to Carlos I. The **Iglesia de Santa María**** on the
same square contains a superb altar screen with graceful Renaissance
capitals and a painting by El Greco, *La Oración del Huerto*.

Accommodation and food in Andújar

Camping Sierra de Andujar; contact the Oficina del Medio Ambiente
(tel: (95) 351–2410) for permits to camp within the park boundaries.

Hotel Don Pedro € *c/ Gabriel Zamora 5; tel: (95) 350–1274; fax: (95)
350–4785.* Plain but well-kept 29-room hotel with air conditioning,
parking and a central location.

Hotel del Val € *Avda Puerta de Madrid 29; tel: (95) 350–0950; fax: (95)
350–6606; www.hoteldelval.com.* On the east edge of town, this modern
79-room hotel has surprising polish and a slick cafetería.

El Toledillo Restaurante € *Carretera a la Virgen km5; tel: (95)
350–5800.* The spectacular terrace where the April *romería* passes is a
fine spot for local cuisine throughout the year.

The tourist office provides a **Ruta de la Tapa** brochure that identifies 10 spots where *tapas* are treated as serious food rather than interchangeable snacks.

BAÑOS DE LA ENCINA❖❖

ⓘ Ayuntamiento *Pl. de la Constitución 1; tel: (95) 361–3004; fax: (95) 361–3455.* Can provide a rough map of town, information on camping and possibly locate Sr Recinte if he's not at home.

☾ Hotel Restaurante Baños € *c/ Cerro de Llaná s/n; tel: (95) 361–4068; www.hotelbanos.com* is the best choice of accommodation in the town.

Below
Baños de la Encina

Baños sits atop a hill overlooking broad, dry country filled with silvery olive trees. The lightly travelled JV5042 road from industrial Bailén is a favourite for hiking, about two hours each way. Baños has been occupied since at least the Bronze Age, as attested by cave paintings found nearby in La Moneda and the crude mining operation now being excavated at Peñalosa. Only scholars can visit these sites, but the town itself is a gem. The **castillo**❖❖❖ is possibly the best preserved Moorish frontier fortress in Andalucía. With a vast keep to protect an entire community during a siege, it has 14 towers of hewn stone and thick walls of conglomerate. It was constructed in 968 on orders of the caliph of Córdoba to guard the entrance to al-Andalus from Christian invasions. The town changed hands six times over the centuries, but the castle was never severely damaged. Hours are by chance, but if the doors of the double-horseshoe arch are closed, knock at c/ Santa María 10, where the window grates are covered with flowers, to ask for the

gatekeeper. The elderly but agile Antonio González Recinte will produce the ancient crank key, open the fortress and provide excited commentary on both castle and the town. There is no formal admission, but a tip of €1 per person is in order. On August evenings, music and dancing take place within the castle walls.

Just below the castle in the town's main square is the **Iglesia San Mateo**✢, with its Gothic nave, Renaissance portal and octagonal pinnacled tower. Easily visible from the battlements of the castle is the **Ermita Cristo del Llano**✢, also open by chance, which has a stellar vault modelled on those in Granada's Alhambra (*see page 234*).

La Carolina✢

Orellana Perdiz €
*Autovía Andalucía
km265; tel: (95) 366–0600;
www.orellanaperdiz.com*
This roadside hotel, restaurant and leather shop is next door to a *ganadería*; the bullring is next door.

Often serving as a staging point for hikers investigating the ridges of Parque Natural de la Desfiladera de Despeñaperros, La Carolina is a 'new town' established by Carlos V in the late 18th century to make the Sevilla–Madrid bullion road more bandit-proof. Laid out on a grid and named after the king, La Carolina does not fit the mould of an Andalucían town. The surrounding hills are dotted with *ganaderías* that breed fighting bulls.

Linares✢

The Greeks and Romans established communities at Linares to mine silver and lead and the town remains a prosperous industrial community. The main reason for stopping is to see the **bullring**✢ where famed matador Manolete was fatally gored in August 1947. Walk around it to see the two monuments: a profile relief on the ring below a tiled reproduction of the poster announcing the fatal *corrida* and a bronze bust under a small tree where his aquiline profile overlooks the ring pensively. Then have a drink at the **bar for bullfighting aficionados**✢✢ set into the walls of the plaza, where extraordinary photographs record the grace, anxiety and flourish of the sport.

Accommodation and food in Linares

Hotel-Restaurante Cervantes € *c/ Cervantes 23; tel: (95) 369–0500.* Reasonably close to the bullring with clean, traditional rooms and simple fare.

Peña Taurina Palo Moreno € *Pl. de Toros; no tel.* Some of the oldtimers drinking here could have been young men in the stands on that fatal day in 1947. They know their matadors, but you may have to ask around before someone identifies Hemingway in one of the old photos.

PARQUE NATURAL SIERRA DE ANDUJAR✦✦✦

ⓘ Park Information
J5010, km14.2; tel:
(95) 351–2410.

This park contains the largest tracts of natural forest in the Sierra Morena mountain range, making it a favourite for long-distance hikers. Preservation of the forest is largely funded through the hunting preserves within its boundaries. Hikers should dodge the hunting grounds and beware of fighting bulls grazing in fenced areas of scrub forest.

The quintessential flora of the region is the polymorphic evergreen oak, *Quercus ilex*. The top branches of this tree are covered with smooth leaves, but those on the lower branches are prickly, leading the red deer and wild boar to fatten up on acorns and ignore the leaves. Although hikers are unlikely to see more than tracks, these hills are the last stronghold of the Andalucían wolf and one of the largest territories of the Iberian lynx. Golden eagles are common. The *embolsos*, or reservoirs, of the Río Jandula east of Virgen de la Cabeza are also excellent fishing spots.

In the middle of the park is the **Ermita de Nuestra Virgen de la Cabeza✦**. According to tradition, the figure of the virgin was discovered here in 1227 by a shepherd from Colomera (Granada). Over the centuries a cult following has developed across Spain, with organised penitential brotherhoods making an annual pilgrimage by

Below
The Andalucían landscape
viewed from the walls of
Baños de la Encina

tens of thousands to pay their respects to *La Morenita*. Festivities begin on the last Thursday of April with the laying of flowers before the figure of the Virgin. Over the next three days, pilgrims arrive from Andújar, 32km away, in what is the second-largest religious pilgrimage in Andalucía.

Accommodation and food in the Parque Natural Sierra de Andújar

Hotel La Mirada € *Sanctuario Virgen de la Cabeza; tel: (95) 354–9111.* Less austere but still simple accommodation geared more to hunters and hikers than pilgrims. Large restaurant with ambitious menu.

Restaurante-Bar Los Pinos €€ *Carretera Sanctuario Virgen de la Cabeza km14.2; tel: (95) 354–9023; fax: (95) 354–9079.* Local herbs are used as seasoning for traditional mountain cooking. The complex also offers 14 wheelchair-accessible bungalows, each with three bedrooms.

PARQUE NATURAL DESPENAPERROS✦✦

The chief appeal of this segment of the Sierra Morena lies in its historic significance and precipitous landscape. The battle of **Las Navas de Tolosa✦**, a site 2km north of La Carolina on the N-IV, marked the beginning of the end for Moorish domination of Andalucía. In 1212 Christian armies led by Pedro II of Aragón, Alfonso VIII of Castilla and Sancho 'el Fuerte' of Navarra, pushed toward al-Andalus. For a thousand years the only known pass between Andalucía and central Spain had been the narrow cut north of Las Navas. On the south side of the pass the army of Granada waited under orders of Mohammed II al-Nasir. According to the legend, a shepherd – variously identified as Martín Alhaga or as San Isidro in disguise – alerted the Spanish commanders and guided them through an alternative pass. The surprise was complete and the army of Granada was routed. Ever since, the mountain pass where Mohammed's troops lay in wait has been known as **Desfiladera de Despeñaperros✦**, or 'pass of the fall of the dogs'. The N-IV autovía traverses the pass with hairpin bends and switchbacks.

Several excellent hikes of varying difficulty can be made in the park, which is closed to vehicles. The small village of **Santa Elena✦** makes the best base. From the crossroads village of Aldea Quemada, 24km from the east end of Santa Elena, the simplest route is a 2-hr round trip over easy terrain along a well-marked path to the **Cascada de la Cimbara✦**, a waterfall which lives up to its name only in spring. Other longer hikes depart from the Las Correderas turn-off on the N-IV autovía a few kilometres north of Santa Elena. Details are available from both the hotel and campsite.

**Hotel-Restaurante
El Mesón
Despeñaperros €** *Avda
Andalucía 91, Santa Elena;
tel: (95) 366–4100; fax:
(95) 366–4102.* Good
dining and simple rooms
looking across a long valley
to the famous pass. The
hotel serves as a *de facto*
information centre for the
park.

**Camping
Despeñaperros €** *Avda
Andalucía s/n, Santa Elena;
tel: (95) 366–4192.*

Right
Baños de la Encina

Suggested tour

Total distance: 144km, 208km with detour.

Time: 6–8 hours.

Links: This route connects to Córdoba (*see pages 188–201*) on the west and to the Renaissance Cities (*see pages 212–23*) through Ubeda on the east.

Route: Begin at **ANDUJAR** (76km east of Córdoba on the N-IV) with a walk around the central square.

Detour: The J5010 at the east end of town winds 32km up mountain roads to the Santuario Virgen de la Cabeza, where a nondescript modern church has replaced the ancient hermitage destroyed in the Civil War.

The N-IV continues east 23km to **Bailén***, home of brick and industrial tile companies. The turn-off at km300 leads to a country road, the JV5042, for the 11km drive through olive groves to **BANOS DE LA ENCINA** . At Baños another small road, the JV5040, reconnects to the N-IV at km288. Continue north 2km to the turning for **Guarromán***, where those in the know go for a local pastry called 'hojaldres Moreno'. The huge ones (half a metre across) can be purchased at Café-Bar Zona Servicio Los Ríos; the main pastry shop with smaller portions lies 200m further along in town.

Baños de la Encina

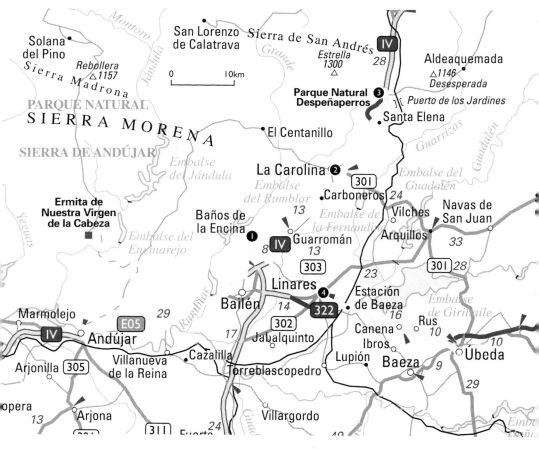

Balneario San Andrés N322
(Carretera Córdoba-Valencia, km137), Canena; tel: (95) 377–0209; open daily 0900–1400 and 1700–2000. Thermal spa.

In 18km, the bullring of **LA CAROLINA** ➋ appears on the right side of the N-IV at a highway turn-off. After passing more bull-breeding farms, the N-IV becomes a less formal road, where virtually every roadside rest stop is filled with makeshift stands selling olives, cheese, honey and ceramics. In 5km, at km265, is the poorly marked turning for the memorial marking the battle of Las Navas de Tolosa. A little further on, at km259, turn off for **Santa Elena***, a handsome village that is the best base for walking explorations of the **PARQUE NATURAL DESPENAPERROS** ➌. The N-IV cuts through the actual pass for the next 10km.

Backtrack on the N-IV for 26km to Guarramón and the A303, which leads through marshy farmland to **LINARES** ➍. From here, the main N322, leads east for 14km to the dusty village of **Canena***, topped with an incredible Renaissance castle, and famed since Roman times for its spa, now called **Balneario San Andrés**. Just 13km further east is Ubeda, the best base for touring the Renaissance cities.

El Bañuelo *Carrera Darro 31; open Tue–Sat 1000–1400.*

Museo Arqueológico € *Carrera Darro 41; open Tue 1500–2000, Wed–Sat 0900–2000, Sun 0900–1430. Free with EU passport.*

Walking Tours (€€) of the Albaicín led by university students leave from the Real Cancillería next to Pl. Nueva on Fri–Sun at 1200, 1600, 1800 and 2000 (*tel: (67) 054–1669*).

Sights

Albaicín**
When the Nasrid court moved into the Alhambra in the 13th century, the old residential *medina* stayed behind, perfectly poised on the opposite bank of the Río Darro to admire the glories of the new palace on the facing hill. The Muslim past is palpable here as the Albaicín's jasmine-scented streets follow an organic logic of their own, and the *barrio* has acquired a substantial Muslim and Sufi population for whom Granada's first modern mosque is being built. The neighbourhood's original mosques have been converted to churches that maintain only fragments of their origins – a courtyard here, a minaret there, sometimes an ablutions fountain.

The eastern edge of the Albaicín follows the Río Darro, where gourmet shops, boutiques and restaurants dominate. About halfway down the street is **El Bañuelo****, 11th-century Arabic baths with four vaulted chambers – one for undressing, one for conversation, a third room with marble floor for napping and massage, and finally the ablution chamber with terracotta floor heated from beneath. Close to the baths is the Casa de Castril, a striking 16th-century palace housing the **Museo Arqueológico****. Exhibiting finds from Granada province, the museum chronicles the Iberian, Roman and Moorish eras. The upper level features exquisite *azulejos*, ceramics and wood carving from the late Moorish period – an artistic style quite distinct from the achievements of the earlier Caliphate period.

Lined with many inexpensive restaurants, **Plaza Larga*** near the top of the hill is the *barrio's* social centre. At one corner stands the **Arco de las Pesas***, a Moorish gate at the end of the remaining walls of the Moorish fortifications. Callejón de San Cecilio wends its way downhill to **Plaza San Nicolás***, a broad and pleasant space that faces the Alhambra. From the **Mirador San Nicolás**** at the foot of the square, views of the Alhambra are unparalleled.

La Alhambra and El Generalife***
As the outlying reaches of al-Andalus fell to the Christian reconquest in the 13th century, Islamic Spain became increasingly concentrated in the kingdom of Granada, where the Nasrid dynasty held on for 250 years until Granada became the last Muslim city to fall in 1492. The Nasrid kings drew on the best architects and finest artisans of al-Andalus to build a palace city atop La Sabika hill that still casts a spell over everyone who sees it. Touring the complex takes at least three hours, and savouring it can stretch the experience to a full day.

The oldest extant portion is the **Alcazaba**✦✦, which dates from the 13th century and was built on the ruins of earlier fortifications. Napoleon's troops destroyed much of the fort, but surviving ramparts and watchtowers provide a feel for how the hill was guarded. Views from the Torre de Vela, the highest point of the Alhambra, are stunning. To the west lies the ravine of the Río Darro, the sprawl of the city and the countryside beyond. Towards the north is the sugar-cube jumble of the Albaicín and the hill of Sacromonte. To the east stand the palaces of the Alhambra with a backdrop of snowcapped Sierra Nevada peaks. When the Catholic monarchs took the city in January 1492, they raised their flags and cross from the tower. Later they had a bell installed to signal the irrigation schedule to the valley below.

The **Palacio Nazaries (Casa Real)**✦✦✦ is the brightest jewel of the complex. Built primarily during the rule of Mohammed V (1354–91), its restrained and simple exterior in no way prepares visitors for the richness of the internal decor. The artists must have abhorred blank space, as virtually every surface is adorned with carved plaster in lacy and delicate abstract patterns and Arabic inscriptions. Floors and many walls are covered with exquisite mosaic tiles, and most ceilings are either ornate plaster or carved wood. Ponds and fountains provide both the sound and sight of water to virtually every chamber, and light and shade are patterned in ways that continually delight the eye.

Below
The Alhambra gardens

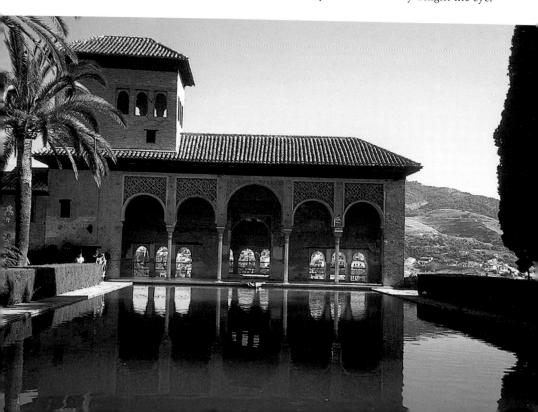

Capilla Real € c/
Oficios 12; open Mar–
Sept Mon–Sat 1030–1330
and 1600–1900, Sun 1100–
1300 and 1600–1900; Oct–
Feb daily 1030–1300 and
1530–1830.

**Casa-Museo Federico
García Lorca (Huerta
de San Vicente)** €
c/ Virgen Blanca s/n; open
Tue–Sun 1000–1300 and
1800–2000 (summer);
1000–1300 and
1600–1830 (winter).

Just as he permitted the desecration of Córdoba's mosque with a cathedral (*see page 193*), Carlos demolished a large section of the Casa Real to build his own palace, begun in 1526 and never finished. The architect Pedro Manchuca was a pupil of Michelangelo, and this Renaissance structure is admittedly beautiful, if rather like a zebra in a herd of thoroughbreds. The unusual circular courtyard is surrounded by a dual arcade of columns with graceful, broad arches. Much of the palace has been turned over to the **Museo de la Alhambra**✦✦, which explores the artistry of the Muslim era with objects found at the Alhambra and elsewhere in Granada and Córdoba, and the **Museo de Bellas Artes**✦. The fine arts museum is a chronicle of royal taste over the centuries, with some superb baroque paintings and many dreary nudes.

The Renaissance palace has elegant symmetry, but it is an alien building for life in Granada's swelter. The **Generalife**✦✦✦, the summer palace of the Muslim rulers, on the other hand, belongs to the land and climate. Sitting on the slopes of the Cerro del Sol facing the Casa Real, the palace buildings tucked away in one corner almost seem an afterthought to the beautifully laid out courtyards filled with pools and fountains. Crisply trimmed hedges turn the gardens into outdoor rooms. A 700-year-old cypress tree in the Patio de los Cipreses is identified as witness to the trysts between Zoraya and the head of the Abencerrajes clan, which led to the bloodbath in the lower palace. Such strife seems far removed from this tranquil setting.

Capilla Real✦✦✦

Across a small plaza from the cathedral, the Capilla Real is the essential Christian religious building to visit in Granada. It stands as an exuberant late-Gothic tribute to Isabela and Fernando, whose coffins lie in the crypt with those of their daughter Juana la Loca (Juana the Mad) and her husband Felipe el Hermoso (Felipe the Handsome). Whether the earthly remains of the monarchs themselves are still here is open to question, as the tombs and coffins were opened and desecrated by Napoleon's soldiers in 1812. The most striking works in the chapel are the marble effigies of the four monarchs, commissioned by Carlos V to make up for what he pronounced 'too small a room for so great a glory'. The central altarpiece, currently under restoration, tells the monarchs' version of the fall of Granada, depicting Boabdil handing over the keys to the city. The gilded *reja* (grille) in front, the crowning achievement of Maestro Bartolomé de Jaén, depicts the life and death of Christ in a sequence of scenes at the top. The sacristy contains Fernando's sword and Isabela's crown and sceptre as well as her personal collection of Flemish art.

Casa-Museo Federico García Lorca✦

The spirit of poet and playwright Federico García Lorca (1898–1936) haunts much of the city – the theatre in the Alhambra Palace Hotel where his first play was produced, the Restaurante Sevilla where he often dined, the Hotel Reina Cristina where he was seized by right-wing thugs and delivered to his death. Some of his happiest and most productive times were spent in the **Huerta de San Vicente**, the 'country house' on the south side of the city that his father purchased in 1925. Lorca spent summers here for the next decade, writing some of his best poems and most important plays. The Casa-Museo sits in the middle of a rather new and splendid park of roses. The half-hour guided tours in Spanish show Lorca's writing desk, his piano, portraits of friends and family members and some of the writer's sketches for theatrical productions. The house now lies well within the busy city, about a 15-min walk from the cathedral.

Below
Granada's Cathedral
and Capilla Real

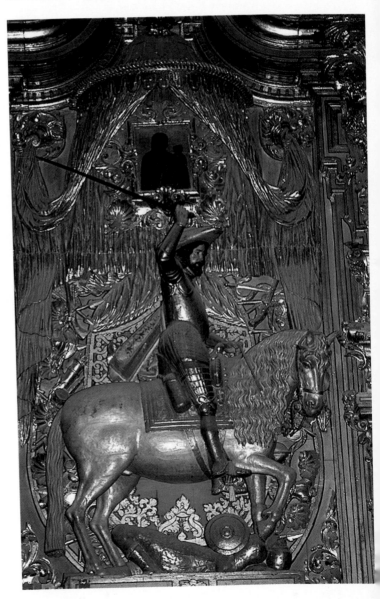

Cathedral €
ⓘ *entrance on c/ Gran Vía Colón; open Mon–Sat 1000–1330 and 1600–1900, Sun 1600–1900.*

Museo de Zambra de María la 'Canastera'
Camino del Sacromonte; tel: (95) 812–1183; www.granadainfo.com/ canastera; open Mon–Fri 1700–1900, Sat–Sun 1200–1500.

◭ Fiesta de Reconquista
tel: (95) 822–5990
takes place 2 Jan.

Fiesta Internacional de Música y Danza *tel: (95) 822–2111.* Late June–early July, features performances at the Alhambra and other monuments.

Cathedral⁺⁺

Building work on Granada's blocky cathedral began in 1521 on the site of the main mosque. Left unfinished (it lacks one of the planned towers), the cathedral has a Renaissance plainness that contrasts with the elaborate façades of the city's Moorish monuments. The painted

Right
Santiago the Moorslayer
in the Cathedral

stonework and towering pillars give the interior a spacious majesty, and stained-glass windows around the base of the central dome let in enough light to rescue the voluminous interior from gloominess. The most notable side chapel depicts Santiago the Moorslayer on a horse, and similar images of San Miguel and Santiago throughout the building drive home the point of the Christian triumph at swordpoint.

Sacromonte**

Granada's large gypsy population used to be concentrated in Sacromonte on Valparaiso hill above the Albaicín. Once a poor neighbourhood, it is now showing signs of incipient gentrification, taking advantage of the unusual lodgings and extraordinary views. Many of the houses along the Camino de Sacromonte are dug into the side of the hill, with exterior profiles following geomorphic shapes and interiors generally having rounded ceilings covered with plaster and whitewash. A number of flamenco-ish shows and disco-bars now hold forth in some of the larger 'caves' in the first half-km of the main road, and they can be good fun if one's expectations are not too high. This *barrio* is no more dangerous than any urban neighbourhood, but visitors should be careful of their belongings. One very pleasant opportunity to visit a traditional dwelling is to walk up in the afternoon to the **Museo de Zambra de María 'La Canastera'***. *Zambra* is what purists prefer to call the Gypsy version of flamenco music and dance, and Enrique Carmona 'El Canastero' keeps his mother's home as a shrine to one of Granada's leading *zambra* singers and dancers of the 20th century. There's no fee, but Sr Carmona is pleased if visitors purchase a drink or perhaps a cassette of his mother's recordings.

Entertainment

The Peña Platería (Patio de los Aljives 13) is a private club for flamenco enthusiasts in the Albaicín off c/ San Juan de los Reyes between c/ Grajales and c/ Frailes de la Virgen. Performances take place most Saturday nights throughout the year and nightly during June and July (closed Aug). Individuals with a genuine interest are often admitted. Of the various flamenco nightclub shows, or *tablaos*, the one that gains at least grudging respect from serious musicians and dancers is Jardines Neptuno (€€€ c/ Arabial s/n; tel: (95) 852–2533). The many shows held in the 'gypsy caves' of Sacromonte make up in atmosphere what they might lack in polish or authenticity. Shows start around 2200, but be prepared to spend plenty for drinks.

The **Plaza de Toros** is located at the west end of the city, entered from *Avda Dr Olóriz*. Most *corridas* take place in early May during the Cruz de Mayo festival and in early June around the Corpus Christi festival. Tickets are available at the ticket office at *Av. Oloriz 25, tel: (95) 827–2451*.

Accommodation and food

Camping Sierra Nevada € *Avda de Madrid 107; tel: (95) 815–0062; www.campingsierranevada.com.* Located northwest of the city centre, this first-class campsite includes an excellent pool and lies on a city bus line.

Carmen de Santa Inés €€ *Placeta de Porras 7 or San Juan de los Reyes 15; tel: (95) 822–6380; fax: (95) 822–4404; e-mail: sinascar@teleline.es; www.carmensantaines.com.* Operated by the same management as the Palacio de Santa Inés, this hotel occupies an Arab house 'enlightened' in the 16th and 17th centuries. The nine rooms overlook either the garden or the Alhambra.

Casa del Aljarife €€ *Placeta de la Cruz Verde 2; tel: (95) 822–2425; e-mail: most@wanadoo.es.* Delightful small hotel with just four rooms, located in the heart of the Albaicín. The 17th-century house has been sensitively restored and there is a shady central courtyard and a roof terrace for catching the rays.

Hostal Britz € *Cuesta de Gomeréz 1; tel: (95) 822–3652.* Excellent-value small hostel within walking distance of the Alhambra. Rooms are basic but comfortable with brightly tiled en-suite bathrooms and a communal TV room.

Hotel Alhambra Palace €€–€€€ *Peña Partida 2-4; tel: (95) 822–1468; fax: (95) 822–6404; www.h-alhambrapalace.es.* Opened in 1910, the Alhambra Palace has become a landmark in its own right, a striking example of a pseudo-Moorish confection. The public areas remain a grand stage set for local society; the rooms are comfortable but unexceptional.

Hotel América €€ *Real de la Alhambra 53; tel: (95) 822–7471; fax: (95) 822–7470; e-mail: reservas@hotelamericagranada.com.* With only 13 rooms inside the walls of the Alhambra practically next to the *parador*, this small inn overstuffed with cushions and knick-knacks offers a striking modest deal. Rate includes breakfast and taxes.

Palacio de Santa Inés €€ *Cuesta de Santa Inés 8; tel: (95) 822–2362; fax: (95) 822–2465; www.palaciosantaines.com.* This stunning hotel with just 6 double rooms and 5 self-catering suites occupies a 16th-century palace on the river looking out on the Alhambra. Its patio contains faded but glorious frescos attributed to Alejandro Mayner, a disciple of Raphael.

Parador de Granada €€€ *Alhambra; tel: (95) 822–1443; fax: (95) 822–2264; e-mail: info@parador.es; www.parador.es.* One of the most luxurious hotels in the *parador* system occupies a converted monastery in the Alhambra grounds.

Bodegas Castañeda €–€€ *c/ Almireceros 3; tel: (95) 822–3222.* Excellent *tapas*, salads, filled jacket potatoes and traditional cuisine. Booking is recommended for the evening.

Café-Pastelería López-Mezquita *c/ Reyes Católicos 39; tel: (95) 822–1205* has been serving superb *tapas* and exquisite pastries since 1862. Its only shortcoming is that it closes at 2100.

Restaurante-Asador Corral del Carbón €€ *c/ Mariana Pineda 8; tel: (95) 822–3810* features grilled meats, especially lamb and sausages. It's wonderfully redolent of old Granada, down to the signed photo of Federico García Lorca at the bar.

A good selection of riverside cafés and bars are found along Paseo Padre Manjón north of the Museo Arqeológico at

the edge of the Albaicín looking across at the Alhambra. Pl. Larga and surrounding streets in the Albaicín are also filled with a range of restaurants and bar-cafeterías, and two good casual dining spots sit just above the Mirador San Nicolás; one of them, **Café-Bar Kiki**, specialises in regional foods from the Alpujarras. Stop for dinner around sunset; by the time the meal is finished the Alhambra will be awash with night-time illumination.

Shopping

Granada is rife with opportunities to purchase souvenirs, from T-shirts to local pottery or jewellery imitating Moorish and Spanish Baroque styles. Shops with better quality goods can be found along the riverside edge of the Albaicín and behind the cathedral.

Artesenía Corral Carbón *c/ Mariana Pineda s/n. Open Mon–Sat 1030–1330 and 1700–1900, Sun 1000–1330*. Artists' studios share the oldest surviving Moorish building in Granada with the tourist office and city arts foundation, just a block from the cathedral.

Guitarrerías are found in the greatest concentration along *Cuesta Gomérez*, including the shop of the fine composer and guitarist Antonio Morales at No 9.

Suggested tour

Total distance: 8km, 14km with detours.

Duration: One full day and an additional morning.

Route: Begin at the **ALHAMBRA ❶**, queuing early for the first tickets. The Casa Real is nearly 1km from the entrance, so move swiftly to enter during your time slot. The perimeter of the entire grounds is about 3km. Visit the Casa Real, the palace of Carlos V and then the Generalife before returning to see the Alcazaba. The austere **Puerta de la Justicia*** built by Yusef I exits the grounds. Cuesta de Gomérez leads downhill through the **Puerta de las Granadas****, which features three pomegranates (*granadas*) carved in stone, to Pl. Nueva – about 1km.

Turn right, cross Pl. Santa Ana and walk along Carrera del Darro to reach **El Bañuelo**. Continue up the street to tour the **ALBAICIN ❷**. About 1km from Pl. Santa Ana, the street changes its name to Pas. del Padre Manjón and concludes at the rising embankment of c/ Chapiz. Turn left on Chapiz and climb the hill.

Detour: Near the crest of the hill, turn right on to Camino del Sacromonte, which leads along the hillside past the caves of **SACROMONTE ❸**.

Chapiz eventually winds into **Plaza Larga**. Pass through the **Arco de las Pesas** and immediately turn left, following c/ Panaderas and Callejón de San Cecilio to Pl. San Nicolás. Sunset from the Mirador San Nicolás is quite an event, as the buildings of the Alhambra reflect a golden glow.

The next morning, begin at **Plaza Isabel la Católica***, a few blocks south of Pl. Nueva, where an army of women with 'lucky' rosemary sprigs are stationed around the **CATEDRAL ❹** and **CAPILLA REAL ❺**. The nearby **Corral del Carbón****, one of the oldest standing Muslim commercial buildings in Granada, is home to the Artespaña crafts shop.

Detour: The main street, **c/ Reyes Católicos**, also has good shops of a less touristy sort on the 0.6km stretch south to Puerta Real. The street changes name here to c/ de Recogidas, then to Neptuno in 2km. The Huerta de San Vicente and **CASA-MUSEO FEDERICO GARCIA LORCA ❻** is only a block further on in the middle of the large park.

Also worth exploring

In Fuente Vaqueros, 16km northwest of the city, the **Museo Lorca**, the house of Lorca's birth, is located just off the main square and is filled with memorabilia of his entire life. Viznar, 10km northeast of the city, has a large **Parque Federico García Lorca** dedicated to all those who died in the Civil War. The trench where Lorca was shot and buried with three others is marked with a granite memorial.

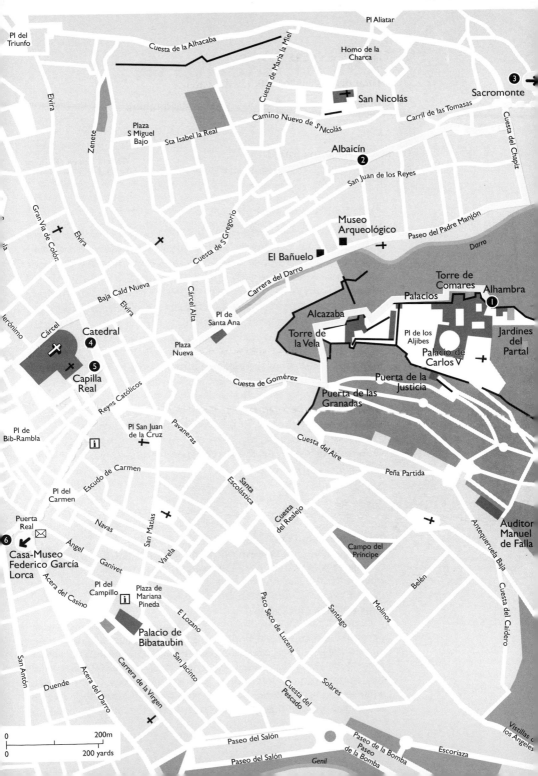

Pl del Triunfo

Pl Aliatar

Cuesta de la Alhacaba

Cuesta de María la Miel

Homo de la Charca

San Nicolás

Sacromonte **3**

Elvira

Plaza S Miguel Bajo

Sta Isabel la Real

Camino Nuevo de S Nicolás

Carril de las Tomasas

Cuesta del Chapiz

Zenete

Albaicín **2**

San Juan de los Reyes

Cuesta de S Gregorio

Museo Arqueológico

Paseo del Padre Manjón

Darro

Gran Vía de Colón

Elvira

El Bañuelo

Carrera del Darro

Torre de Comares

Palacios

Alhambra **1**

Baja Cald Nueva

Cárcel Alta

Alcazaba

Pl de los Aljibes

Jardines del Partal

Jerónimo

Cárcel

Catedral **4**

Pl de Santa Ana

Torre de la Vela

Palacio de Carlos V

Elvira

Plaza Nueva

Puerta de la Justicia

Capilla Real **5**

Reyes Católicos

Cuesta de Gomérez

Puerta de las Granadas

Pl de Bib-Rambla

Pl San Juan de la Cruz

Pavaneras

Cuesta del Aire

Peña Partida

i

Escudo de Carmen

Santa Escolástica

Pl del Carmen

Navas

San Matías

Varela

Cuesta del Realejo

Auditor Manuel de Falla

Puerta Real

Ángel

Ganivet

Campo del Príncipe

Antequeruela Baja

6 Casa-Museo Federico García Lorca

Acera del Casino

Pl del Campillo

Plaza de Mariana Pineda

E Lozano

Paco Seco de Lucena

Santiago

Molinos

Belén

Cuesta del Caidero

San Antón

Duende

Acera del Darro

Carrera de la Virgen

San Jacinto

Cuesta del Pescado

Solares

Palacio de Bibataubin

Viscillas los Ángeles

0   200m

0   200 yards

Paseo del Salón

Paseo del Salón

Genil

Paseo de la Bomba Paseo de la Bomba

Escoriaza

Las Alpujarras de Granada

Ratings

Nature and
wildlife ●●●●●

Architecture ●●●●○

Gastronomy ●●●●○

Shopping and
crafts ●●●●○

Outdoor
activities ●●●●○

History ●●●○○

Entertainment
●○○○○

Museums ●○○○○

South from Granada over the 3000-m peaks of the Sierra Nevada lie the green valleys of Las Alpujarras, isolated from the rest of Spain until the mid-20th century by poor mountain roads. The Alpujarras remained a stronghold of Moorish culture into the early 17th century, when their inhabitants were expelled and the area was repopulated with northern Europeans. But culture dies hard, and while nominally Christian, the villages retain a striking similarity to Berber settlements of North Africa, with terraced vineyards and olive groves and a profusion of wild mulberry trees, descendants of the groves the Moors planted in the 10th century to feed their silkworms. The western half of this corridor, Las Alpujarras de Granada, is greener and more picturesque by far than Las Alpujarras de Almería to the east. Stunning mountain scenery, plentiful wildlife and welcoming villages make the region a popular summer retreat for Granadinos.

HIGH ALPUJARRAS✦✦✦

The three mountain villages of Pampaneira, Bubión and Capileira squat like white birds' nests along the east wall of the Barranco de Poqueira ravine northeast of Lanjarón. Their nearly perfect medieval Moorish cast makes the trio a popular tourist destination, especially on summer weekends, when their altitude guarantees a modicum of relief from the lowland heat.

From a distance the houses resemble those of all the white towns of Andalucía, but close up they display an indigenous architecture found only in the Alpujarras, the Rif mountains of North Africa and certain parts of the Himalayas. Broad and squat, their walls are thick slabs of stone, traditionally left a drab grey but nowadays covered with whitewash. Their roofs are timbered with whole chestnut logs, topped with sheets of slate that are sealed with *launa*, the crumbly grey mica

Nevadensis *c/ Verónica s/n, Pampaneira; tel: (95) 876–3127; www.nevadensis.com.* Provides information on Parque Natural Sierra Nevada, arranges guided hikes and horse-riding expeditions and sells maps and books on the region. Terrific exhibits elucidate Alpujarran culture and history.

Kiosco Chuly *Avda Sierra Nevada s/n, Capeleira; no tel.* Kiosk at end of car park sells maps and provides useful guidance in planning hiking excursions.

clay of the region that becomes watertight when tamped down. By tradition, *launa* is only laid during the waning of the moon. These roofs are generally treated as terraces or patios, with one building's roof providing the entrance patio to the next house up the hill.

The most intrinsically interesting of the three villages is **Pampaneira**✦✦✦, which has a distinct village centre and a lively industry of hand-weavers and other craftspeople. One shop, La Rueca (*c/ José Antonio 4*), sells beautiful weavings, most from locally produced wool, made on the looms in the upstairs workshop. **O Sel Ling**✦ ('Place of Clear Light'), a Tibetan Buddhist monastery (*tel: (95) 834–3134*), perches high on the opposite side of the gorge. Although principally operated as a meditative retreat, the monastery sometimes receives visitors. It can be reached from the turn-off marked 'Ruta Pintoresca' opposite the wayside chapel of Ermita del Padre Eternal on the GR421, 5km south of Pampaneira.

Bubión✦ lacks a real village centre, though it is hatched with superb hiking trails, and honeycombed with studios of artists and artisans. Furthest up the hill at an altitude of 1440m, **Capileira**✦✦✦ is the logical jump-off for mountain hikes as well as for strolls down the Poqueira valley. Just north of the village the seemingly fine G411 road is barred to traffic, and 3km further on the road surface turns to dirt. The medieval road to Granada through a 3400m pass is still there, but even four-wheel-drive vehicles are banned. Snow always kept the road impassable from Sept–Jun; landslides now rule out Jul–Aug. Intrepid hikers nonetheless use the road for ascents of **Pico Mulhacén**✱✱, the 3482m pinnacle of the Sierra Nevada (*see pages 251–2*).

The villages of the High Alpujarras are so close together that one can sight a path from one to the next. A gentle 3km hike – allow three hours for the return trip with stops to look around and have lunch – involves simply stringing together the villages by the obvious footpath that crosses the ravine.

Accommodation and food in the High Alpujarras

Finca Los Llanos €–€€ *Carretera Sierra Nevada s/n, Capileira; tel: (95) 876–3071.* Double rooms and suites with and without self-catering in a tasteful new construction at the top of town. A good restaurant serves Alpujarran specialities.

Hostal Mulhacén € *Avda Alpujarra 6, Pampaneira; tel: (95) 876–3010.* All the modest rooms have beautiful, flower-covered balconies.

Below
Pampaneira

Mesón-Hostal Poqueira €–€€ *c/ Dr Castilla s/n, Capileira; tel: (95) 876–3048.* An outstanding set menu in the attractive dining room, with a very popular, ham-filled bar.

Villa Turística de Bubión €€ *Barrio Alto s/n, Bubión; tel: (95) 876–3111; www.villabubion.com.* Self-catering apartments make an outstanding base for extended exploration of the Sierra Nevada.

Casa Julio € *Avda Alpujarra 9, Pampaneira; tel: (95) 876–3322.* For a protein overload, order the Alpujarran platter with fried egg, grilled pork, smoked sausage, fried potatoes and blood sausage – a sort of all-day breakfast with Alpujarran overtones.

LANJARON**

ⓘ An information kiosk located on *Avenue Alpujarra; tel: (95) 877–0282* supplies maps and information on the area.

ⓑ Balneario de Lanjarón €€€ *Avda Andalucía s/n; tel: (95) 877–0137. From Mar–Dec daily 0800–1400 and 1800–2030,* the thermal spa provides seven kinds of waters, massages and other therapies.

Every visitor to Spain recognises the name of Lanjarón because the local bottling plant puts up 400,000 litres of mineral water per day and sells it all over the country. The town has eight springs, some with carbonates, others with sulphates and varying degrees of sodium and calcium. The Romans came for the cures supposedly associated with these waters, and from Jun–Oct, so do the infirm from all over Europe. In deference to this clientele, many shops along the main street sell walking canes and water glasses that fit inside straw covers. Traditionally, visitors to the spa take their own glass to imbibe the medicinal powers from the tap.

The town also serves as the gateway to the Alpujarras from the population centres to the west, especially Granada. A reasonably charming town of some size, Lanjarón also boasts a significant British ex-pat population, perhaps the result of Gerard Brennan's books. Since many day-trippers to the Alpujarras strike Lanjarón first, a bustling business has grown up at the west end of town selling the local ceramics, basketry and food products of the higher mountain towns to the east. There is one minor historic landmark, the ruins of a Moorish castle where the tatters of the Granada army made its last stand in 1500 and one of the central battles in the Moorish uprising of 1568 was fought.

Accommodation and food in Lanjarón

Hotel Miramar € *Avda Andalucía 10; tel: (95) 877–0161.* Pleasant, unfussy and clean, the Miramar is convenient for the spa, park and restaurants at the west end of town. *Closed Dec–Feb.*

Hotel Nuevo Palas € *Avda Andalucía 24; tel: (95) 877–0111; fax: (95) 877–1283; www.hotelnuevopalas.com.* With liberal use of wood panelling to effect a 'luxury' look, the Nuevo Palas is a pleasant base at the west end of town.

Above
Flower sellers greet
visitors to Lanjarón

Jamones Gustavo Rubio 'El Arca de Noe' *Avda Andalucía 7; tel: (95) 877–0027.* The back of this ham-producer's shop is a delightful wine, cheese and ham bar.

Manolete € *c/ San Sebastian 3 (no phone).* Traditional *tapas* bar frequented by locals and with a good selection of *tapas*, including the all-time favourites *boquerones* (anchovies) and *tortilla* (potato omelette).

The west end of town along Avda Andalucía is lined with shops selling the local hams, cheeses, wines and almond sweets. An exceptional example is **Rincón del Jamón Lanjarón** *Avda Andalucía 38; tel: (95) 877–0054.*

ORGIVA*

Hotel Taray €–€€
Carretera Tablate–Albuñol (A333) km18.5; tel: (95) 878–4525; www.turgranada.com/hoteltaray. Stylish modern comfort in rural setting with superb set menu (€€) in the restaurant.

Camping Orgiva €
Carretera Tablate–Albuñol (A333); tel: (95) 878–4307. Hillside camping located a few km south of town.

The chief reason to visit Orgiva, beyond the fact that the high and low roads diverge here, is to watch the spectacle of the Thursday morning market, when the old-time *campesinos* come to town to hawk their vegetables alongside the counter-cultural refugees from northern Europe selling their macramé, pottery and other crafts. It is a picture of a region where people have headed for the hills to carry on alternative lifestyles, whether the practice of Islam or a belief in crystal power and the transcendental possibilities of meditation. Since the 15th century, Orgiva has been the official capital of Las Alpujarras de Granada, and it is the central spot to catch buses to and from other villages – useful to avoid having to retrace one's steps on a cross-country hike.

Parque Natural Sierra Nevada***

This natural park – one of Andalucía's wildest and offering little for casual users – encompasses almost the entire massif of the Sierra Nevada, which extends from just east of Granada to an area just north of Almería. The highest peaks are concentrated in its northwest corner: the 3470m **Pico Veleta** and the 3481m **Pico Mulhacén**, the latter named after the last-but-one of the Moorish kings of Granada. Muley Hassan, who fought a bitter war for power with his son Boabdil, was so disgusted by the turmoil of court life that he asked to be buried on this mountain where, according to legend, his body still lies, uncorrupted and encased in ice. There are, indeed, perpetual snows on these peaks, which provide a striking backdrop for the verdant Alpujarran valleys. And the melt water, running north toward Granada and south through the Alpujarran villages, guarantees productive agriculture.

Right
Transport in
the Sierra Nevada

The mountain peaks are the primary attraction of the park itself, and there is a time-honoured trail that scales the summit of all the peaks of 3000m or more, the **Ruta de Tres Miles**✧. This arduous journey, which requires good mountaineering skills, a high level of fitness and a willingness to brave the elements, is traditionally staged from the east end of the Sierra Nevada at Jeres de Marquesado and concludes in Lanjarón. Ideally, it should take five days, but most mountaineers push to complete it in three or four to take advantage of concrete shelters along the way. The route is passable only in July and August, and even then hikers should carry an ice axe and crampons and be prepared for overnight freezing temperatures.

TAHA VILLAGES✧✧

◑ Camping Balcón de Pitres *GR421, west of Pitres village; tel: (95) 876–6111.*

Hostal Mirador €
GR421, centre of Pórtugos; tel: (95) 876–6014; fax: (95) 876–6069. Basic rooms above the restaurant side of a bar-restaurant. Fine but hardly sumptuous.

Below
Mountain ham
Opposite
Sierra Nevada hiking trail

Between the High Alpujarras and the truly high village of Trevélez are the least-spoiled towns of Las Alpujarras de Granada, a small cluster of very Moorish communities once part of an administrative unit known as the *Taha,* from the Arabic for 'obedience'. **Pitres**✧ and **Pórtugos**✧ lie on the main high-country road of GR421, while **Mecina**✧, **Mecinilla**✧, **Fondales**✧, **Ferreirola**✧ and **Atalbéitar**✧ lie below the road down steep hills. Like the villages of the High Alpujarras, one can easily see from one Taha village to the next and the hillside paths linking them are fairly obvious, since they are kept up by the steady passage of residents, often as they herd their goats. These paths, in fact, are mostly Roman roads.

A pleasant three-hour saunter around the villages of the Taha de Pitres is best staged from Pitres itself, where there is parking at the Bar-Restaurante La Carretera on the main road. A concrete ramp behind the restaurant descends steeply and turns to a path, with Mecina and Mecinilla visible below – a mere 15 min walk. At the road junction, 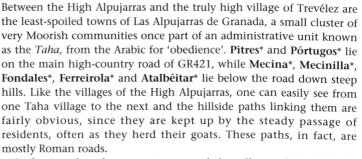 continue offroad towards the church and onto the main street of Mecinilla, passing a modern fountain. Turn left at a group of garages. When the street rises, turn right, passing through a tunnel that connects two houses and turn sharp right again to follow the irrigation channel until it reaches the road. The path continues through orchards into Fondales, a maze of narrow streets where it's usually a good idea to ask directions for the *camino real* mule track towards Ferreirola. In that village, head to the central church and take the north track beside the public washing area. After a fairly steep climb, the path emerges on the road outside Atalbéitar. Have a look, and then continue west on the paved road, watching for the signposted turn-off to the GR7 hiking path, which returns to Pitres less than 1km from the starting point.

TREVELEZ❖❖

Camping Trevélez
*Carretera
Trevélez–Orgiva, km I; tel:
(95) 885–8735;
www.campingtrevelez.org*
Good hillside camping as
base for serious trekkers.

**Restaurante
González Trevélez**
€–€€ *Pl. Francisco Abellán
Gómez s/n; tel: (95)
885–8533.* Ham rules the
menu; the open-air
restaurant has great flair,
while the bar abounds with
local colour.

**Restaurante-Bar
Alvarez €–€€** *on the
same plaza; tel: (95)
885–8503.* Also has roast
chicken for those who
have had enough ham.
Accommodation is also
available. *Closed Fri.*

The three tiers of the village of Trevélez, each on its own terrace, become more 'authentic' and less touristic as one climbs. Most of the shopping and dining are in the lower village. The streets seem chock-a-block full of hams, as this is the foremost centre of mountain ham production in the Alpujarras. Indeed, the town *smells* like ham. Not as rarified as the hams of Jabugo – these, after all, come from white pigs – Trevélez ham is very good indeed. The drive to Trevélez is demanding: it stands at the head of a long and narrow gorge and, at 1500m, is the highest year-round town on the Iberian Peninsula.

Besides attracting visitors interested in buying whole hams close to the source, Trevélez also serves as the base for scaling three major nearby peaks of the Sierra Nevada: Mulhacén, Alcazaba and Puntal de Vacares. From mid-July to late August, Mulhacén is a fairly practical overnight hike, requiring at least six hours to ascend and four hours to descend. Do not take the 'main route' shown on maps toward Jerez del Marquesado, as there are many obstacles. The route followed by pilgrims to the shrine of the Virgin of the Snows works better. It begins at the highest tier of the village and crosses the Crestón de Posteros before linking up with irrigation channels. The Siete Lagunas valley is the traditional place to stay overnight, allowing for an early morning ascent of the summit before the warm air rises from the Alpujarra valley and fog shrouds the cold peak.

Suggested tour

Total distance: 139km, 149km with detour.

Time: One day.

Links: This route connects to Granada (*see pages 232–45*) in the west

Above and opposite
Commerce in the
Alpujarras hills

via the N323 and A348, and to Las Alpujarras de Almería (*see pages 258–65*) to the east on the A348.

Route: This circuit is often treated as a long day-trip from Granada. Begin at **LANJARON** ❶, driving east on the A348 through a landscape of cactus and olives towards **ORGIVA** ❷. After 9km, turn left on to the G421, which begins to climb swiftly with a series of ridgeline switchbacks, passing the small villages of **Carataunas**⁺ and **Soportújar**⁺.

Detour: In 13km, there is a left-hand turn for 'Ruta Pintoresca–Sierra Nevada', which leads 2km to the Tibetan monastery and another 3km before ending at a forest management site that functions as a trailhead for forested mountain hiking.

2km past the detour, the villages of the **HIGH ALPUJARRAS** ❸ become visible from the GR421, which suddenly rounds a bend and passes right through Pampaneira. Although there is one small car park,

it is easier to park above the village along the road and walk down. To continue to the other High Alpujarras villages, turn left on to the G411, and pass through Bubión to Capileira; there is convenient, shady parking on the left before entering Capileira. The G411, which theoretically continues to Granada, is closed just above Capileira, so return to the G421 and turn left to follow a gorge 5km toward the **TAHA VILLAGES ❹**.

The G421 follows a long gorge north 14km to **TREVELEZ ❺**, then carries on down the east bank for another 12km before flattening out and continuing east for 21km through **Juviles⁺** and **Bérchules⁺**. Turn right at the junction, then right again at a stop sign onto the A348 5km to **Cádiar⁺**. The 40-km road to Orgiva follows the south side of a valley, with stupendous views sullied somewhat by bad road surfaces that make looking more difficult. This area is often damaged by landslides and may be under repair. At Orgiva, continue 15km west to return to Lanjarón.

Also worth exploring

The high range of the Sierra Nevada provides Granada with the dubious distinction of the southernmost European **ski resort at Solynieve**, where the downhill skiing world championships were held in 1996. Lifts only run when the ski trails are open, making it hopeless as a base for summer hiking, but skiing sometimes continues into early June and places to rent equipment abound. It's most easily reached by driving southeast from Granada for 47km on the A395.

Las Alpujarras de Almería

Ratings

Gastronomy ●●● ○○

History ●●● ○○

Nature and
wildlife ●●● ○○

Architecture ●● ○○○

Museums ●● ○○○

Outdoor
activities ●● ○○○

Entertainment
● ○○○○

Shopping and
crafts ● ○○○○

The villages of the Almería end of Las Alpujarras see many fewer visitors than those of Las Alpujarras de Granada. Closed in from the moisture of the Atlantic weather patterns by the high wall of the Sierra Nevada and the Sierra Gádor, this string of valleys has a harsh and sometimes forbidding countenance. The 'highways' linking them resemble widened and paved goat paths as they wend their way over the jagged topography of the south face of the Sierra Nevada. Much of the landscape verges on desert, yet masterful terracing and irrigation create surprising oases of green, where the scent of oranges perfumes the acrid air and wine grapes cling tenaciously to the steep hillsides. Some of the best table wines of southern Spain are grown in the area, and the entire fruit industry gives the small towns an unexpected prosperity.

ALHAMA DE ALMERIA ❖

Hotel Balneario San Nicolás € c/ Banos s/n; tel: (95) 064–1361; fax: (95) 064–1282; www.anet.com Old-fashioned hotel with **thermal baths.** The tiled walls and gracious central courtyard make the San Nicolás a true respite for the weary and afflicted. Baths open to non-guests 0600–0900 (€) for a variety of treatments, including massage (€€€).

The springs at Alhama have been famous since the time of the Romans, leading the Moors to found the town to take advantage of the waters' alleged medicinal properties. The local water is bottled and sold in the area as *Agua Mineral Natural Alhama*, but not widely distributed outside Almería province. Alhama is a pleasant enough town, and a good base for spending the day at Los Millares archaeological site, but there is little of interest beyond the charmingly old-fashioned spa.

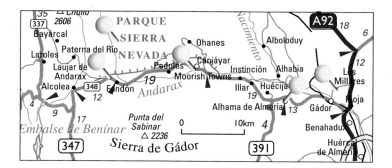

Parque Natural Sierra Nevada❖❖

ⓘ Centro de Visitantes Parque Natural Sierra Nevada A348 west of Laujar de Andarax; tel: (95) 834–0625; open Fri–Sun 1000–1400 and 1600–1800. Provides information on park sites and trails.

While the highest peaks of the Sierra Nevada lie on the Granada end, the arid eastern portion of the park is defined by its river channels: the Río Nacimiento on the northeast boundary of the protected area, and the Río Andarax, which flows east-west through the deep trench valley formed between the Sierra Nevada on the north and the Sierra de Gádor on the south. Lacking the glamorous peaks, this sector of the park is not as well set up for hikers, but there are some refuge huts and campsites that are well marked on hiking maps. Upland hikers may encounter the Spanish mountain goat or ibex (*Capra hispanica*), and the skies are full of kestrels, an adaptable small hawk that feeds on a wide variety of prey.

Laujar de Andarax❖❖

The capital of Las Alpujarras de Almería, Laujar was the last stand of Boabdil, the final emir of Granada, who settled here after he was driven from Granada in 1492. He struck a deal with the Catholic Monarchs to keep an Alpujarran fiefdom, which he intended to rule from Laujar. But within a year the Spanish broke the treaty and Boabdil fled across the Mediterranean to Tunisia. Laujar retained its strong Moorish identity for nearly another century. In 1568, Fernando de Válor, who had adopted the name Abén Humeya, declared himself king of Granada and Córdoba, set up his capital in Laujar, and led the Moorish revolt against Felipe II. In the ensuing bloodbath, Humeya was executed and the last people who would admit to being Moors were expelled from Spain in 1610. The region was subsequently repopulated by Christians from the north, including the soldiers of Don Juan of Austria, and even today many people (not just the tourists) have a Germanic cast to their features.

The original Arab street plan remains, along with the ruins of the Alcazaba at the top of the town. Many of the 17th- and 18th-century houses are built in the Moorish style with central courtyards. But most distinctively Arabic of all are the numerous running water fountains in Laujar – a striking sight for travellers arriving from the desiccated regions of the eastern Alpujarras.

The abundance of water and the surprisingly rich soil has given birth to a burgeoning wine industry in Laujar, which produces both white wines and a 'claret' of blended red and white grapes. Several private residences make small amounts of wine or press their own olives for oil. Wherever there is a sign announcing *se vende aceite* or *se vende vino*, one can simply ring the bell and purchase the local products straight from the barrel. Below the town the valley is planted with extensive orange and lemon orchards, best enjoyed from the *mirador* on the main square.

Accommodation and food in Laujar de Andarax

Hotel Almírez € *Carretera Laujar–Orgiva km1.6 (A348 west of town); tel: (95) 051–3514; www.hotelalmirez.com.* Comfortable property on the edge of town combines lodging with a cafeteria and restaurant (€).

La Molineta € *Paraje del Batán s/n; tel: (95) 051–4315.* Camping on the east side of town is near the Río Andarax. Reservations are necessary during winter months.

Nuevo Andarax € *c/ Casnalejas 27; tel/fax: (95) 051–3113.* This establishment offers beautiful scenery, rooms with terraces and a good restaurant.

Laujar is far and away the best place to sample the peculiar cuisine of this arid portion of the Alpujarras. One of the chief local specialities is *ajillo cabañil*, usually made with goat meat and washed down with the young local claret. Another country food typical of the region is a turnip stew called *guiso de nabos*.

Cooperativa Valle de Laujar *2km west of town on C-348.* A place to taste and buy wines as well as a local liqueur made from grape juice, coffee and anis. The cooperative also sells local goat cheeses.

LOS MILLARES**

Signage leading to this major archaeological site, which was discovered in 1891 during excavations to lay the railway line between Almería and Linares, is absolutely terrible, but it's worth persevering. Railroad engineers Louis and Henri Siret were the first to begin excavating the site, which has since been dated as representing the period from 2700 to 1800 BC, between the Neolithic period and the Bronze Age. Los Millares is generally called a Chalcolithic, or Copper

Los Millares *A348 km 24; tel: (67) 790–3404; open Wed–Sun 1000–1400.*

Age settlement, based on the preponderance of stone and copper (but no bronze) tools. The site represents the oldest metal-working culture known in Spain.

The excavations reveal that Los Millares was a large and complex community for its time. A series of defensive walls enclosed circular huts, a foundry, a grain silo and a simple aqueduct that brought water from Alhama. The 2000 occupants were hunters and farmers, raising sheep, goats and pigs and hunting for wild boar and deer. The climate was substantially more temperate and moist 5000 years ago and, in addition to livestock, the people of Los Millares raised vegetables and cereals, probably barley. The dry bed of an alternative path of the Río Andarax passes directly through the site, and appears to have been more or less navigable at the time of the settlement, since there is evidence that copper ore was transported by river from the Sierra de Gádor for smelting here.

The most notable part of the excavated area is the Necropolis, where more than 100 tombs have been discovered and carefully excavated.

Right
Public fountain in Laujar de Andarax

Suggested tour

Total distance: 78km, 96km with detour.

Time: One day.

Links: Connects to Las Alpujarras de Granada (*see pages 246–57*) on the west via the A348, and to Almería and Environs (*see pages 266–73*) on the south via the N340. The route is popular with people travelling from Almería to Granada.

Route: The road through the central valleys of the Alpujarras of both Almería and Granada, the A348, begins about 10km north of Almería off the N340 Guadix–Granada road. The turn-off is marked as 'Parque Natural Sierra Nevada'.

The landscape begins on this eastern end as lumpy folded terrain, with a brown surface like a loose bag of potatoes. But the wind-eroded bones of the land soon show through as the surface becomes more jagged and the land is lifted to greater altitudes. In 10km, after passing

Above
Rocks of striking hues in the
Alpujarras de Almería

limits of the village of **Gádor**, watch carefully for very small signs to **LOS MILLARES** ❶.

Continue west on the A348 4km to the spa town of **ALHAMA DE ALMERIA** ❷. By this point the flat river valley north of Almería has given way to a limestone shelf, often tilted and cracked, on the north bank of the Río Andarax. Throughout the area different geologies are signalled by changes in the rocks. While the predominant bedrock is limestone made reddish by substantial iron inclusions, occasional purple patches indicate concentrations of manganese. The **MOORISH TOWNS** ❸ begin 26km west, and it's worth taking the turn-off into **Canjáyar** for a look around.

Detour: At Canjáyar, an innocuous sign indicates the turning to **Ohanes**, only 9km away. That 9km requires the better part of an hour's driving, as the road slithers around the mountainsides like a serpent, twisting and turning and seeming to shoot out over cliffs. Moreover, it rises very quickly the whole way to Ohanes. It is a beautiful and terrifying ride, made all the stranger by the discontinuities in rock types. In one area a chalky white limestone stands on one side of the road, a rusty lime from another period on the other. At points along the way, the roadside mountain walls turn to a peculiar puddingstone of limerock with large boulder inclusions – not the most stable stone for a mountain road. This serpentine road, the AL441, passes above Ohanes and returns to the A348 in another 9km. It is lined almost every centimetre of the way with fruit or olive trees, and irrigation channels run along both sides of the road – a thousand-year-old legacy of Moorish horticulturalists.

If not detouring, continue west on the A348, having a look at some of the smaller agricultural villages before entering **Fondón** in 24km. Along the way note the frequent signs for *secaderos de jamón,* the establishments that capitalise on the low humidity of this region to air-dry mountain hams.

It is only another few kilometres into **LAUJAR DE ANDARAX** ❹ and the information centre for the **PARQUE NATURAL SIERRA NEVADA** ❺.

Almería and environs

The city of Almería is a lush and green oasis on the Atlantic, but its interior countryside consists of sweeping emptiness – so desolate that the desert scenes for *Lawrence of Arabia* and *Patton* were filmed here. The rocky desert landscape bakes in the sun with less than 100mm of rain per year. Yet grapes, olives and oranges flourish under irrigation, hinting at the region's fertility before the great climatic changes of the late Middle Ages. The mountains north and east are virtually barren, save the spring wildflower bloom, and deep gullies caused by sudden downpours scar their surfaces. Excellent, newly paved roads ease access to this startling world of high desert, and distances between oases are relatively short. The best season for touring the drylands is spring, when vestiges of winter water coax the tenacious wildflowers, broom and rosemary into delicate bloom.

ALMERIA✧✧

ⓘ Oficina de Turismo de la Junta de Andalucía *Parque Nicolás Salmerón at Martínez Campos; tel: (95) 027–4355; fax: (95) 027–4355; www.andalucia.org; open Mon–Fri 0900–1900, Sat–Sun 1000–1400.*

Oficina de Turismo Municipal *Av Federico García Lorca; tel: (95) 028–0748; www.almeria-turismo.org; open Mon–Fri 1000–1300; Sat 1000–1300.*

The capital of Andalucía's poorest province is a busy port and ferry terminal, making for a lively mix of Arabs, Africans and Spaniards along its seaside promenade. One of the wealthiest ports in al-Andalus in the 11th century, Almería was ravaged by pirates after the 1489 Reconquest and was nearly levelled by an earthquake in 1522. Most of its buildings now date from the late 19th century. In the poorer *barrios*, streets may suddenly end in dirt alleyways and Almería has a persistent core of beggars, rather than the industrious freelance parking attendants found elsewhere. Yet the city can seem wonderfully atmospheric with the patina of age that chic interior designers try so hard to replicate.

The tourist office map outlines the main attractions in the historic centre; many small streets are omitted but street signage is good. The city is justifiably proud of its **Alcazaba✧✧✧**, the largest in Andalucía (*€ open daily mid Jun–Sept 1000–1400 and 1700–2000; rest of the year*

Ferries to Melilla, the Spanish toehold in northeast Morocco, depart daily. Contact **Transmediterránea** *Parque Nicolás Salmerón 19; tel: (90) 245-4645; www.transmediterranea.es* and **FerriMaroc** *Parque Nicolás Salmerón 14; tel: (95) 027-4800; www.ferrimaroc.com*

Peña El Taranto *Pl. Flores 2; tel: (95) 023-5057* presents flamenco concerts in the old Arab cisterns, Los Aljibes, on c/ Tenor Iribarne between Pl. Flores and Pl. San Pedro.

Fiestas de la Virgen de la Mar *tel: (95) 027-4355.* Last week of August; fiesta processions with carnival giants, pilgrimage to the catedral and flamenco festival featuring the *taranto*, Almería's indigenous form of flamenco.

Below
Almería's Alcazaba

0930–1400 and 1630–1900). Begun in 955 by Córdoba caliph Abd al-Rahman III, it rivalled the splendour of the Alhambra in Granada. Earthquakes and time have stripped that grandeur to the heavy bones of a military fortification. The exterior compound, now filled with terraced gardens, was a camp where townspeople took refuge during times of siege. The middle compound, reserved for officials and visiting Moorish kings, had the usual amenities, including a mosque and baths. This area is partially destroyed but a courtyard with bubbling fountains and lagoon retains its serene grace. The interior compound includes a fortress added by the Catholic monarchs; its thick defensive walls are the best preserved of the site. With great views of the city, the harbour and the surrounding hills, the Alcazaba is a favourite spot for watching the sunset.

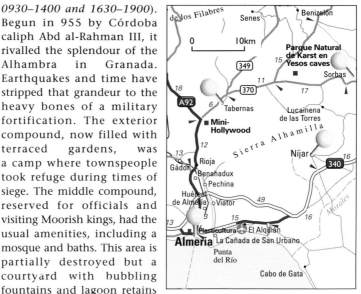

Plaza de la Constitucíon✦✦ (Pl. Vieja), just off c/ Mariana on the way to the Alcazaba, is a tranquil three-storey enclosed square with an arched arcade at ground level and bougainvillaea climbing the walls. The central monument honours all men and women who have died for liberty. A few blocks downhill, the **Cathedral**✦✦ (€ Pl. Catedral; open Mon–Fri 1000–1700, Sat 1000–1300) was built on the site of a mosque destroyed in the 1522 earthquake. Begun only two years later, the cathedral's fortress-like style reflects the uncertainty of the times. Corner towers were constructed for the cannons and the windows are small and recessed to resist attacks by North African pirates. The plain exterior belies the ornate interior.

The friendly and helpful Almeríans often steer tourists away from 'unsavoury' areas, notably the *mirador* at the top of the city and the old gypsy quarter. Just use caution when visiting. The **Mirador de San Cristóbal**✦, visible from the Alcazaba and reached via c/ Antonio Vico, also has broad views of the surrounding city and landscape, as well as of the Alcazaba. The *mirador*, however, attracts many fewer visitors than the Alcazaba and locals consider it a hangout for delinquents. The gypsy district of **Barrio de Chanca**✦, west and downhill from the cathedral, can be reached by following the narrow twisting streets from the cathedral and passing the **Templo de San Juan**✦, built on the site of a mosque. A *mihrab* stands on one wall, but San Juan is only open for services. An easier approach is along the waterfront Parque Nicolás Salmerón to Avda del Mar. The neighbourhood begins several blocks up Avda del Mar at Las Llanas. Clearly an impoverished area, La Chanca's residents have a particular flair for decorating their doors with tiles and mosaic patterns.

The lush **Parque Nicolás Salmerón**✦✦, a leading promenade, is dotted with playgrounds and at weekends fills with families and children in their best outfits. The other choice for an evening promenade and *tapas* is **Paseo de Almería**✦✦, lined with shops and restaurants, clearly preferred by locals over the grander **Rambla de Belén**✦.

Accommodation and food in Almería

Gran Hotel Almería €€–€€€ *Reina Regente 8; tel: (95) 023–8011; fax: (95) 027–0691; www.granhotelalmeria.com.* Modern 117-room hotel with pool and garage near the harbour, a short walk from the historic district.

Hoteles Torreluz €–€€€ *1, 3 and 5 Pl. Flores. Four-star: tel: (95) 023–4999. Three-star and two-star: tel: (95) 023–4399; www.amhoteles.com.* The venerable Plaza Flores, convenient to all the city sights, contains this three-hotel complex ranging in price and luxury, and a variety of affiliated cafés and restaurants.

Bodegas Las Botas € *c/ Pérez 3; tel: (95) 026–2272.* A good place to sample sherry from the cask along with a nice range of *tapas*.

Opposite
The drama unfolds
at Mini Hollywood

Restaurante Valentín € *c/ Tenor Iribarne 2; tel: (95) 026–4475*. Formal, excellent fish restaurant sits a street away from the Paseo de Almería, where its brassier offspring, Marisquería-Freiduría Alcázar, reigns supreme on Pl. San Pedro. *Closed 1–14 Sept.*

Desierto de Tabernas❖❖❖

Mini Hollywood €€€ (additional €€€ for Reserva Zoológica) *N340 km364; tel: (95) 036–5236; open summer 1000–2100 daily; winter 1000–1700, closed Mon.* Western shows at 1200 and 1700 (and 2000 from mid-Jun–mid-Sept).

Texas Hollywood €€€ *N340 km367; tel: (95) 016–5458; open Jul–Sept daily 1000–2100, Oct–Jun daily 1000–1900.* Western shows at 1430 and 1730.

Western Leone €€ *A92 1 km north of N340; tel: (95) 016–5405, open daily 0900–2100.* Western shows daily Jul–Sept at 1200, 1500, 1730 and 2000.

Beginning only 24km inland from Almería, the Desierto de Tabernas is a rare example of true desert in western Europe. The rugged mountains, multi-coloured sands and sparse vegetation of succulents and cactus attracted movie-makers in the 1960s and 1970s, most notably the *auteur* of the spaghetti western, Sergio Leone. Local residents were given non-speaking parts as Indians, outlaws and US cavalry riders. When the film industry lost interest in westerns, the locations served sporadically for action films starring men with strong chins and women with heaving bosoms. Now that the moviemakers are gone, some old western sets are entertainment centres.

Mini Hollywood❖ supplied the set for Main Street in *A Fistful of Dollars*, *The Magnificent Seven* and *The Good, the Bad and the Ugly*, among others. Of the three western attractions, it is the best known and best maintained, although details tend more to theme park expediency than to authenticity. A plodding western melodrama of rough justice is enacted twice a day. The best part of a visit is the small museum of antique projectors and movie posters in Spanish and English. For an additional charge, this park also offers a less-than-thrilling photographic safari through a private zoo. Only a few kilometres away, **Texas Hollywood**❖ has a more spectacular setting, with film sets that include a Mexican town and Indian village as well as a western town. The rough road into the site can be hard on low-slung automobiles. **Western Leone**❖, the newest entry and run by the director's family, also hires out saddle horses.

NÍJAR✦✦

Feria de Otoño is held 20–25 Sept.

Hostal Montes € Avda Federico García Lorca; tel: (95) 036–0157. Small hostal on the main street with modest rooms.

La Curva € c/ Parque s/n; tel: (95) 036–0172. Traditional tapas bar and restaurant also offers croissants in the morning, perhaps a sign of encroaching gentrification.

A mountain-top spring made Níjar an ancient oasis in the high desert, and townspeople still fill their jugs from the **Moorish-era public fountain**✦ in the square by the cathedral. Níjar artisans have drawn on local clays and minerals since Moorish times for a rustic pottery splashed with bold blues, greens and yellows in floral and abstract designs. Most of the stores selling this pottery are located along the main street of the new town, **Avda Federico García Lorca**✦✦ (as opposed to the white warren of the casco antiguo). Níjar is also known for its rugs, bedspreads and curtains tightly woven from colourful cotton rags, and many modern weavers now string their looms with naturally dyed wool from local sheep and goats. One shop selling both traditional woven rugs and typical pottery is **La Jarapa** (c/ Federico García Lorca 23). **La Tienda de los Milagros** (c/ Lavadero 2), the studio of British ceramic artist Matthew Weir, is off the main drag on the Pl. Mercado. Weir creates his own interpretations of traditional designs and glazes.

In 1928, a local scandal inspired Lorca to write his most famous play, *Bodas de Sangre (Blood Wedding)*. Francisca, an heiress with a modest dowry, was being forced against her wishes to marry a labourer named Casimiro, but instead ran away with her cousin. Casimiro's brother pursued them, killed the cousin and was convicted of murder, leaving everyone involved humiliated. Francisca lived as a recluse in Níjar until her death in 1978.

SORBAS✦✦

Oficina de Turismo c/ Terraplén; tel: (95) 036–4476; open Thur–Sun 1030–1430. Information about Parque Natural de Karst en Yesos.

Pensión Sorbas € N340, km 170; tel: (95) 036–4160. Modest rooms, some with shared bath.

Restaurante Sol de Andalucía € N340, km 170; tel: (95) 036–4160. Game specialities. Closed Mon.

Like Níjar, Sorbas has a long-standing ceramic tradition, and a local school encourages its survival. More sombre than Níjar's gaudier glazes, Sorbas pottery matches its surroundings. The village hangs above an ashen gorge in a dark, stony desert that could have inspired the phrase, 'dark side of the moon'. The location is best appreciated from the A370,

Plasticultura

The parched limestone soils of Almería are underlaid by impermeable volcanic rock that traps water, and in the last few decades growers have taken to covering hectare after hectare with plastic greenhouses. By infusing fertiliser into water pumped from deep wells, they have turned a barren wilderness into one of Europe's most intensive horticultural zones, with large harvests of tomatoes, peppers, watermelons and courgettes. Capital of plasticultura is El Ejido, bypassed by the N340 west of Almería.

Opposite
Sorbas, famous for pottery

half a kilometre beyond the turn-off. Three ancient *alfarerías* still operate in the lower village, one still using its original Moorish kiln. Work is for sale, often at bargain prices.

Sorbas, however, serves principally as a staging ground for excursions into the dramatic mineral landscape of **Parque Natural de Karst en Yesos**✦✦✦, where aeons of water erosion created deep gorges and flat-topped humps that resemble volcanic cones. The region is pocked with subterranean chasms filled with stalactites. The landscape can be viewed from the A370, but for a closer look take the AL140 toward Los Molinos de Agua, east of Sorbas. At the crest of a hill, a track to the left leads to a peak above the gorge for a 360-degree view. Visits to the caves by foot or motorbike can be arranged by the local tourist office.

Suggested tour

Total distance: 116km (134km with detour).

Time: 4 hours.

Links: Connects to the Costa de Almería (*see pages 274–81*) at Almería or Níjar.

Below
Sorbas

Route: Leave **ALMERIA** ❶ east from the port on the N344, following

signs to Murcia and the airport. The N340 joins the N344 at the airport roundabout in 12km. Follow signs straight ahead (*not* left) towards **NIJAR** ❷ , turning at km479 on to the AL102 for a 3.5km drive into this hill town. The road passes over flat, arid land of crumbled limestone.

In Níjar, take the high road toward **Lucainena de Las Torres**, marked AL100 on signage but AL102 on all maps. This spectacular drive through the Sierra Alhamilla twists and turns as it follows barren, scrubby ridges. Rosemary, broom and wildflowers bloom here in the spring but otherwise the desert only supports cactus and wild olive. Manganese deposits are evident in purple-tinted pockets of stone, and small bits of quartz and mica hint at the volcanic and metamorphic bedrock.

All along the 20km route to Lucainena are reminders that this desert bloomed before the climatic changes that began around AD 1200. Subtle remains of ancient terraces curl around the hills and some modern olive-growers have begun to use the old Moorish terraces and irrigation systems. Lucainena is a tiny town with a *mirador* overlooking a dry river valley. In 5km the AL100 ends at the A370 highway on the green side of the mountain range.

Detour: Turn right on the A370 and drive 9km to **SORBAS** ❸ , sometimes called 'little Cuenca', high on the edge of a limestone cliff.

Drive west on the A370 through the **DESIERTO DE TABERNAS** ❹ . Multiple ranges of mountains spread to the north and west, rising a dark, cool blue in the arid air. At km500, pass the turn-off for Guadix and return 17km to Almería.

Also worth exploring

At km471 of the A370, the recently restored ruins of a Moorish castle where Fernando and Isabela were based for the siege of Almería stand high on a *mesa* in **Tabernas**.

The Costa de Almería

Ratings

Beaches	●●●●
Gastronomy	●●●●
Nature and wildlife	●●●●
Architecture	●●○○○
Entertainment	●●○○○
History	●●○○○
Shopping and crafts	●●○○○
Museums	●○○○○

Although the first 40km northeast of Almería consists of an extended *litoral* of brown sand beaches and vast salt flats, the topography changes rapidly to jagged limestone peaks, then to the ominous black volcanic mountains of the Sierra del Cabo de Gata crashing into turquoise seas. But wherever an ancient river has cut through the hills, there are white sand beaches surrounded by high cliffs and jutting capes, and along these beaches human settlements have taken hold over the centuries. The parched interior, caught in the rain shadow of the Sierra Nevada, receives less than 100mm of rain per year. This aridity produces monumental deserts, often only a few hundred metres from lush little ports. The Parque Natural Cabo de Gata-Níjar encompasses almost the entire region, providing an infrastructure to preserve the undeveloped areas and to improve the roads, scenic routes and interpretative signage.

CARBONERAS❖

ℹ Oficina de Turismo *Pl. Castillo s/n; tel: (95) 045–4059.*

☾ **Fiestas de San Antonio** *tel: (95) 045–4059.* Celebrations 13–16 Jun include re-enactment of the capture of the town by the Christians.

Charcoal burners reduced the once densely forested hills around Carboneras to a near-desert. Surprisingly, some of the forest fauna survived the transition and even today road signs entering Carboneras warn of deer crossing the road. The town's smoky plumes still make it visible from many kilometres away, but now the smoke rises from tall lime-slaking chimneys that serve the concrete industry. The surge of construction along the Andalucían coast – most of it in concrete and whitewash – could be said to be simply a matter of rearranging the limestone that forms the bedrock of the entire region. Because Carboneras was isolated from inland Andalucía by the surrounding mountains, it became a

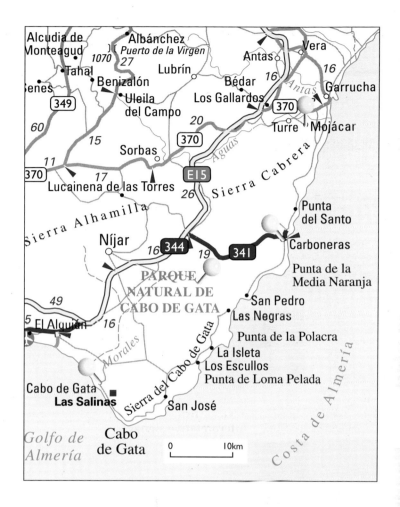

storehouse of contraband and provisions in the 1568 Morisco uprising in the Alpujarras. That same isolation has made it a modern-day coastal retreat from the excesses of the Costa del Sol. Construction is relatively recent – most since the 1980s – and echoes Arabic structures with a modernist accent.

From Easter to early September the town centre often seems deserted, but everyone can be found down at the beach next to the fishing port, where they are likely to be sitting beneath umbrellas and feasting on a juicy white-fleshed fish called *galán* that is mainly found along this coast and in the Balearic islands. The port district has recently been overhauled, with some tasteful new flat construction that fits in well with the fine formal gardens behind the **Castillo de San Andrés**∗, built by the Marqués del Carpio in the 16th century.

Accommodation and food in Carboneras

Hotel Don Felipe €€ *c/ Sorbas s/n; tel: (95) 045–4015; www.hoteldon felipe.com.* Small but nicely appointed hotel a block from the beach.

Hotel El Dorado €–€€ *Playa de Carboneras; tel: (95) 045–4050; fax: (95) 013–0102; www.eldorado-carboneras.com.* Nicely landscaped beachfront hotel with 17 rooms and adequate bar-restaurant (€).

MOJACAR❖❖❖

❶ Oficina de Turismo
Pl. Nueva s/n; tel: (95) 047–5162; www.mojacar.es; open Mon–Fri 1000–1400, 1700–1930; Sat–Sun 1030–1350.

❷ Pl. de las Flores has a wide variety of shops selling handicrafts.

❸ Fiesta de Moros y Cristanos *tel: (95) 047–5162.* Weekend nearest 10 June, dances, processions and costumed re-enactment of the Christian Reconquest of Mojácar.

Mojácar consists of two virtually separate towns: **Mojácar Playa❖❖**, the 10km sprawling beach strip where motels and trinket shops jostle each other along both sides of the road, and **Mojácar Pueblo❖❖❖**, an Arabic mirage sprouting from the rock of a mountain top 2km inland. The beaches are long, clean and unshadowed by high-rise development. The arid climate guarantees maximum sunshine most of the year.

Much of Mojácar's old town is under renovation. In the 1960s, facing a city where whole *barrios* were deserted, the mayor came up with a novel idea to reverse its decline: He simply gave away houses to artists. As is often the case, the artists made the charming village fashionable and real estate developers and speculators have followed on their heels, gutting the medieval quarters to fill them with all the modern conveniences. Isolated as this area is, Mojácar now has not one but two local Internet providers, and the newcomers have adopted the *indalo* figure so thoroughly as to make this Neolithic drawing Mojácar's own smiley-face cliché.

The crumbling old castle, barely recognisable as a fortress, has become a private arts centre complemented by a fine bar-restaurant with a handful of guest rooms, usually reserved for visiting artists. Hardly a street in the old town is on the same level, making it both a visual delight and a challenge to walk. The homes display their Arabic origins conspicuously – even self-consciously – with domes and arches, lattices and patios. Every whitewashed wall, it seems, is dotted with geraniums. Public activity tends to centre on the **Plaza de las Flores****, just inside the old Moorish gate, by the public fountain and the mirador, which has breathtaking views across the parched landscape.

Accommodation and food in Mojácar

Camping Cantal de Mojácar € *Carretera Garrucha–Caboneras; tel: (95) 047–8204.*

Hotel Mamabel's € *c/ Embajadores 3; tel: (95) 047–2448; www.mamabels.com.* Just four rooms with sea views from the old city, Mamabel's fills quickly. But there's usually plenty of room in the excellent restaurant (€€), which gives a welcome contemporary twist to the area's traditional fish cuisine.

Hotel El Moresco €–€€ *Avda de En Camp s/n; tel: (95) 047 8025; fax: (95) 047–8262.* Modern hotel with Moorish styling in a spectacular setting just below the old town's *mirador*. All 147 rooms have small private terraces sharing the view and there's a great swimming pool on the 8th floor.

Parador de Mojácar €€ *Playa de Mojácar; tel: (95) 047–8250; fax: (95) 047–8183; www.parador.es.* Modern hotel of sumptuous comforts and pleasant grounds across main road from beaches. Excellent restaurant (€€–€€€) serves many local fish specialities.

El Almejero *Esplanada del Puerto, Garrucha; tel: (95) 046–0405.* Overlooking the fishing boats at the Garrucha end of Mojácar's beach, El Almejero prepares superb local shrimp (*gambones de Garrucha*) and specialises in whole fish baked in salt.

Parque Natural Cabo de Gata-Nijar***

This vast natural park consists of three distinct geographic regions: the Estepa Litoral (the litoral stretching east of Almería city), the small but ecologically critical district of Las Salinas (salt marshes and salt flats declared a waterfowl preserve, mostly to protect the flamingos), and the black-rock landscape of the Sierra del Cabo de Gata mountain range, formed by now-extinct volcanoes. Driving from coastal village to coastal village often means crossing through the mountainous desert to reach a passable inland road, and a chance to appreciate the elemental vistas.

ℹ Centro de Interpretación Las Almoladeras *Carretera Almería; tel: (95) 016–0435. Semana Santa and Jul–Aug daily 1000–1400 and 1700–2100, rest of year Tue–Sun 1000–1500.*

The flora of the natural park is unusual, characterised by the dwarf fan palm, which grows no more than 1m tall and is Europe's only native palm. Its fibres are used to make mats and brooms and the tender shoots commonly appear in local salads. The jujube bush (*Zizyphus lotus*), found only in North Africa and along this coast, is a thorny shrub with criss-crossed and intertwined branches and roots that penetrate tens of metres down to reach bedrock water sources.

Most visitors enter the park from Almería city, coming past the **Las Almoladeras visitor centre◆** for an orientation to the geology, flora and fauna of the region. The road continues through San Miguel de Cabo de Gata and past the salt flats of **Las Salinas de Acosta◆**, where commercial producers of sea-salt share the lagoons with the flamingos that feed on the larval shrimp. The road passes the tiny fishing village of **La Almadraba de Monteleva◆**, which is simply another spot on the long beach where the fishing is good by net and rod alike. Ultimately, the Cabo de Gata road ends at the **Faro de Gata◆◆**, an unremarkable lighthouse in a very remarkable location. The road rises sharply and begins to corkscrew around the high cliffs en route to the light – then ends rather abruptly in a few km. The forces of nature have overwhelmed mere human activity, so the road leading on to **San José◆◆** is closed. Authorities have been promising for years to repave and reopen it, but for the time being it serves mainly as a well-marked, strenuous walking path between the lighthouse and the fishing village turned counter-cultural enclave.

The pebble beaches and small fishing villages of **Los Escullos◆** and **La Isleta del Moro◆** are not to be missed. Perch on the dock with a beer, watch the retired fishermen play dominoes and it is possible – perhaps even desirable – to imagine living a simple life here forever. **Las Negras◆** offers similar pleasures in a dramatically different setting beneath looming black volcanic cliffs. There is a coastal walking path leading north towards **Agua Amarga◆**. It is heavily travelled, at least for the first 4km to reach Playa de Cala San Pedro, where nude sunbathers stretch out on a large strip of dark sand by a ruined fort.

Accommodation and food in the Parque Natural Cabo de Gata-Níjar

Camping Cabo de Gata € *Ruta de Playa, Ruescas-San Miguel de Cabo de Gata; tel: (95) 016–0443.* Good camping 1.5km from the beach with restaurant and pool.

Camping Los Escullos € *0.5km north of Los Escullos; tel: (95) 038–9811; www.losescullossanjose.com.* Full-service camping village where the desert meets the ocean.

Camping Roquetas € *Carretera Los Parrales s/n, Roquetas de Mar; tel: (95) 034–3809; www.campingroquetas.com.* Good camping 500m from rocky beaches.

Hostal Isleta del Moro € *Isleta del Moro; tel: (95) 038–9713; fax: (95) 038–9764.* Comfortable rooms with private baths over excellent bar-restaurant (€); in a minuscule fishing village, offers a true getaway.

Hostal Puerto Genovés € *c/ Arrastre s/n; tel: (95) 038–0320; www.puertogenoves.com.* Eighteen simple air-conditioned rooms with baths, 100m from beach.

Hotel Las Salinas de Cabo de Gata €–€€ *La Almadraba de Monteleva 20; tel: (95) 037–0103; fax: (95) 037–1239; www.hotellassalinas.com* is the most upmarket hotel on Cabo de Gata.

SAN MIGUEL DE CABO DE GATA[*]

Rarely called by its full name, Cabo de Gata functions as a beach community for Almería city dwellers, who have built a handsome and unassuming community of one- and two-storey holiday homes at the edge of two long, straight brown-sand beaches. The town still has a substantial contingent of in-shore fishermen who have their own dedicated areas of the beaches. Between high tides they can usually be found sitting cross-legged on the beach untangling and repairing their nets.

Accommodation and food in San Miguel de Cabo de Gata

Hostal Las Dunas € *c/ Barrionuevo 58; tel: (95) 037–0072.* Fresh, clean and friendly small hotel 50m from beach.

Restaurante Mediterráneo € *end of c/ Iglesia; tel: (95) 037–1137.* Good local seafood fresh from the waters 20m away. Also has a few single and double rooms with shared bath (€).

Above
Watchtowers near
Carboneras

Suggested tour

Total distance: 221km, 265km with detours.

Time: One long day without stops.

Links: This route is a popular day tour from Almería.

Route: From Almería port district follow signs for Cabo de Gata for 14km to the visitor centre for the **PARQUE NATURAL CABO DE GATA-NIJAR** ❶ at Los Almoladeras. When the road ends in 2km, turn right toward **SAN MIGUEL DE CABO DE GATA** ❷ for the first good look at the tranquil littoral beaches. Follow signs for the Faro de Gata (lighthouse). Just east of town are the Salinas de Acosta, shallow salt ponds and man-made empoundments where brine shrimp flourish and substantial flocks of greater flamingos breed and raise their young from April to August. The large white heaps behind chain fences along the road are of sea salt destined for further refinement and gourmet packaging as *sal de mar.* The wide spot in the road 2km ahead is the village of La Almadraba de Monteleva, a place to slow down en route to the lighthouse. Tour buses stop about half a kilometre before the light, as it is the last place where they can turn round. After seeing the light, ignore the sign indicating that the road is closed and continue 2km towards San José until reaching the bar across the road. There is a spot to park here, and the walk up the road a kilometre or so is well worth the effort for the extraordinary views of cliffs towering above the ocean.

Backtrack to Cabo de Gata and follow signs for 12km to San José. Backtrack again for 2km to the 10km coastal road to Los Escullos and La Isleta, two of the least spoiled and prettiest villages on the Andalucían coast. The road turns inland to high limestone ridges with good views of the sea for the 3km drive through **Rodalquilar**✢ and on to Las Negras.

Detour: The 11km cliff-line hike to San Pedro provides far-reaching views and a good sampling of local flora. Below the cliffs lie stunning sandy beaches in coves guarded on each side by towering rocks. Paths, sometimes the semblance of a road, lead down to the beaches.

Head inland 10km towards **Fernán Pérez**✢ to turn right on to a dirt road that bumps along for 10km until connecting with the local paved road that goes 8km to Agua Amarga.

Detour: A rough but scenic cliff-top road goes 6km south past several ruined Moorish watchtowers to San Pedro.

Follow signs north through high desert on the west side of the hills to **CARBONERAS** ❸. Join the scenic and well-maintained N341 north along the shore 24km to **MOJACAR** ❹, noting the watchtowers and defensive forts built along the waterfront. To return to Almería, drive north along the beach 2km to turn left on the AL152; drive 13km west to the N344 highway, which goes southwest 85km to Almería.

Also worth exploring

Parque Natural Cabo de Gata-Níjar includes within its boundaries all the waters from San Miguel de Cabo de Gata around the cape north to Agua Amarga. The southern and western portions of the park offer particularly good snorkelling and scuba diving. Inquire at the docks in San José about renting gear or arranging boat trips to isolated coves.

Language

Getting around

¡hola! – hello
¡adiós! – goodbye

sí – yes
no – no

abierto – open
cerrado – closed

izquierda – left
derecha – right
todo recto – straight ahead

entrada – entrance
salida – exit

empujar – to push
tirar – to pull

por favór – please
gracias – thank you

ayuntamiento – town hall
banco – bank
barrio – district
cajero automático – automatic teller machine
calle – street
callejón – lane
cambio – currency exchange, change
carretera – highway
casco antiguo – old section of a city
castillo – castle
catedral – cathedral
ciudad – town or city
correos – post office
estación de trenes – railway station
iglesia – church
embalse – artificial lake or reservoir
ermita – hermitage
faro – lighthouse
fuente – fountain
glorieta – roundabout
Judería – Jewish quarter
marismas – marshes
mercado – market
muelle – wharf, pier
museo – museum
mirador – scenic vantage point
palacio – palace, mansion
parada de autobuses – bus stop
parque – park
paseo – promenade
playa – beach
plaza mayor – main square
pueblo – village, town
puente – bridge
puerta – door, gate

puerto – port, mountain pass
ronda – ring road
sierra – mountain range

Eating and drinking

bodega – wine cellar or bar
chiringuita – beach restaurant
freiduría – casual fried fish stand
marisquería – seafood restaurant, often emphasising shellfish
taberna – tavern

desayuno – breakfast
comida – midday meal
cena – evening meal

carta – menu
menú del día – fixed price meal, usually at lunch
tapas – snacks served at bar
ración – meal-sized *tapas* servings
cuenta – bill
entradas – starters
platos principales – main courses

cerveza – beer, usually in bottle
caña/tubo – small/large draught beer
vino blanco/rosado/tinto – white/rosé/red wine

aceitunas – olives
albóndigas – meatballs
almejas – clams
almendras – almonds
atún – tuna
bacalao – salt cod
boquerones – fresh anchovies
calamares – squid
cerdo – pork
chipirones – whole baby squid
chorizo – spicy sausage
cochinillo – suckling pig
conejo – rabbit
cordero – lamb
gambas – shrimp
habas – broad beans
huevos – eggs
jamón serrano – cured mountain ham
langosta – spiny lobster
langostinos – large prawns
mariscos – seafood, shellfish
mejillones – mussels
pescado – fish
pollo – chicken
queso – cheese
salchichas – cured sausages
solomillo – sirloin
ternera – veal
venado – venison

Index

Acknowledgements

Project management: Cambridge Publishing Management Limited
Project editor: Karen Beaulah
Series design: Fox Design
Cover design: Liz Lyons Design
Layout and map work: Concept 5D/Cambridge Publishing Management Limited
Repro and image setting: PDQ Digital Media Solutions Ltd/Cambridge Publishing Management Limited
Printed and bound in India by: Replika Press Pvt Ltd

We would like to thank the following photographers for the pictures used in this book, to whom the copyright in the photograph belongs.

Front cover: Setenil, Peter Adams Photography/Alamy
Back cover: Orange tree, The Travel Library

Patricia Harris (pages 3, 5, 6, 14, 26, 27, 32, 42A, 42B, 45, 46, 52A, 58, 61, 64, 67, 68, 70, 72, 75, 82, 90, 93, 102, 108A, 108B, 118, 121, 125, 126, 128, 130, 132, 148, 156, 158, 164, 171, 176, 180, 183, 195, 202B, 212, 220, 222, 230, 232, 236, 239, 240, 246, 250, 251, 254, 255, 258A, 258B, 261, 262, 266, 267 and 274B); **Nick Inman** (page 19); **David Lyon** (pages 12, 20, 23, 26, 31, 33, 35, 38, 40, 48, 52B, 55, 77, 78, 87, 94, 98, 101, 110, 113, 114,116, 122, 124, 127, 135, 136, 138, 140, 143, 144, 146, 150 153 160A, 160B 166, 169, 170, 173, 174, 185, 186, 188, 191, 192, 196, 199, 202A, 204, 207, 208, 209, 210, 214, 217, 219, 224, 226, 228, 235, 243, 252, 253, 256, 264, 269, 270, 272, 274A, 276, 279 and 280); **Pictures Colour Library** (pages 16 and 57)

Feedback form

If you enjoyed using this book, or even if you didn't, please help us improve future editions by taking part in our reader survey. Every returned form will be acknowledged, and to show our appreciation we will give you £1 off your next purchase of a Thomas Cook guidebook. Just take a few minutes to complete and return this form to us.

When did you buy this book? ....
....

Where did you buy it? (Please give town/city and, if possible, name of retailer)
....
....

When did you/do you intend to travel in Andalucía?..
....

For how long (approx)? ....

How many people in your party? ....

Which cities, national parks and other locations did you/do you intend mainly to visit?
....
....
....
....

Did you/will you:
❏ Make all your travel arrangements independently?
❏ Travel on a fly-drive package?
Please give brief details: ....
....

Did you/do you intend to use this book:
❏ For planning your trip?   ❏ Both?
❏ During the trip itself?

Did you/do you intend also to purchase any of the following travel publications for your trip?
Thomas Cook Travellers: Seville & Andalucía..
A road map/atlas (please specify) ....
Other guidebooks (please specify) ....

Have you used any other Thomas Cook guidebooks in the past? If so, which?
....
....

Please rate the following features of *Drive Around Andalucía and the Costa del Sol* for their value to you (circle VU for 'very useful', U for 'useful', NU for 'little or no use'):

The *Travel facts* section on pages 14–23	VU	U	NU
The *Driver's guide* section on pages 24–29	VU	U	NU
The *Touring itineraries* on pages 40–41	VU	U	NU
The recommended driving routes throughout the book	VU	U	NU
Information on towns and cities, National Parks, etc	VU	U	NU
The maps of towns and cities, parks, etc	VU	U	NU

Please use this space to tell us about any features that in your opinion could be changed, improved, or added in future editions of the book, or any other comments you would like to make concerning the book:

....

....

....

....

....

....

....

....

Your age category: ❏ 21–30   ❏ 31–40   ❏ 41–50   ❏ over 50

Your name: Mr/Mrs/Miss/Ms ....

(First name or initials) ....

(Last name) ....

Your full address (please include postal or zip code):

....

....

....

....

....

Your daytime telephone number: ....

Please detach this page and send it to: The Series Editor, Drive Around Guides, Thomas Cook Publishing, PO Box 227, The Thomas Cook Business Park, 15–16 Coningsby Road, Peterborough PE3 8SB.

Alternatively, you can e-mail us at: *books@thomascook.com*

We will be pleased to send you details of how to claim your discount upon receipt of this questionnaire.